THE ESSENTIAL PRUNING COMPANION

THE ESSENTIAL PRUNING COMPANION

Professor JOHN MALINS

Trafalgar Square Publishing
NORTH POMFRET, VERMONT

FRONTISPIECE:
Yew is very effective when trained to form an arch, although it is not particularly easy to keep in good shape

First published in the United States of America in 1992 by
Trafalgar Square Publishing, North Pomfret, Vermont 05053

ISBN 0 943955 53 X
Library of Congress Catalog Card Number: 91-66168

Colour photographs © Andrew Lawson except:
pp59, 70, 71, 142, 155, 163, 205 (Author)
pp211, 222, 235 (Photos Horticultural)
Line drawings by Maggie Redfern

Printed in Germany

CONTENTS

INTRODUCTION

Most of us think we know what pruning is, but would find it difficult to define. Let us forget a modern use of the word prune to mean 'cut down' in any context, an example of this use being provided by publishers who say 'Prune your manuscript', meaning 'Cut it by half, including your favourite passages.' The verb 'to prune' is derived from the Old French 'prounier', meaning to cut back the vine, and this became 'prouyne' in Middle English. By the end of the sixteenth century 'to prune' was to 'lop off branches, boughs or shoots'.

The introduction to Britain of trees and shrubs from the seventeenth century onward, especially from America, drew attention to their manner of growth and the way

The author in the garden at Tintinhull House

'Poor little tailored bushes'
(*This and the drawing below from* The Pruning Manual *by L.H.Bailey, 1934*)

in which they could be trained for the best effect. Fruit bushes were pruned and trained according to set plans, with splendid results. Scientific study in this century has, in the main, confirmed the principles which trained gardeners had taught from long observation and experience. It is not surprising that the best understood and practised of all pruning tasks is the ancient craft of training the vine.

William Thiselton-Dyer was appointed Director of the Royal Botanic Gardens at Kew in 1885 and found that pruning had been neglected, many trees being 'unshapely'. There was nothing new about such complaints. The Scots gardener, John Reid, in his influential book of 1683 wrote 'Some ignorants are against pruning, suffering their trees to run and ramble to such a head of confusion as neither bears well or fair.' W. J. Bean became Assistant Curator at Kew in 1900 and no doubt put things to rights there, if the work had not been done already. In 1914 he published his classic work *Trees and Shrubs Hardy in the British Isles* in which he wrote 'Of all the arts that go to make up horticulture pruning is the one most frequently misapplied - hard pruning or pruning without aim is worse than none.' Even now, in other places than Kew, there is evidence of ignorance and carelessness where neither should exist. This book aims to help you prune with wisdom and skill.

'A bush that develops its natural and characteristic beauty'

PART ONE

THE
PURPOSE
OF
PRUNING

Why should we bother to prune our plants? Does nature do it? She – or is it He? – does eventually remove dead or diseased branches, but then Nature has plenty of time and is not directly concerned with beauty.

As a tree grows in woodland or plantation, the lower branches are deprived of light and the crown takes more and more of the nourishment from the roots. Eventually these lower branches die and fall to the ground. Examination of timber after felling shows that this process is more cleanly performed in the centre of the plantation than at its margin, where knots in the timber are often found. This is presumably related to the penetration of light and air, which persists to some extent in this outer zone and makes decay a slower process.

Damage, to which the outer zone is specially prone, leads to branches rubbing together, damaging the bark and allowing infection to enter and sometimes spread to the main trunk. So there is every reason to cut back unhealthy limbs as soon as possible.

It is necessary to mention the importance of feeding trees and shrubs with manure and fertilisers after pruning. To remove a substantial number of stems bearing foliage puts a strain on those parts which remain, especially the roots which receive nourishment from the leaves.

The purpose of pruning trees and shrubs may be summarised as follows:

1 To **maintain a good 'natural' shape** by removing over-long or misshapen branches and, by maintaining a single leader to **promote upward growth**, if required at the apex, removing any rivals.
2 To **keep the plant healthy** by removal of diseased or dead wood.
3 To **allow light and air to reach the centre of the plant** by removal of weak or crowded shoots there, thus improving the quantity and quality of flowers.
4 To **remove dead flowers** as soon as they fade before seed formation begins, and so save the energy which would otherwise be spent on reproduction. Dead-heading like this may not be appropriate when fruits are decorative or grown for the table, but in the latter case it is often worth one's while to thin out after the normal 'drop' in early summer, as those that remain will develop better size and flavour with less competition.
5 To **promote replacement growth** by mulching and feeding, especially when pruning has been severe.
6 For wall plants and some climbers, pruning is part of **training** to take advantage of the sun and the extra heat reflected from the wall surface. You should maintain a horizontal position of shoots by tying them to supports. This checks the stimulus to growth and encourages the formation of flower buds.
7 For **fruit trees**, the goal of pruning is to promote the formation of a framework of fruiting spurs (see p206), and to maintain fruit production by selective pruning of trees and bushes.

EFFECTS OF PRUNING
Pruning cuts down the amount of growth that would otherwise be made. Taking away shoots and leaves of trees, shrubs or herbaceous plants reduces the amount of plant food that will be generated in the following season. However, although pruning destroys a number of growing points, it makes available to those that remain nitrogen and other elements essential to the making of cells and utilisation of carbohydrate. As a result, vegetative growth of the remaining shoots is promoted and the reproductive phase slows down. When fruit trees in their early years are pruned too hard new growth is encouraged by fruit buds which fail to develop. Pruning is a dwarfing action, especially in

summer. The notion that the increase in size of a tree after pruning is an optical illusion proves very difficult to accept. It was tentatively hinted at by the great American plantsman L. H. Bailey in *The Pruning Manual* (eighteenth edition, 1934), and has been confirmed by later experiments in the USA and Britain. It does not have any influence on the practice of pruning, but serves to remind us that what seems obvious may be an illusion.

An interesting fact, known to all experienced pruners, is that damage to an apical bud leads to growth of the highest lateral shoots below it. This effect is attributable to hormonal changes, though the diversion of nutrients to a new leader is probably involved also. The knowledge is of value when training a new leader, whether as a replacement at the apex of the plant or as a means of guiding the plant in a new direction - as, for example, when training a climbing rose into a horizontal position on a wall.

WHEN TO PRUNE
It is easier to say when *not* to prune.

1 When the soil is sodden after rain. Standing and walking round a tree or shrub compacts the soil and prevents moisture from penetrating to the roots. In gardens much visited by the public this compacting of the soil and direct damage to the roots near the surface is quite a serious problem, and may require that a precious specimen be roped off.
2 When there is frost, actual or forecast, or icy wind – the only exception is the mature tree, which foresters will prune regardless of frost.
3 When you do not have time to do it properly (stolen from Christopher Lloyd).
4 There are plants which should not be pruned when the sap is actively rising, as they will then respond to cutting by 'bleeding'. This is the exudation from the cut surface of a watery fluid, which is that part of sap which rises in the xylem channel. It is not easy to believe that this is harmless, though it does stop within hours usually or, if not, invariably ceases within a few days. However, some writers refer to 'die back' as a result. The entry here is intended to put minds at rest rather than as firm advice to prune the bleeders in autumn rather than spring. The bleeding tendency is described most often in maples, birch, walnut, poplar, and hornbeam.

Now, at last, when to prune. Common sense suggests that the best time is that which allows the longest period for the development and ripening of new growth before winter. Surely that must be correct for:

1 Flowering plants which carry their flowers on wood formed in the previous year, which should be pruned as soon as the flowers have faded.
2 Flowering plants that carry their flowers on wood formed from early spring onward and have the months until flowering begins to ripen their growth. It is now accepted practice to prune them at the end of winter, hoping that late frosts will not be severe.
3 Deciduous trees which can be pruned at any time, but usually from midsummer until Christmas (with respect for the antibleeding school). An exception to this rule is the genus *Prunus*, in particular plums and a few related species. The reason is silverleaf disease, which is caused by a fungus and declares itself by a change in leaf colour from green to silvery. Next the shoots and branches die and finally fruiting bodies, usually bracket-shaped but sometimes flat, appear on the affected wood, which is purple-tinted when cut. Wounds such as those of pruning provide a route of entry for the disease. There is only a limited period of the year when

infection is unlikely to occur, and that is in summer. Therefore pruning of plums should be carried out in that period (in Britain it is an offence to leave affected wood in place after 15 July). There is no effective treatment for the fungus infection but some experts advise fungicidal applications to wounds and cut surfaces after diseased limbs have been amputated (see *Prunus* in A-Z of Trees & Shrubs).

TOOLS

Of course it is necessary to have the best tools for pruning work. Generally speaking, the best are the most expensive to buy but are also the most enduring and one manufacturer offers spare parts which can keep a much-loved tool in good condition for ten years or more.

Pruning knives

The pruning knife is the badge of the professional gardener but is not much used by amateurs, though available in the major garden centres. It usually has a curved blade and a handle into which the blade folds. The knife is not easy to use without training and practice and it makes untidy cuts when wielded by the inexpert. It is useful in tidying up ragged cuts, which are apt to be made by secateurs, though one seldom sees the infected wound about which dire warnings are given in the literature. A knife must be kept clean and very sharp.

Secateurs

Secateurs also need looking after and that is more difficult. Inevitably the blades are blunted sooner or later, but most problems arise from incorrect use – especially from cutting or trying to cut a stem which is too thick or too hard. To be on the safe side, make 1cm (½in) the maximum diameter of stem you tackle with secateurs, unless you are

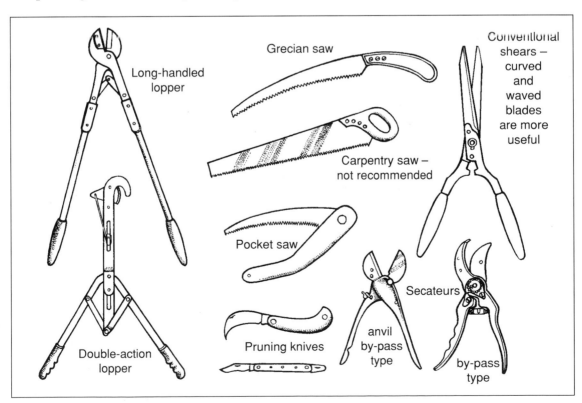

Long-handled lopper

Grecian saw

Conventional shears – curved and waved blades are more useful

Carpentry saw – not recommended

Pocket saw

Double-action lopper

Pruning knives

Secateurs

anvil

by-pass type

by-pass type

familiar with the plant. On some roses 2cm (¾in) would be quite easy to cut, but their old wood at the base would probably not be so amenable.

If you begin to cut and encounter firm resistance, give up at once. On no account use a twisting action, which can only cause an ugly and untidy cut and will probably damage the bearing of the blades and begin to loosen them. Instead, use a lopper or a pocket saw (see below).

The commonest type of secateur is the bypass or side-anvil, with one sharp thin blade and the other stouter, acting like scissors. The blades are curved, which helps to prevent the stem moving out of the jaws as they come together. It is probably wise, if cutting off a small shoot from a branch on the trunk of a tree, to make sure that the sharp blade is against the branch or trunk before cutting. The anvil type has a single blade which cuts onto a surface of soft metal. Both types have ardent supporters and there is evidently not much to choose between them. Some of the bypass models have refinements such as a rotating hand grip, which is comfortable and less tiring for the elderly or those who have a lot of pruning to do.

Secateurs are easy to use and, when carried on a stroll round the garden, can be as threatening as the hoe which gets rid of valuable self-sown seedlings, or the half-moon which insidiously but steadily moves the lawn edge from its intended line; but the vigilant gardener carries secateurs to deal with any unforeseen development.

Long-handled pruners

Long handled pruners or loppers are secateurs with a handle about 45cm (18in) long. They are often not quite strong enough for stems more than 3.5cm (1½in) thick, but that difficulty is partially solved by the double-action lopper. It is really sturdy and long-lived.

The pole pruner has lopper blades at the end of a pole about 3.9m (13ft) long. The cutting blade is operated by a strong wire running from the blade to the foot of the pole. It is not easy to use because a tool of this length is heavy, and awkward to control and to direct into a rather distant space. You think you have at last got it to the correct position and triumphantly bring the blades together, only to find that they are not enclosing the target stem. However, with practice it will deal with an old wisteria climbing to the roof of a house and prevents it getting involved with the gutter. The long slender shoots of summer are easily removed but any stout branches call for a ladder and saws.

Saws

Talking of saws, we left the pruner with his secateurs some way into a stem perhaps 2.5cm (1in) thick. The next stage is withdrawal and, after that, deployment of the pocket saw, which has a straight blade 15cm (6in) long and folds into the handle which is 190cm (7½in) overall. The teeth are not inclined but cut on pulling the tool back towards you. This saw makes a clean job of stems up to 7.5cm (3in) thick or a little more, if you hold the stem with your free hand to prevent it tearing off suddenly.

So we come to another saw which can be recommended wholeheartedly, the Grecian. It has a curved blade with teeth on one side only. These are disposed so that the cut is made as you withdraw the blade, which is an advantage especially when working up a ladder. Cutting is rather slow, but be patient.

For larger branches a bow saw with a narrow nose is very useful as it will fit into quite small spaces, cutting as you push away. After that there is a full-sized bow saw for larger branches. Use a ladder to get as near as possible to the end of the branch, then begin a piecemeal removal, taking off 0.9 or 1.2m (3 or 4ft) at a time and hoping to avoid damage to any underplanting. If the underplanting is

precious the cut pieces of branch can be lowered with a rope.

Shears

Shears are used for hedge-cutting, for topiary and for trimming some shrubs. They should have stainless steel blades and the nut and bolt holding the blades together must be easily tightened. Large shoots tend to move along the blades, narrowing the angle between them, and at the tips it is difficult – often impossible – to make a cut. Curved blades help and, better still, waved blades are quite effective. Shears are satisfactory for trimming compact hedges such as box (_Buxus sempervirens_), _Lonicera nitida_ or low-growing shrubs, for instance _Hypericum calycinum_ or ericas.

Hedge-trimmers

Power hedge-trimmers are driven by electricity or petrol. Electricity may come from

ABOVE:
A border beneath a wall 3.25m (10ft) high. Trained against this wall are two spring-flowering ceanothus and a _Clematis montana_. These plants need quite severe pruning once the flowers have faded. To their right in the picture is the Mexican evergreen shrub _Choisya Ternata_, surprisingly hardy and also flowering in spring. It grows slowly and seldom needs pruning. In the foreground is the hardy perennial _Euphorbia characias_ subspecies 'Wulfenii'. The stems which carry the flowers are cut away when the flowers fade

mains-charged batteries or directly from the mains. The mains-charged battery works with a light cordless machine which is easy to handle and effective for box, _Lonicera nitida_, privet and the trimming of yew. The mains electric machine has a wide price range and a more expensive model will tackle tough and neglected hedges, but its efficiency is limited by the length of the cable which loses power significantly at about 30m (30yd). This may suffice for a small garden, but otherwise a second power point may be necessary.

Finally, it is possible to run an electric trimmer from a 12V car battery. This uses a lot of current and soon exhausts the battery, unless it is possible to park the car nearby with the battery in it and keep the engine running. This system has some supporters.

Petrol-driven cutters are more satisfactory than electric if the hedges are extensive and old, but the machine is heavy and calls for a fit and muscular person (I nearly said man) to operate it. Two hours' trimming at a stretch is the most one can ask, perhaps less when working up a ladder. Using extra-long blades is not helpful unless the operator has acquired the skill needed to make sure of a smooth result.

The noise of these engines is really loud and it is definitely necessary to use earmuffs. In towns the neighbours will not appreciate it, especially at the weekend. An ideal day of gardening does not include engine noise and the whine of electric machines is especially maddening. Earmuffs exclude the many pleasant garden sounds which are part of the essence of gardening and are noticeably ab-sent in Italy, and other countries where the bird population is decimated. Young and fairly young gardeners do not seem to mind the engine noises, but perhaps they are conditioned by exposure to wallpaper noise on radio.

Chain-saws

Chain-saws hardly enter into a discussion of pruning, except of large branches or in the case of a tree falling in your or your neighbour's garden. For everyday use they are exceptionally noisy and quite frightening. We are now in an area which requires professional help – and be sure that the help is professional. Saw-happy cowboys abound.

A final word of caution. For many years the author, in his capacity as a physician, paid a fortnightly visit to a cottage hospital in the Teme valley, an area famous for its fruit. At certain seasons he could be sure that he would find at least one patient per visit with a fracture of thigh, pelvis or arm suffered through a fall from a tree while pruning or picking. These men were not beginners – they were very experienced but somewhat over-confident.

PART TWO

THE
PRACTICE
OF
PRUNING

Abbreviations:
cv - cultivar
var - variety
(D) - dcciduous
(E) - evergreen
(S/E) - semi-evergreen

A – Z
OF
TREES & SHRUBS

This chapter excludes conifers and climbers. See subsequent chapters for information on pruning these plants.

TREES

MAKING THE CUT

A young tree, grown at home or received from a nursery in its first year may be a 'whip', with a single stem and no side branches, or a 'maiden' with side branches known as 'feathers'. If the intention is to grow the tree with a single central leader, attention is focussed on that stem which must be protected from damage and from the competition of laterals forming near it. In the first year it is unlikely that any pruning will be needed but a stake is desirable, not only to avoid damage from wind-rock but also to mark the site of the tree in winter, when it can be forgotten.

In the second year look at the tree often, once a week at least, and make sure that the leader is still intact. If it is damaged or broken remove it completely. If you are skilled in using the pruning knife, this is the best tool to adopt for a job which may be rather difficult to approach without damaging the replacement shoot. If using secateurs, start the cut on the side opposite the bud about level with its lower end, cutting slightly upwards to end 5mm (¼in) above it. Then the next shoot

below is trained to take the place of the lost leader. This may involve tying to a cane placed as near upright as possible.

In autumn cut back the lower laterals by half. Watch still for any lateral threatening the leader, and remove such a lateral if necessary. In the next autumn cut away the lower laterals completely up to a height of 0.9-1.2m (3-4ft) on the tree, and reduce those above this height to half their length. In the next year these can be removed in autumn to leave a bare stem to 1.8m (6ft). From this point pruning can cease apart from general tidying, cutting away diseased or dead wood, and perhaps branches which get in the way of easy progress round the garden.

All the procedures named above are for secateurs, graduating to a pocket saw and finally a bow saw. At this stage we have to deal with sizeable branches, 7.5cm (3in) or more across, and it will be necessary to reduce them piecemeal. Take off about 45cm (18in) at each cut. Start by cutting the underside off the branch until the saw begins to bind, then transfer to the upper side and complete the removal of that section. The initial undercut ensures that the section does not split away and perhaps damage the bark. The final cut is made, not flush with the main stem but half an inch from it. There is a collar at the point where the branch takes off and this produces cambium which helps early

MAKING THE CUT – THE PRINCIPLES

Correct: cut
upwards
to a point
0.5cm (¼in)
above bud

Cut too far
from bud and
sloping
wrong way
(towards bud)

Cut too close
to bud

Rough cut;
too far
from bud

Cut sloping the
wrong way
(towards bud)

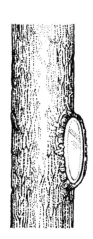

LEFT:
Before the cut

RIGHT:
After the final cut, showing collar

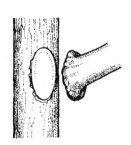

LEFT:
Effect of removing
a large limb with one cut

RIGHT:
A cut flush with the trunk
– best avoided

healing of the wound.

The practice of painting all wounds to avoid infection has now been generally abandoned as experiments have shown no benefit and perhaps occasional harm resulting. Paints make the wound less obvious for the first year. Some old gardeners believe that rubbing earth on them does good.

SHRUBS

The general instructions given above apply equally to the pruning of shrubs – all cuts should be tidy (no whiskers) and encourage healing. Trees and shrubs differ only in the need to give height to the tree by removing the lower branches, to promote flowering on shrubs and, in a few cases, to cut them to the ground each spring to produce young leaves of good form and colour. The frequency and extent of pruning vary from shrub to shrub, and are discussed under individual entries.

Remember always that pruning provokes growth from the stem that is cut. If a shrub becomes lopsided, prune the side which is the weaker and leave the overgrown side alone or prune very lightly (see p22).

A-Z

ABELIA (Caprifoliaceae)
A genus of shrubs most of which are not hardy in Britain without wall protection. They like a good loamy soil.

A. grandiflora (*chinensis uniflora*) (D)
Pallanza, Lake Maggiore, 1886. A shrub 0.9-1.8m (3-6ft) high with arching branches and shining dark green leaves, the flowers in midsummer white, tinged pink, and often continuing until autumn. They are carried on wood of the current year and some shoots may be shortened after flowering, with some of the oldest wood removed. This plant is hardy in all but the severest winters and will grow to 3m (10ft) in the shelter of a wall. None of the species is better or as hardy.

ABELIOPHYLLUM DISTICHUM (*Oleaceae*) (D)
Korea. Needs good soil and yearly feeding. It is best grown against a south-facing wall when it lacks the hot sun of its native region. The fragrant flowers appear in late winter before the leaves. Strong shoots develop to 3m (10ft) in height and are tied to supports. The laterals are allowed to remain and about one third are cut back to 0.5m (18in) after flowering to maintain vigorous growth.

ABUTILON (*Malvaceae*) (S/E)
A. megapotamicum Brazil. Needs a south-facing wall where it will grow to 1.8m (6ft). The flowers appear from late spring for several months; the calyx is red and the corolla yellow, an unhappy combination in this case not improved in the form with variegated leaves. Shoots damaged by frost should be cut back to live wood in spring.

A. × suntense (*ochsenii × vitifolium*) is vigorous and free-flowering deep mauve in spring. It should be dead-headed and cut back after flowering. If the height is as intended, no pruning of the leader is required, but laterals are reduced to 30cm (1ft). If the plant has grown too tall, reduce the leader to the appropriate level; laterals should be reduced as before. It is best grown in the shelter of a wall, as is *A. × vitifolium album* from Chile, which also needs shelter and flowers for at least two months. Pruning is as for *A. × suntense*.

Abutilons usually have a short life, sometimes dying for no obvious reason. They are easily propagated from cuttings.

ACER (*Aceraceae*) (D)
A very large genus, of which only a few can be included. It is said that maples are very easily cultivated, and some are, but it is clear that a few are reluctant to develop in soils which suit most other plants. One must suspect that failure may be due to an alkaline soil and at the Morton Arboretum in Phila-

CORRECTING UNEVEN GROWTH

1 This shrub is overgrown on the right hand side, undergrown on the left. The cure is to prune the weaker side heavily, which will respond with strong growth. The overgrown side should be pruned only lightly, if at all

2 The result: a nicely balanced shrub

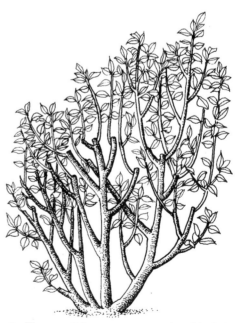

3 Here the shrub has been incorrectly pruned, by cutting back the overgrown side heavily

4 The result is an even more lopsided shrub

delphia a soil pH of 5.5-6.5 is recommended for maples. On the other hand, *The Hillier Manual of Trees and Shrubs* (1991) lists only two maples out of 86 as requiring lime-free or neutral soil.

Acer campestre Europe, N Africa. COMMON FIELD MAPLE is a fine tree, sometimes over 16m (50ft) high, but also serves as a hedge (see Hedges & Topiary). There is usually no difficulty in training a leader and producing a leg of 3m (10ft). The branching tends to be close and this need not be discouraged except in the case of erect shoots towards the end of a branch.

A. forrestii China, 1906, has snake-bark which is revealed by creating a leg of 1.8-2.4m (6-8ft). The young stems are coral red. This tree is almost certainly lime-hating.

A. griseum China, 1901. A small tree occasionally reaching 12m (40ft), with bark which peels to reveal the cinnamon-coloured underbark. The leaves have three leaflets which colour red and scarlet in autumn. It is a most handsome tree, slow of growth and eminently suited to modest gardens. It seems to tolerate any good soil. Arnold Forster (1948) remarks that it needs coaxing in Cornwall, but has no problems in Dorset. It is hardy.

A. japonicum Japan. Favoured for its cultivars, especially 'Vitifolium' with large leaves which produce autumn colours – purple, crimson, scarlet and orange.

A. negundo N America. BOX ELDER is most often seen in its variegated form and, especially if pruned, is likely to produce shoots with green leaves which should at once be removed, but are likely to recur. Don't give up.

A. palmatum Japan, 1820, is a small tree with a round head which has given rise to a large number of clones and cultivars, the best known being the Dissectum group of which the outstanding member is 'Senkaki', the CORAL BARK MAPLE. All the younger branches of this are coral red, and the deeply cut

leaves are pale green turning to yellow in autumn.

A. pensylvanicum MOOSEWOOD. Eastern N America. This is a small tree with brown bark striped with white lines and the cultivar 'Erythrocladum' is even more striking, with young shoots shrimp-pink in winter.

A. platanoides Continental Europe, not Britain. Immensely vigorous. Not suitable for gardens under 4ha (10 acres), but the cultivar 'Drummondii' with white variegation of the leaves is so handsome that it would justify the loss of half a hectare or so.

A. saccharinum Eastern N America, 1725, is very vigorous and very beautiful, not too common a combination. The bark is grey and gave it the name SILVER MAPLE. The leaves are five-lobed and in a mild winter it produces yellow flowers in early spring. The only fault is some brittleness of the wood, not important when it is grown in an open space. As a rule, it makes a well-shaped crown without any training.

Pruning of maples follows the general indications and there are few specific requirements. One should be prepared for the possibility of 'bleeding' if pruning is undertaken early in the growing season, which may be taken to start at Christmas. In some of the trees it is desirable to produce a leg which will display the bark, as has been noted for *A. forrestii* and some others.

AESCULUS (Hippocastanaceae)
HORSE CHESTNUT, BUCKEYE (D)

Deciduous trees or shrubs, all having compound palmate leaves and flowers in racemes. They do well in any good soil, transplant easily and are hardy.

A. × carnea (Hippocastanum × pavia) RED HORSE CHESTNUT is most often seen now as the cultivar 'Briotii' with red flowers. It branches low down and this form can be maintained, if allowing ample space for the effect to be seen. If a leader is maintained it will reach 9-12m (30-40ft) with a leg of 3m (10ft). This

DECIDUOUS SHRUBS, TYPE A

Most evergreen shrubs will develop well if planted in the appropriate soil and will flower within a few years. The same is true of some deciduous shrubs, and nothing is gained by unnecessary pruning.
The following are good examples:

Aronia arbutifolia
Berberis thunbergii
Chionanthus virginicus
Clethra, all deciduous species
Colutea arborescens
Cornus mas, C. florida
Cotoneaster horizontalis
Euonymus europaeus
Fothergilla major
Genista tenera
Halesia carolina
Halimium ocymoides
Hydrangea quercifolia
Ilex verticillata
Jasminum nudiflorum
Ligustrum quihoui
Parrotia persica
Poncirus trifoliata
Prunus mume, P. tenella
Rhus typhina
Salix hastata 'Wehrhahnii'

chestnut is apt to develop burrs on the trunk and main branches. Their nature is uncertain but often healing keeps pace with their development and only leaves an unsightly swelling.

A. hippocastanum HORSE CHESTNUT. N Greece, Albania. The most beautiful of large flowering trees, but only for quite large gardens of not less than 0.2ha (half an acre). When mature, it makes a very large tree with heavy branches. In towns it is a target for collectors of 'conkers' in autumn, and they will stop at nothing. In the nursery stage a central leader must be maintained by removal of any rivals. As the tree grows there is a tendency to produce upright limbs from the laterals and these should be cut away if possible. Longitudinal cracks on the bark are a cause for concern but often they are due to rapid enlargement of the trunk and heal quite quickly. All in all, the Horse Chestnut maintains good health for many years without much attention.

A. indica NW Himalaya, flowers a month later and becomes a very large and graceful tree with no problems, and that includes pruning.

A. parviflora SE USA. Grows to 2.4m (8ft) high but spreads widely and produces suckers. They help to produce a clump which looks splendid in midsummer, as may be seen at Westonbirt in Gloucestershire. The flowers are white. This plant only needs pruning if space is limited.

AILANTHUS ALTISSIMA
(Simaroubiaceae) (D)

N China. The Asian name, meaning TREE OF HEAVEN, suggests that it is not suitable for the garden. Nevertheless, it became very common in London gardens because it proved very tolerant of atmospheric pollution. It can

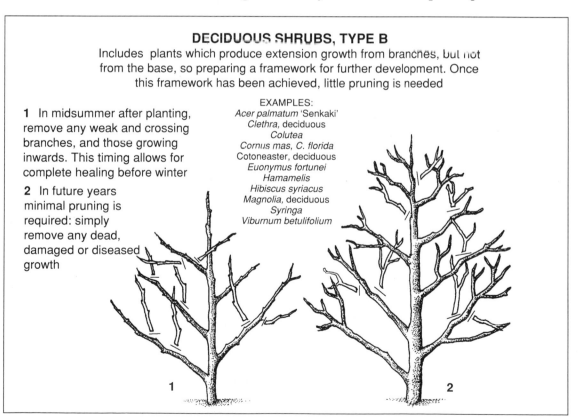

DECIDUOUS SHRUBS, TYPE B

Includes plants which produce extension growth from branches, but not from the base, so preparing a framework for further development. Once this framework has been achieved, little pruning is needed

1 In midsummer after planting, remove any weak and crossing branches, and those growing inwards. This timing allows for complete healing before winter

2 In future years minimal pruning is required: simply remove any dead, damaged or diseased growth

EXAMPLES:
Acer palmatum 'Senkaki'
Clethra, deciduous
Colutea
Cornus mas, C. florida
Cotoneaster, deciduous
Euonymus fortunei
Hamamelis
Hibiscus syriacus
Magnolia, deciduous
Syringa
Viburnum betulifolium

1

2

LEFT:

Abutilon x suntense. A very successful hybrid *(ochsenii x vitifolium)*, vigorous and with the dark mauve flowers produced freely. Lateral growths are shortened by half in spring

RIGHT:

Acer platanoides 'Drummondii' is an elegant tree which develops a broad, spreading head over time. The leaves are margined with cream – occasionally branches revert to green and should be removed

be useful in small gardens if cut to the ground each spring. The emerging buds are reduced to two or three which will produce handsome ash-like leaves 0.9m (3ft) long and give an almost tropical effect.

ALNUS (Betulaceae) (D)

An unfairly neglected genus including several first-rate trees and shrubs. The fact that alders flourish in wet land of very little value may give them a poor reputation but there are great trees such as *A. cordata* and worthy shrubs such as *A. maximowiczii*.

A. cordata Sicily, Corsica. ITALIAN ALDER prefers a good soil and tolerates chalk. It is fast-growing and reaches 21m (70ft) in time. No pruning.

A. glutinosa COMMON ALDER. Europe including Britain. Will make a big tree with a fine bark but is seldom allowed to do so. Some river authorities sadly but understandably cut it to the ground every few years.

A. incana Europe, Caucasus. GREY ALDER is remarkably vigorous and completely hardy. The male catkins are 10cm (4in) long in the late winter and very pretty. The cultivar 'Aurea' has red-yellow young wood, striking all through winter. Pruning is cosmetic only.

A. maximowiczii Japan, is a large shrub with prominent yellow catkins in spring.

So there is a collection of hardy, healthy, undemanding plants, scorning the pruner and enhancing any garden of medium or greater size.

AMELANCHIER (Rosaceae) (D)

A. canadensis Canada. Commonly grown but often confused with **A. laevis** (USA, Canada), both being large shrubs with many white flowers in spring. Unfortunately these are of short duration, but are compensated by a lengthy period of red leaf colour in autumn. *A. canadensis* is a suckering shrub and the oldest stems are cut away in winter. *A. laevis* can be trained to tree form by reducing the side shoots in spring.

AMORPHA FRUTICOSA
(Leguminosae) (D)

SE USA, 1724. No amount of pruning can make it a worthwhile garden plant. It flowers in midsummer and after that untidy shoots can be cut back. It is available from some nurseries.

DECIDUOUS SHRUBS, TYPE C

Includes plants which flower on wood of the previous year, either laterals or small shoots on the branches themselves

EXAMPLES:
Cytisus scoparius and cultivars
Deutzia
Forsythia
Hydrangea macrophylla
(delay pruning until spring, see p78)
Kolkwitzia
Philadelphus
Ribes sanguinem
Stephanandra
Tamarix, spring flowering

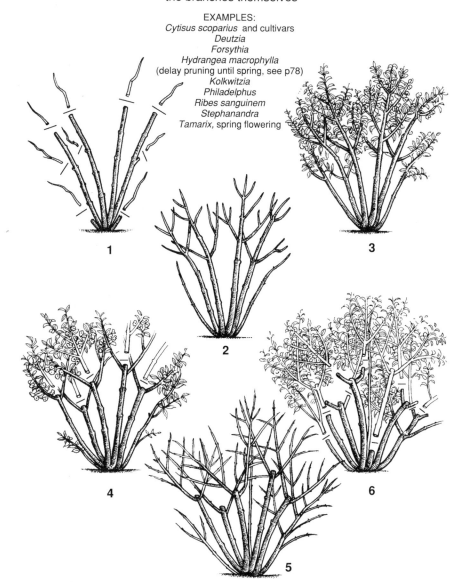

1 A three-year-old shrub at planting. Remove weak shoots, prune strong stems by 15cm (6in)
2 By autumn of the first year stems have grown well and laterals have formed
3 In the second year moderate flowering occurs in early summer
4 Immediately after flowering, cut back the main stems which carried the flowers to strong young growth or buds
5 By autumn the young shoots have grown well. Mulch in winter
6 Repeat pruning after flowering in the following and subsequent summers

ANDROMEDA POLIFOLIA
(Rosaceae) (D) BOG ROSEMARY. Cold areas of N hemisphere. Needs a damp, acid soil and makes an evergreen shrub 0.3m (1ft) high with dark green leaves and clusters of pink flowers in late spring. No pruning needed.

ANTHYLLIS HERMANNIAE
(Leguminosae) (D)
Mediterranean region. A small, deciduous shrub, not more than 0.6m (2ft) high with crooked branches, having grey leaves and yellow flowers in early summer. It needs a sunny place. Discreet cutting back by about half after flowering is indicated.

ARALIA *(Araliaceae)* (D)
Two species with very similar characteristics from different continents.

A. elata JAPANESE ANGELICA TREE. Japan, Korea, Russian Far East, 1830. A deciduous shrub or tree which, if left alone in good conditions, branches freely to become a large crooked shrub or occasionally a tree of character with compound leaves and small, off-white flowers in very large panicles over 0.3m (1ft) long. More or less hardy in most northerly areas, it is remarkable in Cornwall (SW England) where the branches spread 6m (20ft) or more on a tree 9m (30ft) high. Clearly it requires a large and favourable site to avoid the need for pruning, which spoils its shape. However, suckers often form and should be removed.

A. spinosa HERCULES' CLUB. USA. This tree is not so hardy and is rare in cultivation.

ARBUTUS *(Ericaceae)* (E)
A . × andrachnoides, including many plants sold as *A. andrachne*, is most desirable. Not requiring acid soil, it shows tenderness only in severe winters. Growth is quite fast and it should be allowed plenty of space, enough to show the ruddy brown bark and the flowers in late autumn and winter. Pruning is only required for the removal of dead shoots at

---

DECIDUOUS SHRUBS, TYPE D
Includes less vigorous plants which bear flowers on the current year's growth

EXAMPLES:
Caryopteris
Ceanothus deciduous
Spartium junceum

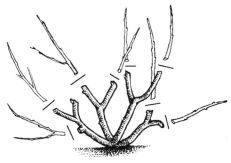

In the first year shorten main shoots by an inch or two in early spring

Strong shoots bear the flowers in late summer

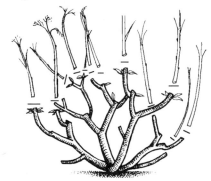

In the following spring the previous year's growth is cut back by one half. All weak growth is removed and in subsequent years all wood produced in the previous year is cut back to two buds

the centre, which hide the bark. Damage from frost or storm may be dealt with radically; regeneration will soon occur and the new growth is obvious.

A. menziesii W USA, Madrona, is only hardy in southern Britain and is extremely calcifuge. It flowers in late spring.

A. unedo STRAWBERRY TREE Mediterranean, Ireland. A small tree which does well in SW Britain and Ireland where it is native (Killarney). Withstanding gales, it needs no pruning.

ARCTOSTAPHYLOS (Ericaceae) (E)

Western N America. Prostrate shrubs which must have acid soil. All are evergreen and several are worthy of a place in the garden. Most often grown in Britain is *A. uva ursi*, the BEARBERRY, a trailing shrub of the N hemisphere, useful for ground cover. It has plentiful green foliage and small pinkish flowers from early spring, followed by red fruits. It is a good plant for sandy soil. If it encroaches on neighbouring plants, individual shoots may be removed entirely, so preserving an informal appearance.

ARONIA (Rosaceae) (D)

Two species related to *Sorbus* from Eastern N America, c1700.

A. arbutifolia RED CHOKEBERRY is a vigorous shrub 1.6-3m (5-10ft) high. Leaves narrowly obovate, toothed, dark green above, the lower surface covered by a white felt. White flowers appear in late spring and are followed by bright red fruits, then the leaves turn brilliant red until they fall.

A. melanocarpa BLACK CHOKEBERRY is a small shrub with white flowers in spring, followed by black fruits.

These shrubs produce shoots from the base when well manured and, when necessary, old growth can be cut away entirely after the autumn display is over, which may be in midwinter. They do not readily tolerate chalk in the soil.

ARTEMISIA (Compositae)

A genus with many herbaceous species and a few that are woody.

A. abrotanum Mediterranean. Has been in England since the sixteenth century and has been valued for the aromatic scent of its undistinguished leaves. A long-lived plant, it likes a sunny position but does reasonably well in shade. It is hardy and is cut back in spring every year.

A. arborescens Mediterranean, is tender but has choice silver leaves and is worth risking in front of a wall. It is pruned severely in spring. The cultivar 'Faith Raven' is more hardy and a better plant.

A. tridentata W USA. SAGEBRUSH has silvery grey leaves which give out a pleasant aroma even after a shower of rain. It is comparatively hardy and is pruned hard in spring.

ATRAPHAXIS BILLARDIERI
(Polygonaceae) A BUCKWHEAT (D)

Needs a well-drained soil and plenty of sun. It makes a shrub, almost prostrate with pointed leaves and flowers in a cluster in early summer. The sepals persist, enclosing the fruit, and their rose colour has a long season. Some of the older wood can be cut away in spring for the sake of tidiness.

ATRIPLEX (Chenopodiaceae) (D)

Of the GOOSEFOOT family. All tend to sprawl, especially in rich soil, and may be trimmed in spring to produce a regular shape. *A. canescens* and *A. confertifolia* are natives of western America, evergreen and growing to

(continued on p33)

Berberis thunbergii 'Rose Glow' is a very striking shrub, its young leaves being purple mottled with pink. Later in the summer the leaves become a deep purple

DECIDUOUS SHRUBS, TYPE E

Includes plants which flower on the previous year's wood and produce
nearly all their new growth from ground level

EXAMPLES:
Kerria
Prunus tenella
Spiraea arguta

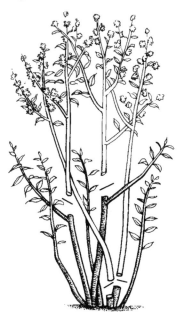

A young shrub at planting.
Remove any weak stems;
otherwise, do not prune

After flowering, cut all shoots to
the base, except for one or two which
have produced strong laterals

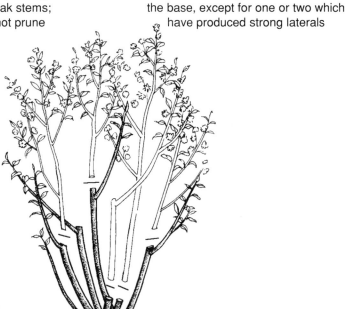

This pruning routine is repeated in subsequent years

1.2m (4ft) or rather more. The flowers are yellow and very small, borne in midsummer. The grey leaves are pleasant.

A. halimus TREE PURSLANE. Europe. The 5cm (2in) long leaves are silvery and of excellent appearance, the flowers negligible, often absent. Though scorched by frost it recovers in spring. Pruning is seldom necessary.

AUCUBA JAPONICA (Cornaceae) (E)

Japan, c1861. The green-leaved form is less common than the yellow-spotted 'Variegata' which came to England in 1783. The former arrived in about 1860 and the females produce scarlet berries, but not regularly. Even without them, the green-leaved form is more stylish and worth a place in the garden. Both forms are hardy and endure the most unfavourable conditions of shade and competition. Dead wood remains on the bush indefinitely without causing any ill effect other than ugliness. Removal with the Grecian saw is easy; otherwise no pruning is needed.

AZARA (Flacourtiaceae) (E)

Chile.

A. lanceolata is moderately hardy and, after a hot summer, produces a spectacular display of yellow flowers in spring, small but crowded in corymbs.

A. microphylla, 1861, is evergreen and also quite hardy, with small dark leaves with fragrant yellow flowers in early spring. Neither of these shrubs needs any routine pruning, but tidying up after an average winter can be tedious.

BERBERIS (Berberidaceae)

This is a good example of the importance of finding out the height and spread to be expected of a plant before deciding to put it in the garden. There are dwarf berberis, others which reach 2.4m (8ft) high but remain neat, and some less high which arch widely.

B. darwinii Chile 1849. This plant is among the evergreens and is very hardy, flourishing in any good soil, including chalk, and producing a fine show of orange flowers in late spring, followed by luminous blue fruits. What more can one say of any shrub? It is admittedly rather untidy and needs some pruning. The temptation to do so after the flowers fade should be resisted if the fruits appeal. They will have disappeared by midsummer and any over-long shoots can then be cut back by two-thirds.

B. linearifolia Chile, Argentina, 1927, is perhaps even better, with flowers of a more refined colour, and is equally hardy.

B. × stenophylla (*darwinii* × *empetrifolia*) makes a dense bush from which emerge arching stems covered with golden-yellow flowers. The fruits can be sacrificed and pruning carried out immediately after flowering, preferably using secateurs and reducing long shoots by a half.

B. verruculosa W China 1904 is notable for its tidy form, reaching 1.8m (6ft) high and 1.2m (4ft) across; it seldom needs any pruning.

B. dictyophylla China. Of the deciduous shrubs, this attracts by its slender branches, covered in their first year by a white bloom. The flowers are pale yellow, the fruits red. Some of the older stems should be cut out each winter, followed by ample manuring. It is not perfectly hardy, and should be put in a sheltered place.

B. × rubrostilla is notable for abundant coral-coloured fruits. It is a hybrid of *B. wilsoniae*, the other parent not determined.

B. temolaica Tibet, grows rather slowly to 2.4m(8ft) with glaucous pale green leaves and pale yellow flowers, not abundant. When fully grown it is a magnificent sight. No pruning needed.

B. thunbergii (D) Japan, 1870. A shrub of dense habit reaching 2.4m (8ft). It is valued for the fine red colour of the leaves in autumn and the bright red berries, but in Britain neither of these is as striking as in the USA and its native Japan. The cultivar 'Rose Glow' is not as large as the type, and has purple

DECIDUOUS SHRUBS, TYPE F

Includes vigorous plants which produce a woody framework and flower on the current year's growth

EXAMPLES:
Buddleia davidii   *Cotinus coggygria*
Cornus stolonifera   *Sambucus nigra* 'Guincho Purple'

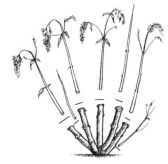

In early spring cut all healthy shoots back to 30cm (1ft). Discard others

By summer the shrub will have doubled in size, and flowers are borne at the end of shoots

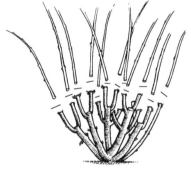

In late winter cut all shoots back to 30cm (1ft) as before. Repeat annually, manuring well in spring

---

leaves with pink and white variegation.

B. wilsoniae W China, reaches 1.2m (4ft) high, rather more across. The flowers and fruits are abundant and the leaves colour well in autumn, in tints too difficult to describe.

BETULA (Betulaceae) BIRCH (D)

Deciduous trees and a few shrubs, nearly all of character and beauty. Most need a good deep loam to thrive but *B. pendula*, the SILVER BIRCH, tolerates a thin sandy site.

B. nigra E USA, 1736. The RIVER BIRCH, does well near water.

B. albo-sinensis China, 1901. Makes a big tree and its trunk of bright orange to orange-red elicited lyrical descriptions from E. H. Wilson, who introduced it to England in 1901. Its var. *septentrionalis,* collected by Wilson in another area of China, was described by him as having 'Bark orange-brown or orange to yellowish-orange or orange-grey . . . singularly beautiful.' The beauty is often marred somewhat by the old bark persisting on the tree.

B. alleghaniensis Eastern N America, c1767. Formerly *B. lutea*, this tree has shining amber-coloured bark and the leaves turn rich yellow in autumn.

B. lenta Eastern N America, 1759. CHERRY BIRCH was considered by Bean to be unsatisfactory in Britain, where it is not common.

B. maximowicziana Japan, 1893, is very vigorous and makes a wide crown. The trunk is orange-brown becoming grey. The large leaves colour well in autumn.

B. medwediewii Caucasus, 1897. Makes a large shrub with stout branches and large terminal buds. Good autumn colour.

B. papyrifera PAPER BIRCH. N America, 1750.

OPPOSITE:
Bupleurum fruticosum is a shapely evergreen shrub which needs little pruning except to keep its development in check. Its yellow umbels followed by buff seedheads give it a long season of beauty

EVERGREEN SHRUBS

These do not need systematic pruning if the space required for the mature plant has been carefully considered. Growths which protrude from the plant in isolation should be removed in spring

EXAMPLES:
Arbutus andrachnoides
Artemisia
Ballota pseudodictamnus
Berberis darwinii
Bupleurum fruticosum
Camellia
Cotoneaster lacteus
Daphne burkwoodii
Eleagnus pungens
Escallonia rubra 'Apple Blossom'
Hebe (many)
Hypericum kouytchense
Mahonia (most)
Olearia macrodonta
Pieris formosa 'Wakehurst'
Rhododendron (many)
Sarcococca

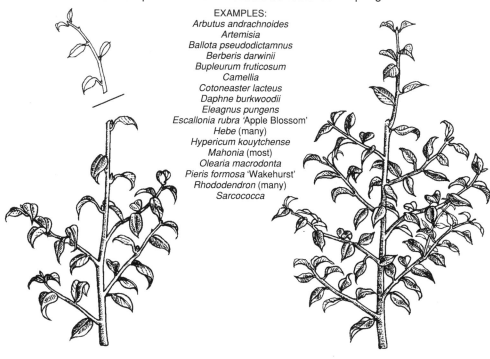

A young camellia with failing leader. In the first spring, cut it back to a healthy bud. Apply a lime-free mulch

By summer there has been considerable improvement all over. Train in the new leader

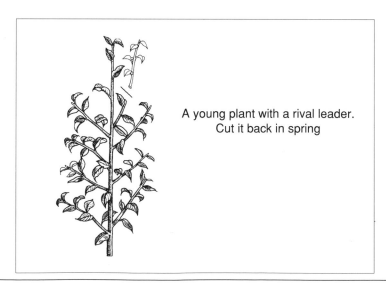

A young plant with a rival leader. Cut it back in spring

Does well in Britain and has clean white bark. Good autumn colour.

B. pendula COMMON SILVER BIRCH. Europe, including Britain. Can be 18-21m (60-70ft) tall under good conditions. It is one of the best birches, particularly in its graceful outline. The cultivar 'Laciniata', SWEDISH BIRCH, with drooping shoots and cut leaves is nearly as good.

B. utilis HIMALAYAN BIRCH. Himalayas, China, 1849. A tree of medium size which has orange or copper-brown peeling bark.

Pruning is mainly directed towards establishing a leader in those specimens that are to become trees. If the leader is broken in the early stages the replacement should be the strongest growing shoot, at whatever level it is situated. Any pruning necessary for birches should be carried out in autumn, as in spring there is a tendency for bleeding to occur (see p12). 'Witches' brooms', of fungal origin, are seen mostly on B. pendula. Their exact nature is obscure but they may be present and multiply for years without affecting the health of the tree (see Glossary).

BROUSSONETIA PAPYRIFERA
(Moraceae) (D)

China, Japan, in early eighteenth century. Makes a round-headed tree and is notable for the variable outline of the leaves, both in size and form. On young trees no two leaves may be identical but the difference becomes less obvious as the tree matures. The male catkins, up to 7.5cm (3in) long, are pleasant and the female has orange-red fruits. Branches often grow from low down and may need removing, or can be allowed to extend, according to the space available.

BUDDLEJA (Loganiaceae) (D)

Medium to large shrubs, a few making small trees, they all like good soil but survive in a feeble state in rough ground. For the gardener they may be classified according to flowering pattern.

1 Those which flower mainly on wood of the previous year; the best known is **B. alternifolia** (China, 1915), which produces arching stems bearing flowers freely in early summer. These stems are cut back after flowering to new growth, which by then is appearing.

2 Those which flower at the end of shoots produced in the current year, including **B. davidii** (China, 1900) and its many cultivars. The shoots are left after flowering until late winter, when all are cut back to 0.3m (1ft). They can be relied on to produce a symmetrical arching bush each year, but must be well manured after pruning.

3 Those which develop strong shoots in one year and flower in the next on buds which develop from these shoots. Such is **B. globosa** (Chile, Peru, 1774), an erect shrub with handsome leaves and, in early summer, globular flower heads. In early spring weak growths may be removed. It is tempting to do no pruning after flowering but the shrub can grow to 6m (20ft) and become gaunt. If that happens it must be cut back drastically, perhaps to 1m (3ft) all over, with the loss of a year's flowering.

BUPLEURUM FRUTICOSUM (E)

S Europe, Mediterranean region, c1670. Hardy if given reasonable shelter from north and east. In thirty years' experience the author has never known it seriously damaged by frost. In spite of this it has a reputation for tenderness and perhaps this is why it is relatively uncommon. It does look as if it should be tender. It will grow to 2.4 or 2.7m (8 or 9ft) high and rather more across. It is pruned in spring, cutting back all shoots to about 0.9m (3ft). More drastic pruning will only produce rather longer and weaker growth.

BUXUS (Buxaceae) (E)

Mainly used for hedging and the edging of

borders but one at least, **B. balearica**, (Balearic Isles, before 1780), makes a tree of character with good bright green leaves. It bears shade, even quite dense, and should never need pruning as its habit is compact.

B. sempervirens COMMON BOX. S Europe, N Africa, W Asia. Can reach a height of 6m (20ft) but is rarely allowed to do so, as it is too slow in growth to encourage its use as an ornamental tree.

B. wallichiana (_Himalayan_) NW Himalayas. Reached a height of about 1.8m (6ft) in fifty years at the Royal Botanic Gardens, Kew but is rather tender, both discouraging features (see also Hedges & Topiary).

CALLICARPA BODINIERI var. _Giraldii_ (_Verbenaceae_) (D)

China, 1800. An erect, deciduous shrub reaching 2.4-2.7m (8-9ft). It must have plenty of sun and a good soil. It is perfectly hardy. The flowers are diminutive and lilac-coloured, borne in midsummer, and are followed by abundant small violet fruits. The plant has at first an upright growth, but shoots extending outward from the base become almost horizontal. Any pruning to

maintain shape is carried out in spring. If the plant seems to be failing and flowering poorly, cut it to 30cm (1ft) from the ground in autumn and manure well. It may soon recover and flower well the next year. The name of the genus, as Greek scholars will recognise, refers to the beauty of the fruits.

CALLISTEMON (_Myrtaceae_) (E)

Natives of Australia, they only flourish in mild maritime climates and even there benefit from protection from the north and east. **C. speciosus** 1825, makes a large shrub or small tree to 4.5m (15ft) high. If given wall protection it should be planted 0.6-0.9m (2-3ft) from the wall, as it has a rounded shape. It does not like chalky soil but otherwise needs only plenty of sunlight. The flowers are borne in spikes 15cm (6in) long, the stamens rich crimson, hence the name _Bottle Brush_ given to the genus. The fruit is a capsule firmly attached to the branch and able to persist for years. The growing point continues to extend beyond this and in the next year produces a stem, leaves and eventually another flower head. For this reason pruning should be withheld except for correcting the shape of the plant.

CALLUNA VULGARIS (_Ericaceae_)

HEATHER, LING (E)

On its native moorlands of Europe (including Britain) it is an untidy shrub up to 0.9m (3ft) high, with long growths which hide the bare stems for a while but eventually become thin with few leaves. Under garden conditions the growth is vigorous at first but in the end results in lengths of bare stem and hardly any leaf.

Pruning can be very effective in maintaining the early state. The procedure consists of cutting back all shoots by at least one half but avoiding the old wood, which does not readily break into leaf. Secateurs produce the best effect but if shears have to be used you should ensure that you do not produce a smooth

Calluna vulgaris: cut back by at least half in spring, avoiding old wood

civilised surface, but something which looks natural. Meanwhile, cuttings should be kept going to provide replacement plants when old age at last prevails. The flowers, in racemes 15-30cm (6-12in) long, vary from white or pink to red or crimson in the many cultivars.

CALYCANTHUS FLORIDUS

(Calycantheaceae) CAROLINA ALLSPICE (D) Carolina, 1726. A good-looking deciduous shrub which has no special needs except for ample sunlight – not unknown in Carolina, but uncommon in Britain. The leaves are dark green and should be evergreen, but drop rather suddenly in autumn. The flowers in early summer are fragrant, reddish-purple and brown. Leaves, wood and even roots have the fragrance of camphor. There is little for the pruner here.

CAMELLIA (Theaceae) (E)

A huge genus of compelling, obsessive interest to many gardeners who have the conditions to grow them well, and of envy to many who have not. They must have a moist, lime-free soil and do well at planting if given some peat or a substitute and leaf mould. They are evergreen shrubs or trees, widely distributed in Asia and first known in Britain at the end of the seventeenth century. *C. japonica* Japan, the COMMON CAMELLIA, was introduced from China in 1739. Others followed and camellias became enormously popular as conservatory plants until the late nineteenth century, when people became bored with them. The introduction of *C. saluenensis* (China, 1924) changed that since it led to the creation of hybrids.

The winter of 1928-9 was very harsh in Britain and showed that camellias are in fact among the hardiest of evergreen shrubs. Their defect is that the flowers are very easily damaged by even minor spring frosts. Therefore a site with minimal risk of spring frost must be chosen.

DEAD-HEADING

Camellias share with rhododendrons the capacity to flower with abandon and produce a lot of seed. It is logical to dispose of any seed that is not needed for reproduction and thus spare the plant the output of energy required in that process. This is achieved by removing the flower heads as the blooms fade, a tedious task with large bushes – desirable, but not vital

As a rule very little pruning is needed. Stems that spoil the shape of the plant may be cut back in the dormant season except for *C. sasanqua* (Japan, 1896) and other autumn-flowering kinds, for which spring is the right time. The object is to produce a dense texture, allowing branches which develop low down to grow. Some plants, when young, flower very freely and may be partly disbudded. On the other hand a worn-out shrub,

DECIDUOUS SHRUBS, TYPE G

Includes plants which flower on the current year's growth and do not produce a woody framework

EXAMPLES:
Ceratostigma
Dorycnium
Fuchsias, hardy
Leycesteria
Perovskia

In the spring after planting, cut back to one or two buds

The plant will flower in late summer to autumn

Prune again to two buds each spring. Leaving the shrub unpruned leads to weak stems and no flowers within a year or two

hardly flowering, may be pruned heavily removing up to half the total plant by cutting back stems by half. With liberal feeding regeneration may occur quite rapidly. Young flower buds damaged by late frost are best left until the level at which live tissue begins is revealed. This can be decided by scratching a small area of bark: the underlying tissue is pale and juicy if alive, brown and dry if dead.

CARAGANA (*Leguminosae*) (D)

C. arborescens Siberia, Manchuria, 1752. This is the easiest to grow and has several interesting cultivars. Young plants left alone for one season may in the spring of the following year be reduced by rather more than a half, to encourage the formation of laterals and build up a sturdy plant. To form a tree, a leader is selected and maintained in the usual way (see p19).

CARPENTERIA CALIFORNICA (*Philadelphaceae*) (E)

This is the only species, discovered by Colonel Fremont about 1850 and first flowered in Britain by Miss Jekyll in 1885. In southern England it is hardy near a south or west-facing wall, preferably 0.6-0.9m (2-3ft) from it to allow the formation of a bush. It is not easy to train on supporting wires. It likes an average soil and should not be too heavily fed, since this encourages the formation of tender shoots. Worn-out shoots may be removed entirely and young shoots from the base encouraged.

CARPINUS (*Carpinaceae*) (D)

Only a few are in cultivation of 45 known species, all from the temperate regions of the N hemisphere. They do well in any good soil, not objecting to lime, and are very hardy.
C. betulus COMMON HORNBEAM a British native, indigenous to eastern England, Essex in particular. It can reach 21m (70ft) high but is usually not more than 18m (60ft). The trunk

becomes fluted, which quickly distinguishes it from the beech. The leaves are ribbed and turn a good yellow in autumn. The fruiting catkins, 7.5cm (3in) long, are conspicuous in summer. The tree is very strong and not inclined to lose major branches. Pruning is only necessary in the stage of maintaining a leader. The cultivar 'Fastigiata' is a medium-sized tree, narrow in its early years and suitable for a garden, later broadening out. *C. caroliniana* Eastern N America, 1812. AMERICAN HORNBEAM does not make as fine a tree in England as in the USA, but its autumn leaves colour well. For hedges see p161.

CARYA (Juglandaceae) HICKORY (D)

Almost confined to NE and central USA; two species from China are not known in Britain and only about half of the American species. *C. cordiformis* BITTERNUT HICKORY. Eastern N America, 1766. A very large tree and, of all the hickories, the hardiest and most vigorous in Britain. Recognised by the yellow scales on the winter buds. Leaves 25cm (10in) long with seven leaflets, as a rule. It is best sown in a pot and later planted out into the permanent position. A leader must be trained and a clean trunk of 1.8-2.4m (6-8ft) exposed, the pruning for this taking place in summer. *C. ovata* Eastern N America, 1629. The SHAGBARK HICKORY is equally handsome but slower in growth. The leaves are 25cm (10in) or more long, with five leaflets, and turn a striking yellow in autumn.

CARYOPTERIS × CLANDONENSIS (Verbenaceae) (D)

The name refers to a group of hybrids from the cross *C. incana × mongolica* of which the original clone is cultivar 'Arthur Simmonds'. The leaves are ovate-lanceolate and the flowers bright blue. The cultivar 'Ferndown' has dark green leaves and flowers of deeper colour than the type, while 'Kew Blue' has even darker blue flowers.

Caryopteris repays annual pruning, which prolongs the useful life of the plant considerably as long as feeding is adequate. It involves cutting back all the shoots into living wood and this is not easy to identify at the end of winter, in which some die-back is inevitable. Therefore be patient; but if your patience fails by mid-spring, but not your courage, cut back boldly and all should be well.

CASSINIA (Compositae) (E)

All are from New Zealand, for our purpose. *C. fulvida* makes a dense evergreen shrub eventually up to 1.8m (6ft) high, with yellow shoots and crowded white flowers in the spring after a frosty period. Though normally erect, wayward shoots may appear and should be removed entire.

CASTANEA SATIVA (Fagaceae) (D)
SWEET or SPANISH CHESTNUT

At its best, this is one of the greatest trees of Britain, not a native but is thought to have been brought in by the Romans and was certainly here before the Norman Conquest. It is only suitable for a large garden and is best in an open position in a park. It is easily raised from seed and self-seeds even in cooler areas. Somewhat intolerant of lime, it does well in light sandy soils.

At first growing slowly, after three or four years it develops rapidly and forms a good leader. A clean trunk up to 1.8 or 2.4m (6 or 8ft) is desirable as the bark is impressive, at first grey and smooth, later deeply fissured and dark brown with spirals of heavy ridges.

No pruning is needed until signs of old age appear with dying branches, which may be removed as the vitality of the tree usually persists and some regeneration can occur. Sucker growth is common at all stages and is coppiced to provide fencing. The timber of large trees is of limited value.

Castanea dentata The AMERICAN CHESTNUT has grown well at The Royal Botanic Gardens, Kew, but in its native North America

An arch of *Ceanothus thyrsiflorus* which is vigorous and hardy with evergreen leaves about 2.5cm (1in) long and pale blue flowers in late spring to early summer. It should be pruned immediately after flowering, cutting the flowered growth back to 2.5-5cm (1-2in) from the old wood, but not into it. The cultivar 'Cascade' is very similar

has been ravaged by a blight, *Endothea parasitica*, which has made it virtually extinct. Other species have not flourished in England, probably because the summers are cool, at least so far.

CATALPA (Bignoniaceae) (D)

C. bignonioides INDIAN BEAN, SOUTHERN CATALPA. Eastern N America, 1726. It likes a deep loam and some sun but not an exposed position, where wind may damage the large leaves. It is perfectly hardy. The flowers are white with yellow and purple markings in midsummer. W. J. Bean found that this tree often declined in its fifth decade and was best in southern England.

Left to develop it quickly branches low down and pruning is directed to achieving a clean trunk up to 1.8 or 2.4m (6 or 8ft). Then a crown is quickly established. If it becomes necessary to cut back damaged branches, regeneration is rapid and soon fills the space. ***C. speciosa*** WESTERN CATALPA. Central USA, 1880, seems to have several advantages over *C. bignonioides*: it makes a taller tree, its flowers have few purple spots and its timber, at least in the USA, is extremely durable and resistant to moisture.

CEANOTHUS (Rhamnaceae)

A genus containing Californian evergreen and deciduous shrubs of great beauty with a variable flowering habit. They flourish in good soil, well drained and neutral.

The evergreens are moderately tender though most will survive and flower well when grown against a south or west-facing wall, on which they should be trained fanwise

to create a framework.

C. thyrsiflorus 1837. Perhaps the hardiest evergreen, and best in its form 'Cascade'. The nomenclature of the evergreens is confused and it is advisable to see a plant in flower before buying it, unless you know the nursery to be wholly reliable. Immediately after flowering the shoots are pruned to two or three buds from the old stem. Use secateurs if possible – no, on reflection, use secateurs always, shears leave an untidy surface. *C. floribundus* × *C. indigo*, named *C.* × *burkwoodii* or 'Somerset'. A splendid hybrid of uncertain origin. It is evergreen with shining light green leaves and flowers of rich blue in midsummer. It is pruned in spring, cutting back to two to three buds as with many evergreens.

The deciduous shrubs derive from a French cross – *C. coeruleus* × *C. americanus* – and are almost hardy, including 'Gloire de Versailles' with powder-blue flowers; 'Indigo', deep blue; and 'Topaz', indigo. These are pruned severely in mid-spring to two buds.

CELTIS (*Ulmaceae*) NETTLE TREES (D)
C. australis S Europe, N Africa, Asia Minor, 1796. The best known, this is not a success in Britain, presumably due to lack of sun to ripen the wood. It flourishes in Italy and Spain and makes a good street tree of moderate size. The leaves turn bright yellow in autumn. The fruit is reputed to be the lotus of the ancients, making those who ate it forget their own country; not necessarily a bad thing.
C. sinensis Japan, 1910. Grows well, if slowly, in milder areas and makes a pleasant tree with leaves of shining green. If pruned or otherwise damaged, it regenerates freely.

CERATOSTIGMA (*Plumbaginaceae*) (D)
C. willmottianum China, Himalayas. Introduced by E. H. Wilson, of course, in 1928 and he gave seed to Miss Ellen Willmott. A deciduous shrub to 1.2m (4ft) high. Flowers bright blue in summer and into autumn. The semi-woody stems usually die right back and can be cut off, but in mild areas they survive and should be hard pruned to a few inches in spring.

CERCIDIPHYLLUM JAPONICUM
(*Cercidiphyllaceae*) (D)
Japan and China, 1881. It has been placed among *Magnoliaceae*, then with the *Trochodendraceae* and finally as a separate family within the magnolia alliance, perhaps most nearly related to the genus *Liriodendron*. Let us hope it will now settle down. It is an exceptionally handsome tree when doing well, which is not often the case in Britain where its young growth is often ruined by frost. Therefore it should thrive more on a

southern slope, but the soil would need to be retentive. A clearing in woodland suits it best. Evidently a continental climate produces the best trees, as in Germany and the Arnold Arboretum in the USA. After early training the tree should not be pruned but allowed to develop its natural shape.

CERCIS SILIQUASTRUM
(*Leguminosae*) (D)
E Mediterranean, sixteenth century. A deciduous tree, not often much over 6m (20ft) in Britain. It needs a deep loam and plenty of sun, so that here it gives the best performance in East Anglia, notably in Cambridge. This is still inferior to that in Mediterranean countries.

It is not easy, but desirable, to train a single leader. If attempts fail, branches should be shortened and some removed to make a stronger framework. The tree is seldom killed by frost but may be damaged enough to require extensive removal of small branches. It is very prone to attacks by the coral spot fungus (*Nectria Cinnabarina*). As soon as it is recognised – that is easy, as the small but prominent spots are of bright coral colour – the affected branch should be removed at a point 15-30cm (6in-1ft) away from the spots on the healthy side, and burnt. If the main trunk is involved there is little chance of a cure and the tree must be sacrificed. A replacement should be planted on a different site. If all goes well the clusters of rosy lilac flowers on the leafless shoots in spring will be a reward, and the purple pods in summer an additional bonus.

CESTRUM PARQUI (*Solanaceae*)
Chile, 1787. A deciduous shrub to 3m (10ft) high with long upright shoots from ground level. Lanceolate leaves. Flowers yellow, rather than yellowish-green as often described, in panicles, from early summer to autumn (in 1990 still in perfect flower in early November in Somerset). It is hardy

with wall protection and can be cut to the ground in early spring.

CHAENOMELES (Rosaceae) (D)

Three species, natives of China and Japan, two of which one might expect to be readily available whereas, in fact, *C. japonica* is moderately so and *C. speciosa* mainly by a large number of cultivars, of which 'Nivalis', 'Crimson and Gold' and 'Knap Hill Scarlet' easily predominate.

C. japonica c1869. Remains one of the best, growing to 0.9m (3ft) in height and, like the other species and cultivars, needs a good loamy soil and a sunny position, and does best against a wall. Pruning is aimed at first at producing a framework of short branches. Any shoots coming forward from the wall are stopped during the growing season at four or five leaves, unless they are needed for extension of the bush. The sublaterals which may form are stopped at two leaves, and this is repeated if more growth occurs. The whole procedure is continued each year until spurs form and flowering is established. Thereafter, the shoots which have flowered are shortened to three buds and in late summer any branches which point outward are shortened by half, or rather more.

C. speciosa Before 1800, is more vigorous and can reach 3×3m (10 × 10ft), so space must be allowed. The pruning in the early stages is the same as for *C. japonica*, but in maturity nothing more than the shortening of over-long shoots is necessary. Of the forms of *C. speciosa*, the following are worthy of notice: 'Moerloosii', which flowers white with pink overlay; and 'Nivalis', with flowers pure white. A good form of *C. × superba* is 'Crimson and Gold', bearing large flowers with crimson petals and golden anthers.

CHILIOTRICHUM DIFFUSUM
(Compositae) (E)

Chile, Argentina. Discovered in 1774 during Cook's second voyage, but not cultivated in Britain until 1927. It is a variable plant in its form and hardiness, which is normally greater than that of its relations the olearias. Grows slowly in good soil and the flowers in midsummer are white and daisy-like. Pruning is not needed if an area 0.9m (3ft) wide is allocated.

CHIMONANTHUS PRAECOX
(Calycanthaceae) WINTER SWEET (D)

China, 1766. An upright shrub to 1.8m (6ft) with no special soil requirements. It is commonly grown against a wall to gain the extra warmth reflected by the structure. It is hardy but flowers more freely in this situation and is prized for its strong scent in midwinter. Pruning consists of shortening the secondary shoots to two buds to promote spur formation. This is done as soon as the flowers have faded to give as much time as possible for the new wood to mature before the next winter.

CHIONANTHUS (Oleaceae) FRINGE TREE (D)

C. retusus (China, 1845) and **C. virginicus** (E USA, 1736) are alike, needing a deep, loamy soil and full exposure to sun. They are hardy in Britain but fail to produce the very striking display of flowers which makes them precious in the USA; lack of heat is probably the reason. Nevertheless, they are handsome at all times and are among the latest shrubs to come into leaf. *C. virginicus* often makes a small tree, and if it shows the vigour to do so a leader may be trained. However, it may be impossible to control the upward inclination of the branches. If so you should give in and await developments.

CHOISYA TERNATA (Rutaceae) (E)

MEXICAN ORANGE FLOWER. 1825. A rounded shrub with almost every virtue one could wish, and one of the greatest garden plants. It accepts an average soil and appreciates full sun. If in the shelter of a wall, it should be planted 1.8m (6ft) from it. The leaves are

obovate dark green and are said to have an unpleasant odour when crushed, so just don't crush them. The flowers are white in corymbs in late spring. The plant is hardy in an average winter but is often damaged, though not severely, by early spring frosts. It regenerates vigorously when the damaged shoots are cut away.

CISTUS (Cistaceae) ROCK ROSE (E)

A very attractive genus, moreover useful, an adjective usually reserved for unattractive plants. Rock roses like a dry, sunny position, are not affected by drought and, although the flowers last for less than a day, they are produced in a steady succession daily through midsummer.

Few are really hardy but *C. laurifolius* (SW Europe, 1731) and *C. × corbariensis* (*populifolius × salviifolius*) have maintained this reputation. The former is rather untidy but reaches 1.8m (6ft) in a few years; the latter does not exceed 0.9m (3ft) and is neat. Both bear white flowers. Of others *C. × cyprius* (*ladanifer × laurifolius*) with large flowers, white with a red blotch near the base of each petal, is one of the best and quite hardy. Another is *C. × skanbergii* (*monspeliensis × parviflorus*) with grey-green leaves and pale pink flowers on a beautifully smooth shrub.

The half-hardy shrub *Cestrum parqui* is, in fact, hardy against a south-facing wall. It is deciduous and can be cut down in winter, often growing to 1.8m (6ft) by early summer. The leaves are lanceolate and rather striking. The flowers are yellow or greenish-yellow and appear in midsummer, often carrying on into autumn. This picture was taken in October at Tintinhull

Pruning has a limited place with this genus, which does not break freely from mature stems if damaged. Any cutting back of the tips should be left until spring. Have a replacement ready from a cutting, which will root readily.

CLADRASTIS (Leguminosae) (D)

C. lutea YELLOW WOOD. SE United States, 1812. A tree of moderate size with a spreading crown and not requiring more than average soil. It bears long drooping panicles of white flowers in early summer. The leaves turn a good yellow in autumn.

C. sinensis CHINESE YELLOW WOOD. 1901. A very graceful tree with compound leaves of light green in early summer. The flowers are white tinged with pink in summer but may take over ten years to appear. Both these trees have a reputation for brittleness, but during twenty-one years – including several severe storms – there has been no evidence of that in a *C. sinensis* known to the author. Pruning is rarely needed.

CLERODENDRUM TRICHOTOMUM (Verbenaceae) (D)

China, Japan, c1880. Clearly the best of this genus and var. *fargesii* is only marginally more hardy. The type is hardy enough and undemanding. Up to 6m (20ft) high. Fragrant white flowers enclosed in maroon calyces appear in late summer, followed by blue fruits which regrettably turn black eventually. Flowering is improved by cutting back the wood of the previous year to the last pair of buds in spring. It is important that ground for 1.8-3m (6-10ft) around the tree should not be cultivated or disturbed in any way, as any damage to roots near the surface leads to a forest of suckers which may be impossible to control.

CLETHRA (Clethraceae)

All, evergreen or deciduous, must have acid soil, pH 5-6, and are not worth attempting without it. The evergreen species are tender and in northern regions only flourish in maritime climates.

C. alnifolia Eastern N America, 1731. Deciduous and hardy, especially the cultivar 'Paniculata' which produces fragrant white flowers in late summer.

C. barbinervis Japan, 1870. Rather less hardy but has very pretty flowers on an elegant bush.

C. delavayi China, 1913, is considered the finest of all but of doubtful hardiness.

Pruning is directed to the tendency to develop growths from the base of the plant, which make it possible to thin the older shoots at ground level and remove some of the suckers. This is done in the dormant period.

COLLETIA ARMATA (Rhamnaceae) (D)

Chile, 1882. Of more botanical than garden interest, but it is moderately hardy and grows well in full sun. The young branches are in fact flat triangular spines and leaves are few, especially on old plants. The flowers are white and tubular, each 3mm (⅛in) long, produced in late autumn or early winter. This plant might in ten years make an impenctrable hedge. Pruning is only needed to remove dead wood.

COLUTEA ARBORESCENS (Leguminosae)

COMMON BLADDER SENNA (D)

Mediterranean Europe, seventeenth century. It will grow well in any soil that is not boggy. It lost caste when it colonised the railway cuttings of suburban London but has considerable merit. It makes quite a tidy shrub and the pea flowers, of a good yellow from early summer for several months, are borne freely to make an attractive picture. Then the inflated pods follow, 7.5cm (3in) long and light brown. It self-seeds readily and can be trained to tree form, reaching 1.8-2.4m (6-8ft).

C. orientalis is similar, with brown copper flowers which sound exciting but are not produced in sufficient numbers to justify growing it – in England at least.

Pruning of these plants consists of cutting away weak growths in spring, nothing more. If you think the author has a soft spot for *C. arborescens*, you may be right.

COMPTONIA PEREGRINA (Myricaceae)

SWEET FERN (D)

Eastern N America, 1714. Dear to English gardeners because it was named for Henry Compton, Bishop of London (1632-1713), a lover of trees who planted many in the gardens of Fulham Palace. It is a shrub up to 1.2m (4ft) high, with alternate leaves, tapered at both ends and cleft into lobes. Unfortunately, it is completely calcifuge and also needs hot summers, so that it is seldom successful in Britain as it is, for instance, in Pennsylvania and Delaware.

CONVOLVULUS CNEORUM
(Convolvulaceae) (E)

S Europe, c1640. The only woody species in cultivation in Britain and only hardy in the South West though often planted elsewhere with some success against a south-facing wall. Flowers white tinged with pink, and beautiful. It makes a shrub 0.6-0.9m (2-3ft) high. Long, old growths should be completely removed in spring.

CORIARIA TERMINALIS
Var. *xanthocarpa* (Coriariaceae) (D)

Tibet, China, 1897. Unlike the other members of the genus in cultivation, this one is hardy at the Royal Botanic Gardens, Kew, and produces flowers of both sexes on terminal racemes, which in the fruiting stage become yellow. The pruning consists of cutting back in spring any shoots which have been damaged by frost, and removing some of the older growths entirely. The coriarias have a dubious reputation for being poisonous to animals, perhaps man as well, except *C. terminalis* which seems to be harmless.

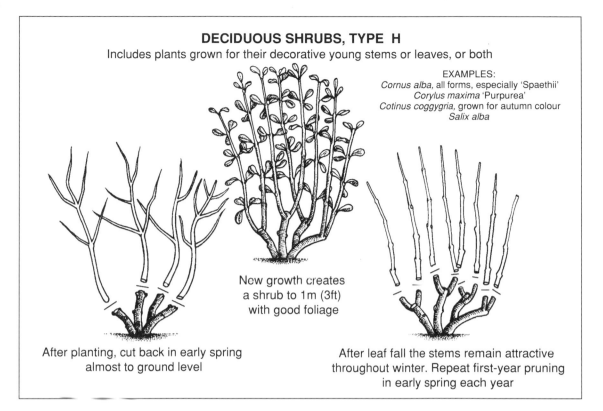

DECIDUOUS SHRUBS, TYPE H
Includes plants grown for their decorative young stems or leaves, or both

EXAMPLES:
Cornus alba, all forms, especially 'Spaethii'
Corylus maxima 'Purpurea'
Cotinus coggygria, grown for autumn colour
Salix alba

New growth creates
a shrub to 1m (3ft)
with good foliage

After planting, cut back in early spring
almost to ground level

After leaf fall the stems remain attractive
throughout winter. Repeat first-year pruning
in early spring each year

CORNUS (Cornaceae)
CORNEL, DOGWOOD (D)

A very large genus with variable characteristics, here presented in alphabetical order of the more important members.

C. alba China, Siberia, 1741, produces stems which become a fine red in autumn and through winter. When first planted it should be left unpruned for a whole season. In the following spring, when growth is apparent, it is cut almost to ground level. Shoots of several feet will follow and the pruning is repeated each year thereafter. If good feeding is applied regularly in late spring the process can be continued for years.

The cultivar 'Elegantissima' has leaves with a margin of creamy white, the centre grey-green, the stems in winter red. Cultivar 'Sibirica' has the considerable advantage of being less vigorous than the type, making pruning less arduous. The colour of the stems is bright red. 'Spaethii' has red bark and mid-

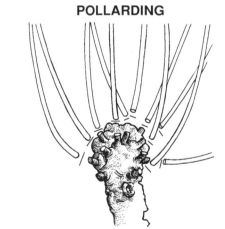

POLLARDING

Plants of Type H may be pollarded by cutting back the year's growth by half rather than to ground level. This can be repeated for several years and will build up a woody base, from which new growths will arise in spring and may be cut back to their origin. Manuring is desirable, as this process eventually exhausts a plant which is not fed

Choisya ternata, an invaluable evergreen shrub, hardy with some shelter and producing its white flowers in spring without fail. It grows slowly, but if pruning is needed it regenerates quickly

green leaves which develop irregular areas of yellow which can occupy the greater part of the leaf area, and only start to fade as the leaves become ready to fall. To add to this the foliage is never scorched by sun and the plant also tolerates considerable shade. The pruning is exactly that of *C. alba* itself.

C. alternifolia Eastern N America, 1760. Has alternate leaves, as does *C. controversa* (see below), the only other member of the genus in cultivation with this leaf pattern. *C. alternifolia* 'Argentea' is a favourite variegated shrub, usually growing slowly with tiered horizontal branches and reaching 1.5-1.8m(5-6ft) high. The leaves are small and have a creamy margin. No pruning needed.

C. capitata BENTHAM'S CORNEL. Himalaya, 1825. A tree which only reaches more than a few feet in the most favoured areas. It is comparatively hardy in some shade but then does not flower (yellow bracts of some beauty).

C. controversa Japan, China, before 1880. A deciduous tree reaching 12-15m (40-50ft) in as many years. The branches are horizontal in tiers, leaves alternate and flowers white in cymes about 13cm (5in) across. It does well in average soil, as does the cultivar 'Variegata' which has lanceolate leaves with a yellow-ish-white border of irregular outline. These trees may lose their leaves in a spring frost but manage to produce a second series in a short time.

C. florida E USA, 1730. FLOWERING DOGWOOD makes a small tree to 6m (20ft) high in Britain, where it arrived in 1730. It has never been really successful here, probably due to a combination of spring frost damage and poor ripening of the wood.

C. kousa Japan, Korea, China, 1875. Grows well in good soil and, like *C. florida*, owes its beauty to the four bracts that surround the otherwise inconspicuous inflorescence. The variety *chinensis*, not botanically distinct, is more vigorous and has larger flowers. In both cases the branches are almost horizontal but the outline of the tree is upright and does not demand a great deal of space. Pruning is seldom needed.

C. mas CORNELIAN CHERRY. Native of Europe. In Britain for centuries, it is not difficult to grow but a decision has to be taken at an early stage whether to train it as a tree or allow its tendency to branch low down. If it does make a tree it is still desirable to retain the lower branches to some extent, as the abundant display of yellow flowers in late winter on the leafless stems is best admired at eye level. The fruit is bright red but not regularly borne. This plant, whether tree or shrub, needs plenty of room and ideally should have an evergreen background, of holly perhaps.

C. nuttallii PACIFIC DOGWOOD. Western N America, 1835. It is extremely fine in its na-

tive habitat but unfortunately is not successful in most of Britain, and only at its best on
the Atlantic coast where the climate resembles that of its home. It flowers when quite
young but is reported to deteriorate without
warning and die for no apparent reason. The
flowers in late spring are small, purple, and
surrounded by a whorl of bracts which are
white, sometimes pink-flushed. In Cornwall,
at Lanhydrock, it is unforgettable when
flowering in May. Pruning is cosmetic only.

COROKIA COTONEASTER
(Cornaceae) (E)
New Zealand, 1875. Will do well with the
protection of a south-facing wall in most
parts of Britain, but should be planted at
least 0.6m (2ft) from the wall. Any light soil
will do. It can reach 2.4m (8ft) and is a rounded
bush. The branches are twisted, covered with
a white felt at first, later becoming almost
black. The leaves are spoon-shaped and the
flowers bright yellow in late spring. A problem with pruning is that the leaves are so
sparse that it is difficult to tell live from dead
tissue. Remember the pruners' rule: 'When
in doubt, do nothing'.

CORONILLA *(Leguminosae)*
C. emerus SCORPION SENNA. Central and
southern Europe. Makes a shapely deciduous shrub of more than 1.8m (6ft) high in
good ordinary soil. Regular pruning involves
the removal of old and unhealthy growths in
winter.
C. glauca S Europe, 1722. Evergreen but
needs shelter and a sunny position as it is
liable to injury in any period of frost. Damaged or failing growths can be cut back in
spring.

CORYLOPSIS *(Hamamelidaceae)* (D)
They need acid or neutral soil and some
exposure to sun.
C. pauciflora Japan, 1862, makes a dense
shrub with long shoots and a neat surface

over 1.8m (6ft) in diameter. Yellow flowers
appear in early spring and last six weeks or
more. If grown in full sun the leaves may be
scorched.
C. willmottiae China, 1909. A larger shrub
and more beautiful in its growth and flower
form. Pruning may be needed to control
overlong shoots.

CORYLUS *(Corylaceae)* (D)
All do well in good loam and tolerate chalk.
C. avellana HAZEL or COBNUt. Native of Europe, including Britain, W Asia and N Africa.
A shrub or tree to 6m (20ft) but normally a
thicket maintained by sucker growth if it is
not cut down for peasticks, making walking-
sticks, or even water divining. If the plant
becomes ungainly it may be cut entirely to
the ground and will quickly renew itself.
C. colurna SE Europe, W Asia, 1582. When
young the TURKISH HAZEL is an exceptionally
graceful tree but as it matures becomes less
so, for instance the old tree at Syon House by
the Thames which is almost unique in Britain
for its size. However, in the continental climate of Vienna old trees are very fine. At the
nursery stage *C. colurna* easily forms a leader
and the lateral branches distribute themselves evenly. No pruning is needed.
C. maxima FILBERT. S Europe, 1759. Little different from the cobnut. The cultivar
'Purpurea' is well worth having if you like
purple-leaved trees.

COTINUS *(Anacardiaceae)* (D)
C. coggygria Central and S Europe, c1656.
VENETIAN SUMACH, native of middle and
southern Europe to the Himalayas and China,
should not be planted in rich soil which
somehow inhibits its flowering. It makes a
large rounded bush, very suitable for a big
'herbaceous' border. The orbicular leaves
are of a pleasant green turning yellow, less
often red, in autumn. The inflorescences, 15-
20cm (6-8in) long, develop in midsummer
and last till autumn; they are light brown at

first, finally turning grey. The cultivar, 'Foliis purpureis' includes several forms with purple leaves, one of the best defined being 'Notcutt's variety'. If you dislike purple leaves the plain form is more attractive than it sounds, in fact some gardeners find it one of the most decorative of garden shrubs in its quiet way.

Pruning of all these plants can be planned in one of two ways.

1 A strong branch system is built up from ground level. Once this has grown to 1.2 or 1.5m (4 or 5ft) there is no further pruning and the inflorescences cover the bush.

2 The framework is confined to two or three main stems from ground level. These are allowed to branch until the shrub is 0.6-0.9m (2-3ft) high, after which the young wood of each is reduced to the two lowest buds in spring. This encourages growth and a display of foliage but the inflorescences will not be formed on the young wood.

COTONEASTER (Rosaceae)

A large genus mostly with a pleasant character of growth and foliage; also fruits, in some. They do well in almost any soil if not waterlogged and are easily propagated.

C. bullatus (D) China, 1898. Of graceful habit with good corrugated leaves, little flower beauty but clusters of strong red fruits which are attractive to birds.

C. conspicuus (E) Tibet, 1925, is a low, spreading shrub, excellent in flower and fruit.

C. distichus (D) 1825. Reaching 1.8m (6ft) and notable for its abundant bright red fruits, which birds ignore. It also retains its leaves until spring.

C. horizontalis (D) W China, c1870. Despised by some but is a great plant, bearing its fishbone-like stems quite low in open ground but standing quite vertical without support against a wall. This is useful if any work has to be carried out on the wall, as the shrub can be pulled away and later replaced. Pruning

for *C. horizontalis* and others of the same character involves the removal of whole stems or none, otherwise the splendid form of the ranks of branches is disturbed if not ruined.

C. lacteus (E) China, 1973, reaches 3m (10ft) high and is then striking, especially when flowering (white) in midsummer.

C. salicifolius (E) China, 1908. Grows to 7.6m (25ft) and spreads widely, needing plenty of room. The bright red fruits are only 5mm (¼in) wide but numerous enough to be spectacular. As with *C. horizontalis*, attention should be given to the natural form of these large shrubs and cutting away of short lengths of stem avoided.

Fireblight is most important in this genus and must be taken seriously.

CRATAEGUS (Rosaceae) HAWTHORN (D)

A large genus, though many of the species are suspected of a hybrid taint. The majority come from eastern and central America and a few from Europe and Asia Minor. All are easily cultivated in good loam and tolerate lime. They are best raised from seed but are still grafted sometimes, especially the less common sort. Therefore if you buy an unusual thorn keep a lookout for suckers at a grafting level, just above ground, and remove them forthwith.

C. crus galli COCKSPUR THORN. Eastern N America, 1691. A small tree with a broad top, branches armed with thorns 7.5cm (3in) long, flowers white in early summer and profuse. Fruits, ripening in early autumn, persist until spring. It is perfectly hardy.

C. × lavallei 'Carrierei'. A fine tree to 6m (20ft). Handsome leaves, white flowers in early summer and orange-red fruits up to 2.5cm (1in) wide, persisting through the winter.

C. monogyna COMMON HAWTHORN. Perhaps a British native, certainly European, and certainly was common in hedges recorded in Anglo-Saxon charters. It remains the best plant for a 'working' hedge to contain stock and keep out humans (see 'Hedges & Topiary' p161). As a tree it is easily trained to make a leader and then to have a bare trunk to 1.2-1.5m (4-5ft) and a dense crown, covered in mid-spring with fragrant white flowers. There are many records of hawthorns living to be more than three hundred years old and, in medieval times, they were planted as signposts for travellers in places where they could be seen for a mile or more.

C. oxyacantha MAY. Similar to the last, but not as effective as a hedge.

C. pedicellata NE North America, 1683. A tree to 6m (20 ft) bearing white flowers in late spring, followed by scarlet fruits 15mm (¾in) long, ripe in early autumn. Var. ellwangeriana is said to be even better.

C. phaenopyrum WASHINGTON THORN. SE United States, 1738. A tree to 9m (30ft) with a rounded crown on a thin trunk. Shoots with thorns 7.5cm (3in) long, glossy leaves like a maple and white flowers abundant in midsummer. Fruit scarlet, persisting until spring. The leaves turn scarlet and orange in autumn, perhaps never as brilliant in Britain as in the USA.

The tree forms of *Crataegus* need very little attention after their early training. Remov-

OPPOSITE:
Cornus controversa 'Variegata' has the tabular leaf form of the type, but the leaves are longer and narrow with an irregular yellow border. It is subject to damage from spring frosts, but soon makes good with fresh growth. No pruning needed

BELOW:
Cornus alba 'Spaethii' is grown for its unusual leaf variegation, green and yellow in various proportions – leaves can be anything from wholly green to wholly yellow. These colours do not fade until the leaves are about to drop, and they are never scorched by the sun. Pruning is simple – cut the stems to ground level every spring and manure liberally

ing laterals to produce a bare trunk is important if the tree is near a path or in a cultivated area, as the spines are sharp and not obvious.

CRINODENDRON HOOKERIANUM (Elaeocarpaceae) (E)

Chile, 1848. An evergreen shrub which is too demanding for any but maritime-climate areas of Britain. Not only is it strictly calcifuge, but it must have some shade and is tender. However, if these requirements are met, it is dazzling. The lanceolate leaves are handsome and from the terminal leaf-axils the crimson corolla of the flowers hangs down. Cutting out dead growths in winter is the only attention it needs.

CYDONIA OBLONGA (Rosaceae)

COMMON QUINCE (D)

Native country unknown, probably Near East and Central Asia, in Britain for centuries. A low tree of character, usually to 4.5m (15ft), with branches which crowd together, often crossing. The leaves are dark green above, pale below and turn a good yellow in autumn. The flowers in late spring are white, each at the end of a twig. The fruit is golden and pear-shaped. In the cultivar 'Maliformis', which Philip Miller (1691-1771) took as the type of C. oblonga, the fruit is apple-shaped.

The quince tends to sucker and that needs watching. One should also inspect the crown for crossing branches but their removal, considering the density of the crown and perhaps the need for a ladder, is daunting. To encourage you it is worth pointing out that the quince was the 'Golden Apple' of the Ancients, who considered it the emblem of love and happiness. It was brought to Rome from Greece before the birth of Christ and spread through the West. Chaucer spoke of it as growing in England in his day. Cotignac, a sweetmeat of which it was the basis, was offered to Joan of Arc when she entered Orleans. The seed coat contains a gum with demulcent properties which accounts for its value in making jellies, jam and marmalade (its Portuguese name is _Marmelo_, hence marmalade. A quince cheese made in Spain is called _Membrillo_. It must be pink, the golden form is made with apples and no good). Apple pie is still improved with quince.

CYTISUS (Leguminosae) BROOM (D)

This shrub varies from 0.3 to 3.6m (12in-12ft) in height, some also spreading widely.

C. albus A spreading dwarf shrub less than 0.3m (1ft) high. White flowers in clusters during early summer. The plant grown in gardens for many years as C. _albus_ is now C. _multiflorus_, see below.

C. ardoinii S France, 1866, is only a few centimetres high, of neat habit with golden flowers. Pruning is best avoided.

C. battandieri Morocco, c1922, is like no other broom, with a tree-like form when grown in the open. It is usually hardy. It survived unharmed in an open site in Worcestershire in the bitter winter of 1962-3. The leaves are covered in silky hairs, the flowers fragrant and golden yellow in early summer. The horizontal lower branches tend to die back and, if they do, should be removed at once. Old wood and any wayward shoots can be cut away in spring.

C. × burkwoodii is a hybrid growing to 1.2m (4ft) high, with cherry-red flowers, the wings dark red, edged yellow. A robust shrub, in early summer flowering well in partial shade.

C. × kewensis is a low dense bush, suited to the rock garden, with creamy flowers in spring. No regular pruning.

C. multiflorus Spain, Portugal, N Africa, c1752. Grows to 3m (10ft) or more and carries white flowers along the previous year's wood in late spring. It is not essential to prune it, but if it becomes necessary the operation should be carried out immediately after flowering.

C. × praecox is a group of hybrids of which the original clone is C × _praecox_ 'Warminster'.

In habit it resembles *C. multiflorus* but the growth is more dense and the flowers, of creamy yellow, are very abundant in late spring. The cultivar 'Andreanus' is like the type except in the flowers, which have wing petals of a rich red-brown and the standard petals yellow but lined with that colour. No regular pruning.

C. scoparius Europe. COMMON BROOM is at its best in thin sandy soil, as are most brooms, and under these conditions may live for several years without becoming untidy and will display yellow flowers in abundance for many weeks. Hybrids of this broom are legion and include cultivar 'Andreanus', with brownish crimson wing petals, yellow standard petals stained with the former colour; 'Burkwoodii', cerise and maroon; 'Cornish Cream', cream and yellow; and 'Johnson's Crimson', clear crimson.

Pruning for the bushy brooms is definitely valuable. They flower on the wood of the previous year and as soon as the pods start to develop the flowered wood is cut back by two thirds, being careful to avoid cutting into the old wood (which has no young shoots). This saves the energy of the plant and prevents it becoming leggy. It also lessens the incidence of black-fly aphid infestation, which involves the pods.

DABOECIA (Ericaceae) (E)

The genus has two species.

D. azorica Azores, 1929. Requires a lime-free soil and does not exceed 0.3m (1ft) in height, but spreads widely. The flowers are carried in an erect raceme in early summer, and are of a rich crimson shade. It is moderately tender and should have some shelter.

D. cantabrica ST DABOEC'S HEATH. Western Europe, and found wild in Connemara, western Ireland. Its character is very similar to *D. azorica* but the rose-purple flowers appear intermittently from early summer until autumn, and it is more hardy. There are several cultivars and hybrids. Some *D.*

cantabrica × *azorica* were raised by Jack Drake of Aviemore and one with his name is considered by him to be the best, and more hardy than *D. azorica*. Both these plants and their offspring benefit from pruning in early spring, cutting down the flower spikes and about half the growth of the previous year.

DANAE RACEMOSA (Liliaceae) (E)

Asia Minor, Iran, c1713. The ALEXANDRIAN LAUREL is the only species of its genus, resembling *Ruscus* and like it having 'leaves' which are flattened branches – phylloclades – which serve the leaves' function. It makes an elegant shrub to 1.2m (4ft) and tolerates shade, while its growth is slow, never calling for pruning beyond the removal of any leaves which have become ragged or unhealthy.

DAPHNE (Thymelaceae)

A wonderful genus with a widespread origin from Japan to Britain, whose only fault lies in the reluctance of some of the species to do well in spite of apparently correct culture. They like neutral or limey soil, retaining moisture but draining well, and most are sun-lovers (not an easy prescription to satisfy).

D. bholua (D) Himalaya, c1935, is a plant which seems to improve with every introduction, at least in hardiness, though variations in flower colour are disturbing. No pruning is needed if space is reserved for a plant 2.4m (8ft) high.

D. × *burkwoodii* (*caucasica* × *cneorum*) (D) was raised by Albert Burkwood in his garden at Kingston-on-Thames, England. Only three seeds formed but all germinated. Albert kept one, whose descendants are correctly 'Albert Burkwood', and gave the other two to his brother Arthur, who worked at Scott's Nursery in Somerset. One died but the other survived and was named Somerset by Arthur. Both clones are wonderful and almost identical, except that Somerset is said to be rather the larger. Experience of this plant in Somer-

set, SW England, confirms that it is fully hardy and in full sun maintains a good rounded shape to a little over 0.9m (3ft) for up to ten years. The surface is covered with very fragrant pink flowers in late spring. Pruning is only to remove dead shoots and inevitably mars the outline for the time being. Propagation from cuttings is very easy, and it is prudent to have a young plant to hand.

OPPOSITE:
One of the purple forms of smoke bush, *Cotinus coggyria* is set off here by the scarlet autumn leaves of *Acer palmatum*. See p53 for pruning alternatives

BELOW:
***Cotoneaster horizontalis* is fan-shaped in habit and has glorious scarlet foliage and red berries in autumn**

D. cneorum (E) C and S Europe, c1750. The GARLAND FLOWER is a prostrate shrub with long leafy branches and is very free-flowering. It seems to have no special soil needs but is far from easy to cultivate and therefore, for amateurs at least, layering of some shoots is well worth while.

D. laureola (E) S and W England, is included only as a British native and evergreen, excelled at all points by *D. pontica* (see below).

D. mezereum (D) Europe, perhaps including Britain, Siberia. An erect slender shrub to 1.2m (4ft) with fragrant purple-red flowers on wood of the previous year in late winter, before the leaves appear. One of the difficult daphnes to grow well, though sometimes self-seeding freely. It needs moisture and does well in limey soil, but sometimes dies quickly for no obvious reason – perhaps a virus infection.

D. neapolitana (E) Perhaps still called *D. collina* var *neapolitana*. A plant with most of

the virtues of *D. ×burkwoodii* – easy to grow, hardy and comparatively long-lived, a shrub to 0.9m (3ft) with dark green leaves densely arranged, and fragrant purple flowers from early spring for several weeks.

D. odora (E) China, Japan, 1771. The cultivar aureo-marginata is, surprisingly, more hardy than the type and this makes it desirable though the yellow and white marginal variegation is rather feeble. More important, the flowers, though not very pretty, are extremely fragrant and appear in midwinter, lasting for two months.

D. pontica (E) Asia Minor, 1732. This shrub is 0.9-1.2m (3-4ft) high and wide-spreading, with light green leaves making a dense surface. The greenish-yellow flowers are inconspicuous but fragrant and appear in midspring. This plant likes at least moderate shade.

In general the advice to those who plan to prune daphnes is, 'Don't'.

DAPHNIPHYLLUM MACROPODUM
(Daphniphyllaceae) (E)

China. Hardy, and makes a stylish rounded shrub to 1.8 or 2.4m (6 or 8ft), with inconspicuous pale green flowers and black berries. It would be an insult to the handsome foliage of this shrub to suggest pruning. It is hardy.

DAVIDIA INVOLUCRATA
(Davidiaceae) (D)

W China. DOVE or HANDKERCHIEF TREE is usually grown in the form of the variety 'Vilmoriniana', which is probably more hardy and easier to establish than the type. Any good soil suits it. The display of large white bracts in late spring is very fine. It readily develops a leader and a trunk which should be, in the end, clean to 1.8m (6ft). In a dry summer the leaves on many of the branches fall early and may give the impression that the tree is dying, but in the next spring the shoots develop normally. It is vulnerable to spring frosts and should be planted in a sheltered place, fully exposed to the sun. No routine pruning.

DECAISNEA FARGESII
(Lardizabalaceae) (D)

W China. An upright shrub producing young shoots from the base and not branching freely; the young shoots are subject to late spring frost damage. The leaves are pinnate, 0.9m (3ft) long, the flowers yellow in racemes followed by dull blue fruits 7.5-10cm (3-4in) long. It likes a rich loamy soil. No pruning, nor is it recommended except for the warmest eastern areas of Britain.

DENDROMECON RIGIDA
(Papaveraceae) (E)

California. Likes a sandy loam and some lime, with full sun. A south-facing wall is desirable as it is far from hardy and will climb for several feet. The flowers are reminiscent of poppies and bright yellow. When grown in pots the shrub is planted against the wall and the shoots are trained fan-wise. Later more vigorous growths appear from which the flowering laterals form. The early shoots can then be cut back.

DESFONTAINEA SPINOSA
(Potaliaceae) (E)

Andes; introduced by Lobb from Chile, 1843. It has succeeded most in the British Isles on the west coast of Scotland and in Northern Ireland. In England there are few plants of any great size but it is said to be hardy in the Home Counties. George Brown in his book of 1977 writes that the shrub 'is so difficult to please and to grow successfully that one is rightly hesitant to prune it', and experience confirms this. It does not tolerate chalk and needs more than average rainfall, with which it may make a shrub 3m (10ft) high. The leaves are very like those of the common holly. The flowers have a scarlet corolla, with five yellow lobes; the calyx is green.

DESMODIUM PRAESTANS
(Leguminosae) (D)
China, 1914. A large shrub whose rounded leaves are covered in silky hairs which give it a silvered appearance. Purple flowers appear in late summer. It needs a south-facing wall and plenty of sun. It is evidently too tender to be long-lived and is rare in cultivation, sometimes lingering for years without flowering. No regular pruning indicated.

DEUTZIA (Philadelphaceae) (D)
Shrubs from China, Taiwan or Japan except *D. pulchra* from the Philippines. One would not guess at a glance that they are related to *Philadelphus*. They like a rich soil, retentive of moisture, and are mostly lime-tolerant. They are nearly all winter-hardy but some are lured into growth by any warm spell in spring, with loss of all bloom for that year should the weather turn wintry again. This is one reason for cutting back the shoots which have borne flowers as soon as they fade, in order to allow the maximum period for ripening the wood for the next year's flowering.
D. corymbosa China. A vigorous shrub, reaching 2.7m (9ft) high. Flowers with a scent like hawthorn, petals white, anthers yellow, in early summer.
D. × elegantissima A Lemoine series of hybrids, the typical form an erect shrub with flowers rose-pink, in corymbs.
D. longifolia China. A shrub 1.6m (5ft) high. Flowers in panicles, purplish-rose, paler at the margins of the petals, in early summer. A good doer.
D. reflexa China. Grows 0.9m (3ft) high. Flowers in corymbose panicles, white, in late spring or early summer.
D. × rosea cultivar 'Carminea' reaches 0.9m (3ft) high. Flowers rose-pink, bell-shaped, in large panicles. It responds well to annual removal of the older shoots.
D. scabra Japan, China has special virtues. Flowering in early summer on one-year-old wood, it escapes the effect of late frosts in most years. The flowers are borne on erect panicles up to 15cm (6in) long, are pure white and very striking.
D. setchuenensis China, 1895. A fine plant but the variety 'Corymbiflora' is finer. It grows to 1.8m (6ft), with graceful shoots arranged closely together. The leaves are oval-lanceolate with fine teeth. It flowers in early summer in corymbs 7.5-10cm (3-4in) across, making a splendid picture of pink-white which may last from six to eight weeks. Pruning involves cutting back the flowered shoots to their origins as soon as the bloom fades. Be ready to wait for five to six years for a young plant to give of its best.

Apart from the pruning already mentioned, removal of old and failing branches is helpful.

DIERVILLA (Caprifoliaceae) (D)
All are natives of eastern USA.
D. sessilifolia A small stoloniferous shrub, usually not more than 0.9m (3ft) high. Yellow flowers borne in cymes, from early summer for several weeks. A good plant, widely available. It superficially resembles *Weigela*, a genus now separated. Diervilla should be pruned in spring, cutting back the shoots to about 0.3m (1ft). New growth comes from the base.

DIOSPYROS (Ebenaceae)
China, 1904. No routine pruning needed.
D. kaki CHINESE PERSIMMON (D) China, 1796. A tree to 12m (40ft) high, with shining dark leaves and producing its fruit with fair regularity if trained against a wall, at least in milder areas. Even without fruit it is a handsome tree and easy to grow. It is vulnerable to spring frost when young but later becomes hardy.
D. lotus (D) China, c1597. The DATE PLUM is perfectly hardy and in Britain reaches 9m (30ft) or a little more. Female plants produce fruits which are like tomatoes but yellowish and too bitter for eating. It also is handsome,

with lustrous leaves.

D. virginiana (D) Eastern N America, 1629. PERSIMMON is a fine tree to 18m (60 ft), tender at first but perfectly hardy in a few years. The pale yellow fruit is much favoured in its native region and was made famous in Britain through Joel Chandler Harris' book *Uncle Remus*, perhaps no longer available. This tree should be trained to have a clean trunk of 1.8m (6ft) and the lower branches will hang almost to ground level.

DIOSTEA JUNCEA (Verbenaceae (D)

Andes, 1890. A tall, slender shrub with rush-like shoots resembling a Spanish Broom. Flowers pale lilac in early summer, not conspicuous. The lower part becomes bare and it is best planted among evergreens to conceal this; they should be 2.4m (8ft) high at least.This is a rare plant.

DIPELTA (Caprifoliaceae) (D)

A genus of Chinese origin.

D. floribunda China, 1902, is the most effective of these plants, easy to grow and hardy. Notable for the bracts which surround the flowers in a shield-like form. The peeling bark on the older stems is attractive. The main branches are upright but the laterals arch over as flowering begins, robbing the centre of light and causing die-back, which calls for prompt removal of affected branches. At the same time it may be helpful to cut back some old branches as new growths are readily produced from ground level.

DISANTHUS CERCIDIFOLIUS (Hamamelidaceae) (D)

E China, 1893, is not worth attempting to grow except in a lime-free soil. It makes a shrub of 2.4m (8ft) high and has flowers of no account, but leaves like those of the Judas tree which give one of the best autumn displays, mainly red and purple. It seems to favour woodland conditions but should be given ample space and allowed to develop

branches which will droop to ground level. No routine pruning.

DORYCNIUM HIRSUTUM (Leguminosae) (D)

Mediterranean, c1683. Hardly a shrub, but does form a woody base and then becomes quite hardy if grown in a sunny position in light soil. It is a magnificent plant with grey hairy leaves, white flowers tinged pink, and reddish fruit pods, the whole a perfect colour composition not above 0.3m (1ft) high. In spring the stems of the previous year are cut back to the younger basal shoots.

DRIMYS (Winteraceae) (E)

D. lanceolata MOUNTAIN PEPPER. Tasmania, New South Wales, 1843. A medium-sized shrub. Does well in any good soil which is not dry. Young stems and petioles crimson for a year or more. Leaves aromatic, peppery. Probably hardy if sheltered from northeast winds. Creamy flowers in late spring.

D. winteri Chile, 1827. A large shrub or tree of upright habit, capable of reaching 16m (50ft). It must have moisture and tolerates chalk. The grey bark is aromatic, the leaves 20cm (8in) long, dark green above, glaucous beneath, the flowers fragrant, ivory white. It is hardy if grown in the form generally known as var. *latifolia*. It should be planted near to but not less than 0.9m (3ft) from a wall. Var. *andina* is a truly dwarf form, usually not

Deutzia setchuenensis corymbiflora **is very floriferous and valuable as a flowering shrub in midsummer. Prune back the flowered branches**

more than 0.9m (3ft) high. Pruning is seldom called for except to give extra space. The bark of *D. winteri* was brought to England by Captain William Winter, who was with Drake on his voyage round the world. Winter had found this bark useful to his crew: 'instead of spices with their meat and as a medicine very powerful against the scurvy.' It is not possible to say whether his observation was well grounded. Vegetable matter, especially leaves, had been used long before Drake's voyage.

DRYAS OCTOPETALA (Rosaceae)
MOUNTAIN AVENS (E)
From mountainous places in the northern hemisphere, including Britain. A prostrate evergreen to 7.5cm (3in) high with woody stems. White yellow-centred flowers appear at the end of spring. No pruning indicated.

EDGEWORTHIA CHRYSANTHA
(Thymelaceae) (D)
China, 1845. A shrub to 1.8m (6ft), young shoots having silver, later glabrous olive, alternate leaves. The inflorescence forms in autumn but does not expand until late winter in a terminal cluster with a yellow calyx. The stems weaken with age but new shoots appear at the base of the plant and can replace any that are removed in late summer.

EHRETIA (Ehretiaceae)
A genus mostly tropical with three species more or less hardy in Britain. G. D. Ehret, for whom it is named, spent most of his life as a botanical artist in London.
E. dicksonii (D) China, c1905. A tree to 12m (40ft), vigorous with downy shoots. The large hairy leaves, up to 20cm (8in) long, are striking; the white flowers in late spring, less so. It is 7.6m (25 ft) high at Tintinhull, Somerset, and has not suffered any damage from high winds though exposed. Pruning has not so far been necessary.
E. macrophylla Himalayas, 1897. A slow-growing shrub with leaves almost round, hairy on both sides. Hardy with some protection from north and east.
E. thyrsiflora (D) China, Japan, 1900. Hardy when adult, reaches 9m (30 ft) high and is a tree rather than a shrub. The leaves are large, oval, up to 17cm (7in) long, 7.5cm (3in) wide. The flowers are fragrant and white, borne in midsummer. Mature trees have an impressively corrugated bark.

ELAEAGNUS (Elaeagnaceae) OLEASTER.
These need a light, sandy soil and those with silvery leaves show this colour less well on a heavy one.
E. angustifolia (D) Temperate Asia, sixteenth century. The RUSSIAN OLIVE makes a small tree and produces fragrant but diminutive flowers from late spring to early summer. At this time it can be mistaken for *Pyrus salicifolia* but in midsummer the leaves deteriorate and present a drab appearance. There is often considerable die-back, but with this comes new growth at a lower level and is the time to remove unhealthy branches. The unripe new growth will survive an average winter.
E. commutata SILVER BERRY (D) 1813. An American native which has more conspicuous flowers and makes a shrub about 3m (10ft) high.
E. macrophylla (E) Korea, Japan, 1879. A strong-growing rounded shrub with leaves silvery on both surfaces in spring, fading later. The fragrant flowers appear in autumn. It gave rise to *E. × ebbingei*, the other parent being *E. pungens* (see below).
E. multiflora (D) China, Japan, 1862. Notable for its unusual and beautiful fruits, described as ox-blood in colour. Alas, this picture is short-lived if you have an active bird population around.
E. pungens (E) Japan, 1869. The cultivar maculata must now be the most popular of variegated evergreen shrubs. The large dark green leaves have a deep yellow central area of varying size and shape. The effect is stri-

dent and not to be ignored; could you face it every day of the year as you emerge from your front door?

E. umbellata (D) China, Japan, 1830. A very large and wide shrub – 9m (30ft) high has been mentioned. The flowers, in late spring, are larger than most in the genus.

It may seem rather banal to conclude by remarking that pruning is only directed to controlling the shape and spread of these plants. There is one more exciting task, and that is to watch for signs of reversion in *E. pungens maculata*. It is almost bound to appear sooner or later and in any place on the shrub you may see a branch or branchlet with the foliage of *E. pungens* or *E. macrophylla*. If so, it should be cut off at once and a close watch kept for any recurrence.

EMBOTHRIUM COCCINEUM
(Proteaceae) FIRE BUSH (E)

China, 1846. There have been introductions at intervals since the first by William Lobb in 1846, and that of H. Comber about 1930 has proved hardy and almost deciduous. It has been named 'Lanceolatum' but is now considered to be a form of *coccineum*. Both the plants mentioned demand a lime-free soil and shelter from cold winds, with plenty of light. When suited they give a breath-taking display of crimson-scarlet flowers in late spring. Comber's has an upright habit and will sometimes form a tree but it seems unnecessary to establish a leader by pruning. It shoots from the base and suckers so that a 'thicket' is a possibility. No routine pruning.

EMMENOPTERYS HENRYI
(Rubiaceae) (D)

China, 1907. From all accounts this is a very beautiful tree. It has proved hardy at Kew but has never flowered. It maintains a good leader and the lateral branches tend to be horizontal but not abundant. Pruning seems unnecessary. This plant is not readily available in commerce.

EMPETRUM NIGRUM
(Empetraceae) CROWBERRY (E)

A dwarf carpeting shrub, common in uplands of the northern hemisphere, including Britain. It must have lime-free soil and moisture. The flowers are not easy to detect.

ENKIANTHUS CAMPANULATUS
(Ericaceae) (D)

Japan, 1880. Easily outstanding among the species of the genus. A shrub to 3.6m (12ft) high which dislikes lime but tolerates a neutral soil. The leaves, which tend to be in a cluster, give a fine autumn display of orange and red. The flowers are yellow-veined and edged with crimson. If, for any reason, stems have to be cut back they will 'break' readily. New growth arises from the base in any case.

EPIGAEA REPENS **(Ericaceae)** MAYFLOWER, TRAILING ARBUTUS (E)

Eastern N America, 1736. A creeping shrub with oval leaves of bright green and white scented flowers. Very difficult to cultivate in northern regions as it is vulnerable to spring frosts and hardly deserves a handlight.

ERICA **(Ericaceae)** HEATH (E)

The only heaths are European natives, a few British. They prefer a light, sandy soil with peat but do reasonably well in a neutral medium.

1 Summer-flowering. Prune each spring, making sure to avoid cutting into old wood and therefore not going much below the flowered spikes, which have been left on through the winter as they are decorative. As far as possible secateurs should be used, but if a large area is involved shears can be substituted so long as you make some variation in the angle at which the blades are directed, in the hope of preserving a natural appearance. As the plants grow older take cuttings, and be ready to substitute them as signs of senility appear

in the original stock.

2 Winter-flowering. Some authorities prune every second or third year or even do not prune at all. Experience suggests that cutting back immediately after flowering prolongs the healthy life of the shrub. Be sure that you *do* trim immediately after flowering, since new growth may already have begun. Very vigorous forms of *E. carnea* such as 'Springwood Pink' or 'Springwood White' may be cut back at this time to avoid collision with neighbours. Others in this group are 'Ruby Glow' and 'Winter Beauty'.

3 Tree heaths, **Erica arborea**. Var *alpina* cv 'Backhouse vivellii' is preferred as it is very hardy. This being so it should not need pruning unless damaged by snow or gale.

E. lusitanica does well in mild maritime areas and flowers abundantly but elsewhere is tender unless well protected.

E. terminalis is hardy, flowers throughout the summer and tolerates neutral soil. The flowers are rose-pink and the foliage rather dark green. It is widely available.

ERIOBOTRYA JAPONICA (Rosaceae)
LOQUAT (E)

Makes a small tree given the protection of a wall. It flowers through winter and may produce fruit but this rarely achieves an edible maturity except in the mildest areas. However, the foliage is attractive, the glossy corrugated green leaves sometimes 0.3m (1ft) long. No pruning needed.

ESCALLONIA (Escalloniaceae)

All are evergreen except one, and that one of the best, *E. virgata*. They thrive in any soil and some are hardy in milder regions.

E. langleyensis A hybrid from *E. virgata* and *E. rubra*. Of the group of hybrids stemming from this cross 'Apple Blossom' is as fine as any and 'Donard Seedling' another.

E. × 'Iveyi' This plant is of uncertain parent-age and has been damaged even against a wall, especially by late frosts, but quickly recovers. It is beautiful in leaf and has white flowers.

E. virgata Deciduous, bone-hardy and bears white flowers profusely in early summer.

Pruning of all these shrubs is confined to the occasional removal of a long branch spoiling the shape of the whole. Plants which are cut to the ground by frost must not too readily be assumed to be dead. They may regenerate in late spring.

EUCALYPTUS (Myrtaceae) GUM TREE (E)

A most complex genus which justifies confining attention to the two hardy members which can be planted without much risk in colder areas.

E. gunnii CIDER GUM, a native of Tasmania, has produced trees from 21-30m (70-100ft), but all in mild or maritime regions. It is hardy except in really severe winters but is often damaged by prolonged cold wind. It will grow in most soils but chalk is best avoided.

In the nursery it should be planted out from pots as soon as possible. Later it should not need any support. Should frost damage occur the young plant can be cut back to 0.3m (1ft) and should continue growth. Another form of culture is to cut away all growth to near ground level in spring, the result being the appearance of very large leaves which make an effective ground cover. This can be repeated annually or every other year.

Drimys winteri is one of the most handsome evergreen shrubs for a sheltered corner. The fragrant flowers, opening in early summer, are ivory white. Prune hard in spring

E. parvifolia SMALL-LEAVED GUM is about equally hardy and makes an elegant small tree with a dense crown. No pruning is needed.

EUCOMMIA ULMOIDES
(Eucommiaceae) (D)

This really does look like an elm, and is absolutely hardy and vigorous in good soil. It should be trained to a clean stem up to 1.8m (6ft) as the crown develops quickly once laterals are allowed to grow. Uniquely for temperate climates, it produces rubber, though not of commercial quality. If a leaf is torn in two, strings of rubber can be seen.

EUCRYPHIA *(Eucryphiaceae)*

E. glutinosa (D) is hardy but seems to be lime-hating.

E. cordifolia (E) is lime-tolerant but rather tender. The hybrids are more satisfactory, especially *E. ×intermedia* (E), a tree 2.4-5.5m (8-18ft) high.

E. × nymansensis (glutinosa × cordifolia) (E) gave rise to the selected clones 'Nymans A' and 'Nymans B'. The former, as 'Nymansay', has proved most successful and is hardy in mild, maritime areas.

All eucryphias need sun but also some shelter; not always an easy combination to find. No routine pruning.

EUODIA *(Rutaceae)* (D)

E. davidii and *E. hupehensis* are very similar, both making trees to 15m (50ft) in any soil and are hardy. The small white flowers have a scent which is hard to describe. These trees are somewhat brittle and should be placed in some shelter. No pruning once established.

EUONYMUS *(Celastraceae)* SPINDLE TREE.

Evergreen and deciduous shrubs and creepers.

E. alatus COMMON SPINDLE TREE (D) Japan. Valued for its scarlet leaves in autumn.

E. europaeus (D) Europe, including Britain.

Draws attention by its scarlet fruits.

E. fortunei (E) is a very hardy trailing evergreen, useful as ground cover but when reaching an upright surface climbing by aerial roots as ivy does.

E. japonicus (E) Much used for hedging in seaside resorts (see Hedges & Topiary).

The need for pruning in these and other species is only for restriction and fairly obvious. The deciduous forms are often attacked by black fly, which may be hard to control and involve some cutting back.

EUPATORIUM LIGUSTRINUM
(Compositae) (E)

Mexico. Usually grown as a pot plant in summer. It has survived outdoors in maritime sites and is worth a risk as it is a very shapely plant and bears fragrant white flowers in late summer. If it needs pruning something is amiss.

EURYOPS ACRAEUS *(Compositae)* (E)

Natal, Basutoland, c1945. A truly evergreen shrub, up to 0.9m (3ft) high. Bright yellow flowers. It needs sun and a well-drained soil and has proved hardy in mild areas.

EXOCHORDA *(Rosaceae)* (D)

All like good soil. *A. racemosa* resents chalk. They all are liable to produce sucker growths and these should be removed in winter until a clean leg of 0.3m (1ft) has been formed. They will continue to need attention. After flowering any unwanted shoots can be cut away or rubbed off.

E. macrantha 'The Bride' is the most popular cultivar, the upright *E. korolkowii* the most distinguished.

FABIANA IMBRICATA *(Solanaceae)* (E)

Likes a sandy soil but is only successful in milder areas.

F. i. violacea, reintroduced in the 1920s, is considered superior in all ways to the type, the branches projecting almost at right angles and making the shrub as wide as it is tall. One main leader should be maintained. If any laterals are damaged they can be removed and regeneration quickly begins.

FAGUS (Fagaceae) (D)

F. sylvatica COMMON BEECH is a native of southern Britain and one of the nation's best-loved trees, whether as an isolated specimen or in plantations (many of which date from the eighteenth century and are regrettably reaching their end). When drawn up to a tall smooth column of considerable grandeur the crown is dense and the lower branches die off. When this is detected these branches should be removed so that a healthy wound results. In maturity there is a tendency for large limbs to fall suddenly, leaving an ugly tear on the trunk. Such an event is very difficult, perhaps impossible, to predict and foresters are driven to advise felling when in doubt, particularly when there is public access to the site. In addition there are several fungus infections which may affect the root system and make the tree unsafe. The numerous forms and cultivars present the same problems as *F. sylvatica*.

F. grandiflora The AMERICAN BEECH is not a success in Britain and that is all that can be said, except that the same is true of many trees, notably oaks, from eastern N America. Perhaps lack of hot sun is a factor in its dislike of migration. American tree-lovers seem to consider their beech superior to that of Europe and, once more, that is all that can be said.

F. englerana China. This tree is not controversial; it is a most charming specimen. The foliage, especially when young, has a very attractive light green colour. It tends to branch early and that cannot be rectified.

× FATSHEDERA LIZEI (Araliaceae) (E)

This is *Fatsia japonica* 'Moseri' × *Hedera helix hibernica*. It is a hardy shrub, enduring shade well and showing a tendency to climb. The variegated form has very striking green and yellow leaves. In a confined space pruning to direct growth is effective.

FATSIA JAPONICA (Araliaceae) (E)

Usually a wide-spreading shrub reaching 6m (20ft) if trained up a wall. It has lobed, dark green leaves at least 0.3m (1ft) across and branching panicles of white flowers in autumn. At that time it makes a striking picture. Pruning is often needed in a town environment. Most of the branches arise at ground level and the most prominent can be cut back to their origin.

FEIJOA SELLOWIANA (Myrtaceae) (E)

A large shrub, demanding shelter near, not close to, a wall. Leaves greyish-green, flowers crimson and white. Pruned back directly after flowering each year it will build up a firm structure. Now it has changed its name to *Acca* but still *sellowiana*. It is available commercially.

FICUS CARICA (Moraceae)

COMMON FIG (D)

From W Asia, but grown in Europe including Britain. It will grow in the open in northern latitudes but, except in the mildest areas, must have wall shelter to produce fruit. When cut to the ground by frost it revives in the spring. Garden plants are always females, which can develop fruits without the help of a male. If the shrub becomes untidy, as it usually does, it can safely be cut back to the ground in autumn or winter (see also Fruit Trees & Bushes).

FONTANESIA PHILLYREOIDES (Oleaceae) (D)

Said to have the same character and value as privet which is, of course, cheaper, and much easier to obtain.

FORSYTHIA (Oleaceae) (D)

An important genus which does best in good

soil (but see below) and tolerates lime. In essence, pruning is the same for them all. Most produce shoots from ground level readily and these are the replacements for the oldest stems, which are removed immediately after flowering.

F. × intermedia 'Spectabilis' Understandably the most popular member of the genus. It is likely to produce vigorous growth after pruning and not much flower until another year is past.

F. suspensa is grown against a wall where its main branches can reach 4.5-6m (15-20ft), the laterals being allowed to hang down. Older branches can be cut out after flowering and younger laterals trained in as replacements.

FOTHERGILLA MAJOR
(Hamamelidaceae) (D)

A shrub to 2.4m (8ft), preferring a sandy soil but disliking lime. It flowers in spring before the leaves appear and in autumn the latter turn yellow, then orange and finally red. The growths which occur at the base should not all be removed as they may provide a replacement if a mature branch dies.

Fothergilla Major

Fraxinus Pennsylvanica This young tree was chewed by rams when the trunk was 1.2m (4ft) high. A group of young stems emerged in the following spring. The central, and longest was selected, and all the others were cut away. The rams were also disposed of. The photograph above shows the selected new leader, with all other stems removed; the photograph opposite shows the tree flourishing after 4 years

FRAXINUS (Oleaceae) ASH (D)

A genus of over thirty trees and a few shrubs. Most of the trees are shapely and have good pinnate leaves. They are hardy, tolerant of most soils and fast-growing.

F. americana WHITE ASH. A great tree in the eastern USA and one of the best American trees brought to Britain, notable for its handsome outline and the quality of its timber.

F. excelsior COMMON ASH. A British native which at its best is a really noble tree. That 'best' is most likely in a deep moist soil, often clay, and not excluding lime. It is very fine in the dales and plains of Yorkshire. Its timber is exceptionally tough and durable. If a sizeable branch has to be removed it is usually possible to find a straight length from which a handle can be made for a gardening tool. Though this ash is hardy enough, it sometimes loses its first growth of leaves from a late frost. However, the foliage is quickly replaced.

F. ornus MANNA ASH is a relatively small tree, easily grown and within a few years producing off-white flowers, rather malodorous but pretty, in spring. The lower shoots should be removed gradually to give a clean stem as the branches tend to droop. The crown is dense but should not be thinned.

F. pennsylvanica is less tall than *F. americana* but even more handsome in Britain.

FREMONTODENDRON
(Sterculiaceae) (E)
Makes a shrub or small tree, evergreen or semi-evergreen, needing a light, well-drained, not rich soil. It tolerates chalk. The flowers are golden yellow on leafy spurs. It is not hardy except in the mild areas. It should be pot-grown until planted in its permanent site as it hates disturbance at the root, and should be staked until several feet high. Pruning is not needed.

FUCHSIA *(Onagraceae)* (D)
Best represented in gardens by the hybrids, mostly derived from *F. magellanica*. The oldest is 'Corallina', often grown against house walls in the South West and North Wales. The flowers are reddish purple. In colder areas it is herbaceous. 'Madame Cornelissen' and 'Mrs Popple' are both levelled to the ground in winter but revive in spring and old growth can then be cut away, having served as a marker and possibly provided some protection. 'Riccartonii' is almost hardy, quite so in the mild regions and especially in W Ireland, where it naturalises.

GARRYA ELLIPTICA *(Garyaceae)* (E)
The male form is usually grown for its flowers, which are on pendent catkins up to 15cm (6in) long in cold areas, nearer 30cm (1ft) in warmer places. The flowering shoots should be cut right back once they look shabby. This applies to the shrub when it is grown beside a wall though not trained as a climber. If that is done the whole last year's growth can be

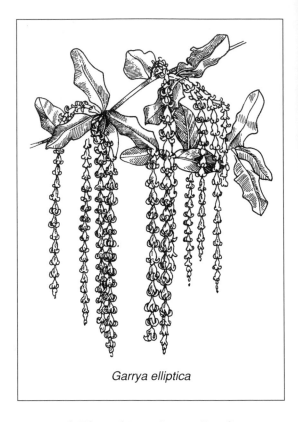

Garrya elliptica

removed. The cultivar 'James Roof' seems a superior plant with much longer flowering catkins. It and the species are widely available in commerce.

GAULTHERIA *(Ericaceae)* (E)
All need an acid soil and moisture, and a sheltered position with some shade. All are hardy and the following are the most favoured species.

G. cuneata W China, 1909. Flowers white, early summer. Fruits white.

G. miqueliana Japan, 1892. Flowers white, fruits white or pink.

G. procumbens N America, before 1762. Flowers pinkish white, fruit bright red.

G. shallon Western N America, 1826. Flowers pink-white, in spring and summer. Fruits dark purple.

All are readily available. Pruning has no role except for restricting the spread of the shrub and is seldom necessary.

GAYLUSSACIA (Ericaceae) HUCKLEBERRY USA, 1796.

G. brachycera BOX HUCKLEBERRY (E) seems to be the only species to have made any mark in Britain. A small neat deciduous shrub. A call for pruning, apart from removing dead wood, is very unlikely.

GENISTA (Leguminosae) BROOM

A large genus of shrubs and trees, mostly deciduous. All but one species have yellow flowers. In many the leaves are so few and small that the green stems fulfil their function. Some are dwarf and, at the other extreme, some are 6m (20ft) or over.

G. aetnensis Sardinia, Sicily. More a tree than a shrub, up to 6m (20ft). Staking in the nursery stage and pruning to a 0.9 or 1.2m (3 or 4ft) leg gives it a good start. Wonderful in flower, golden yellow, it is still handsome with its bright stems at other times. No pruning.

G. hispanica SPANISH GORSE. A small shrub not much more than 0.3m (1ft) high, and rounded. It likes a light soil, not rich, and a sunny position. In early summer it covers itself in golden yellow blossom. If overfed it develops dead patches which spoil its looks. Follow the advice of George Brown (see bibliography): cut away the dead wood and peg down some living stems to fill the gap. Dress with leaf mould to encourage rooting, and watch the results. It works.

G. lydia May suffer in the same way but cannot be pruned effectively.

G. pilosa Europe. Makes dense ground cover, useful for sunny slopes.

G. tenera Madeira, 1777. A large bush and wide, very regular in outline and flowering in summer. It is difficult to get. Try the similar *G. cinerea*, SW Europe.

GINKGO BILOBA (Ginkgoaceae)

MAIDENHAIR TREE

China, 1754. It is best raised from S European seed but is always very slow for the first ten years or more. Perfectly hardy. The fan-shaped leaves are maybe unique and very beautiful. Flowers of no account. After raising it from seed and planting out it is vital to maintain an upright leader. If neglected the growth can be quite irregular and very difficult to straighten. A bamboo stake does help and the tree does respond to pruning by growing, but attention to rival leaders has to be kept up, perhaps for years. It's worth it. (See also Conifers.)

GLEDITSIA (Leguminosae) (D)

They are deciduous and pod-bearing, tender when young but improving later. Fond of good soil and plenty of sun; they should and probably do thrive in East Anglia where the summers are hotter than elsewhere in England.

G. caspica CASPIAN LOCUST. Caucasus, Iran, 1822. A tree to 9 or 12m (30 or 40ft), notable for the number of very big spines on the trunk, a feature which is commended by some writers who probably do not have children. Personal experience was that this tree proved extremely slow in growth and had no redeeming features.

G. triacanthus HONEY LOCUST. Central and eastern USA, 1700. Draws attention by its fern-like leaves which turn yellow in autumn. Happily the spines are smaller than on plants grown on the European continent and not so large in shady places as in sunlight. In addition the fruits are in pods over 0.3m (1ft) long, which rattle in the wind.

G. f. inermis is said to be free from spines altogether and cultivar 'Sunburst' has leaves golden in spring, becoming green later. It is unarmed.

However, only *G. triacanthus* and its cultivars 'Ruby Lace' and 'Sunburst' are widely available. All these plants make a leader readily and need pruning only for cosmetic reasons. Prune in autumn or early winter to avoid bleeding. They deserve to be more widely planted.

GREVILLEA ROSMARINIFOLIA
(Proteaceae) (E)

Only reliably hardy in the mildest places. A handsome shrub to 1.8m (6ft) high. Flowers crimson in racemes. Prune if necessary in spring.

GRINDELIA CHILOENSIS
(Compositae) (E)

A sub-shrub wider than it is high (0.6-0.9m; 2-3ft). It belies its reputation for tenderness and is hardy in the southern half of England. It needs full sun and good drainage. The flowers are rich yellow through the summer. Dead growth can be removed in spring and new growth will soon appear.

GRISELINIA (Cornaceae) (E)

Two species from New Zealand.

G. littoralis 1850. Not hardy except in mild regions. It tolerates chalk and stands up to Atlantic wind. It hardly seems to have sufficient charm for a specimen shrub, though the apple-green leaves are pleasant, but it is an excellent shrub for maritime places and is commonly used there for hedging (see p163).

G. lucida Less hardy but has larger leaves. No pruning problem.

GYMNOCLADUS DIOICA (Leguminosae)
KENTUCKY COFFEE TREE (D)

E and C USA, early eighteenth century. Hardy and likes a rich soil but grows very slowly and very seldom flowers. As so often, this is a tree which does not perform really well in Britain, perhaps from lack of sun. Pruning should ensure a clear trunk of 1.8m (6ft) or a little more. The outer branches above this are somewhat pendulous and bring down the foliage to eye level.

HALESIA (Styracaceae) SNOWDROP TREE (D)

All the species seen in Britain come from SE USA, and like a soil which drains well but does not dry out (not easy to supply). They also hate lime.

H. carolina 1756. One of the most beautiful trees to come from the USA but is by no means common in Britain. It makes a spreading tree to 6m (20ft) and flowers in late spring, in white clusters on the wood of the previous year. It can be kept as a bush as growth often arises low down and can be left to develop.

H. monticola 1897. Much taller and quickly forms a tree if the leader is maintained by regular removal of rivals. It flowers when quite young. _H. monticola_ var. _vestita_ is not significantly different. All three of the plants mentioned are readily available.

× HALIMIOCISTUS
(Cistus × Halimium) (E)

Four hybrids of which only × _H. wintonensis_ is of garden origin.

× **H.** 'Ingwersenii' is a pretty, hardy shrub with white flowers from spring into summer.

× **H. sahucii** Larger, to 45cm (18in), with white flowers in early summer.

× **H. wintonensis** (H. lasianthus × Cistus salvifolius) Flowers white with a maroon and yellow blotch at the base. It is not reliably hardy. None of these hybrids responds well to pruning.

HALIMIUM (Cistaceae) (E)

H. lasianthum Spreads without being more than 0.3m (1ft) high. Flowers yellow with a purple blotch near the base. Perfectly hardy and can be discreetly pruned to restrict spread.

H. ocymoides May be 0.6-0.9m (2-3ft) high with downy shoots and panicles of yellow flowers, each with a purple blotch at the

An informal hedge of _Hibiscus syriacus_ 'Blue Bird' ('Oiseau Bleu') needs full exposure to sun and a fertile soil. It grows slowly and is hardy, but only flowers freely in mild areas, and never as well as in its native France. When a framework has been formed by cutting stems to half their length each spring, the pruning will then cut back all growths to three or four buds from their origin, again in spring

base. It seems hardy and long-lived, not needing pruning if given enough room.

HALIMODENDRON HALODENDRON
(Leguminosae) SALT TREE (D)
SE Russia, 1729. A shrub 1.2-1.8m (4-6ft) high with a spreading habit and springy branches. Flowers pale purple in early summer and grey foliage. Avoid pruning if possible. It has in the past been grafted on *Caragana arborescens* or laburnum and if so a watch should be kept for suckers, which should be easy to identify.

HAMAMELIS (Hamamelidaceae)
WITCH HAZEL (D)
All have very narrow petals up to 2.5cm (1in) long. They like a good average soil, preferably neutral.

H. mollis China, 1874. CHINESE WITCH HAZEL has spreading branches and it may be worth training a leader to raise the plant to 1.8m (6ft) high, so that the midwinter flowers and their scent can be enjoyed.

H. pallida is suspected of being a hybrid. The flowers are described as 'soft sulphur yellow' (Bean) and appear in midwinter.

H. virginiana Eastern N America, 1736. May make a small tree, more often a low spreading bush. The golden yellow flowers appear in late summer and continue until late autumn, and the persistence of the leaves obscures them. This is the *hamamelis* from which the medicinal witch-hazel is produced.

Pruning of any of these plants should be restricted to limiting unwanted spread, and be carried out between flowering and the appearance of the leaves. Those mentioned are widely available.

HEBE (Scrophulariaceae) (E)
Mostly from New Zealand. In this genus intermediate forms abound, probably hybrids, and that makes identification difficult. Variable in hardiness, they are easy to grow and do best in light sandy soil, tolerating chalk. It is impossible to list plants in relation to hardiness since it seems likely that the nature of the soil in which they are grown has a definite effect, that which is over-rich making for tenderness. Many of the large-leaved species, such as *H. speciosa,* are tender and are cut back severely in a frost of any magnitude. They should be left untouched until spring when new growth appears (if the plant has survived) and then pruned. Spring pruning also benefits those which are untidy. The very desirable *H. hulkeana* seems to benefit from removal of the spent flowers, as might be expected, the fruits being substantial.

HEDYSARUM (Leguminosae) (D)
Most are herbaceous but *H. multijugum* (Mongolia, 1883) is a deciduous shrub up to 1.5m (5ft) high with sparse ungainly growth. Flowers magenta in summer. Long branches may be cut back in spring but may also be pegged down at that time to make replacements.

HELIANTHEMUM (Cistaceae) SUN ROSE (E)
Any soil, including limestone, suits them but they must have full sun. They benefit from light pruning with secateurs as flowers fade.

HELICHRYSUM SPLENDIDUM
(Compositae) (E)
S Africa. Hardy and will grow to 0.9m (3ft) high and more across, but is best pruned hard in spring and trimmed lightly in summer. The flowers are unimportant.

HIBISCUS SYRIACUS (Malvaceae) (D)
E Asia, sixteenth century. Not a graceful shrub, with its upright branches often crowded together, but it has the virtue of flowering in late summer. It is hardy except in the north and grows in an average soil but must not be shaded. On the Continent of Europe, as at Versailles, it flowers more profusely than in Britain. Of the numerous vari-

eties the single-flowered are more elegant. Pruning is first directed to dead or diseased wood, which suggests a soil defect or coral spot disease. For a formal effect, even a hedge, cutting back in spring is appropriate.

HIPPOPHAE RHAMNOIDES
(Elaeagnaceae) (D)
Europe, temperate Asia, native to Britain in maritime areas but grows perfectly well inland in average soil. The features are the silvery leaves and the orange berries, ripe in autumn and persisting for months. Pruning is not needed, especially when a clump is formed.

Hippophae rhamnoides

HOHERIA (Malvaceae)
All from New Zealand.
H. lyallii A small tree with grey leaves and fine white flowers. Is hardy except in severe winters.
H. glabrata (D) Much the same.
H. populnea (E) Tender.
H. 'Glory of Amlwch' (D) is thought to be a hybrid *glabrata × sextylosa*. The latter is evergreen and almost hardy in mild regions; 'Glory of Amlwch' is said to be hardier than both, but as a young tree it is tender.

Pruning includes the training of a leader for the tree forms, and clearing dead wood after winter. Coral spot is a problem in damp situations.

HOLODISCUS DISCOLOR
(Rosaceae) (D)
N America, 1827. Makes a large shrub with arching stems, with lobed leaves and panicles of creamy flowers in summer. It needs good soil and an isolated but not shady position. The flowering period is regrettably short. Young canes are produced from the base and the oldest stems may be removed each year after flowering. Some must be left and are reduced to a point at which young shoots are growing.

HYDRANGEA (Hydrangeaceae) (D)
The genus is divided botanically into sections and of the shrubs and trees in cultivation nearly all belong to the section Hydrangea. All the species like a rich soil and some tolerate chalk, and some shade, notably *H. aspera* and *H. involucrata* 'Hortensis' (Bean, 1973, p384; see bibliography).
H. arborescens Can reach 3m (10ft) with loose growth. Fertile flowers of dull white. Far surpassed by *H. a.* cv. Grandiflora, a splendid plant whose stems bend under the weight of the flower head, a fault which is easily corrected by installing at an early stage a circular support such as is used for paeonies. It has pure white flowers (large, sterile) through summer and is hardy.
H. aspera villosa Up to 3m (10ft) and wider across. As originally described had flowers varying from white through pink to purple but Bean (1973, p386) considers that the species is mainly represented in Britain by plants called *H. villosa*. In 1990 *H. aspera villosa* seems to be the correct title. This plant, whatever its name, is most desirable, with rosy flowers bluish-purple and good structure. It is somewhat tender and apt to lose its flower buds in a spring frost.
H. macrophylla A parent of the dozens of garden plants, possibly hybrids and divided for convenience into Hortensias and Lacecaps. The parent itself is of botanical interest only.

HYDRANGEA MACROPHYLLA

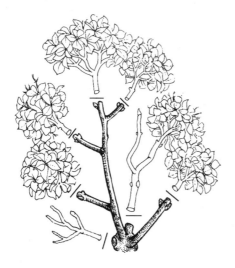

ABOVE:
Flower heads of the previous season are left on the shrub until spring and are then cut away, together with any failing stems. Basal growth of new stems does not always form readily, and manuring is advisable at this time

BELOW:
The result: good flowering, and new growth for next season

Hortensias have flower heads which are globose corymbs: white, pink, red, blue or a combination. Hortensias, mop-headed hydrangeas, reach 1.8m, sometimes in mild areas 3m (6-10ft). They are best suited by a site to the north or west of a wall, or at least a sheltered site with some shade. The flowering stems are cut back to 5cm (2in) from the old wood once the flowers are spent. In cold areas delay this until the following spring.

Lacecaps have large flattened corymbs of fertile flowers. They are mostly vigorous and include 'Blue Wave' and 'Mariesii', whose flowers are blue only in acid soils, otherwise pink or lilac. Pruning is delayed until the point in spring when buds are developing well, or not so well. It is thought that the dead heads provide some frost protection through the winter. In spring cut back to a healthy bud and remove any shoots that look weak. In fact, if treated well with regular manuring, weak and worn out shoots are not very common, and it is often possible to do no more than remove dead flowerstalks.

H. paniculata cv 'Grandiflora', up to 6m (20ft) high, has flowers white to pink, all sterile, in a pyramid. Not surprisingly it requires good loamy soil and a mulch of manure once growth has started. The flowering stem is cut back to two to four buds in early spring.

H. quercifolia OAK-LEAVED HYDRANGEA. SE USA, 1803. Up to 1.8m (6ft) when grown on the north side of a 2.4m (8ft) wall. Leaves like those of the Red Oak in its native America. Flower panicles are erect through summer and sufficiently numerous in the site mentioned above. Also hardy.

H. sargentiana A noble plant when seen at its best; 3m (10ft) high but also quite low when in considerable shade. It needs the best soil. The leaves are large, up to 25cm (10in) long and 15cm (6in) wide, with a hairy covering like velvet on the upper surface. Sterile flowers white on the outer side. Fertile flowers beautiful rosy-lilac. It is subject to damage from spring frosts but recovers quickly,

Hydrangea arborescens 'Grandiflora'. A cultivar from Ohio, markedly superior to the type. Pure white flowers appear from midsummer for many weeks. The plant needs support as its stems extend

though a year's flower may be lost. The woody framework is absolutely hardy.

HYPERICUM (Hypericaceae)

The terminology of this genus has been a minefield, largely resolved by Dr. N. K. B. Robson when at the British Museum (Natural History). The plants are valued especially for flowering in late summer and autumn, but their foliage is healthy and a good green for many months. They like good soil, most tolerating chalk, and are hardy.

H. calycinum ROSE OF SHARON (E) is an excellent ground carpeter in shade, if not dense. Unlike most plants of that description it is beautiful when flowering, which occupies most of the summer.

H. kouytchense (D) China. Semi-evergreen, 0.9m (3ft), with good golden yellow flowers followed by red fruits. Two notable hybrids are *H.* 'Hidcote', quite hardy, and *H.* 'Rowallane' with large flowers. The latter is

not fully hardy but if frosted will usually recover and flower later in the year.

Pruning of *H. calycinum* is simple, consisting of cutting the whole plant almost to ground level. The more shrubby sort can be pruned in spring, removing the dead ends of the shoots and shortening the living portion by a few centimetres to produce a sizeable shrub – or alternatively, and less desirably, cut right back as for *H. calycinum.*

HYSSOPUS OFFICINALIS (Labiatae) (E)

S Europe, West Asia, traditional in Britain by the sixteenth century. An aromatic shrub to 45cm (18in), leaves aromatic, flowers blue, rather insignificant. Cut back in early spring.

***IDESIA POLYCARPA (Flacourtiaceae)* (D)**
Japan, China, 1864. Grows well in neutral or acid soil and readily makes a straight trunk, with horizontal branches in threes. These grow long enough to shade neighbouring areas of the garden and the lower ones may have to be removed. The flowers are tiny but large bunches of red berries may appear in exceptionally hot years. This tree is available but not widely.

***ILEX (Aquifoliaceae)* HOLLY (E)**
All species like a moist, loamy soil, but often the common ones do not get it. They have alternate leaves, flowers of little account except to bees, and the fruit is a drupe (a skin, fleshy layer and store protecting the seed) and not a berry.
I.* × *altaclerensis A group of hybrids between *I. aquifolium* and *I. perado* including 'Camelliifolia', 'Golden King' (golden variegated), and 'Hodginsii', formerly much planted in industrial areas because of its tolerance of a polluted atmosphere.
***I. aquifolium* COMMON HOLLY.** British native. So common that its virtues are often overlooked. It can make a tree to 15m (50ft), a specimen shrub or a splendid hedge (see 'Hedges & Topiary'). After centuries of cultivation it has accumulated a vast collection of varieties and cultivars, of which the best may be 'J. C. Van Thol'.
I. verticillata Of the deciduous hollies, does best in Britain, with scarlet berries which mature before the leaves fall. American hollies such as *I. verticillata* do not flourish in Britain.
   Pruning to shape is best in spring and the wounds are soon hidden. *I. aquifolium* can be pruned at any time but high summer is usually recommended, for no reason that is obvious; perhaps because that is not a busy time.

***ILLICIUM (Illiciaceae)* (E)**
I. anisatum Japan, Formosa, 1790. A shrub or small tree, hardy in milder regions where it may reach 6m (20ft). It prefers an acid soil and some shelter from high winds. Flowers in spring, greenish yellow. The leaves and wood have a strong, elusive fragrance.
***I. floridanum*,** S USA, 1771. As hardy as the former, flowers in late spring, maroon-purple. The whole plant has the same fragrance. Pruning is only necessary to control wayward growth, when it is best carried out in autumn.

***INDIGOFERA (Leguminosae)* (D)**
The shrubs able to survive in northern temperate regions lose all their shoots in winter if unprotected, but do survive. All they ask is a sunny position, and they seem to tolerate a moderately limey soil.
I. amblyantha China, 1908. Hardier than most. The pinnate leaves are pleasant and the flowers, in racemes, are rosy pink and appear throughout the summer.
I. potaninii China, 1825. Has a similar habit of growth and flowering, both preserving a short woody branch system. Pruning in early spring removes the dead part of the shoots and 2.5-5cm (1-2in) of the new growth.

***ITEA ILICIFOLIA (Escalloniaceae)* (E)**
China, 1901. A superb evergreen shrub up to 3m (10ft), doing well in good soil with some shelter. In Somerset it flourishes a few feet away from the north side of a 2.4m (8ft) wall and, in ten years, has never shown a sign of frost damage. The leaves are holly-like but no more than those of *Quercus ilex*. The pendulous racemes of greenish white flowers hang vertically, 0.3m (1ft) or more long, quite crowded, and make a memorable picture. No doubt in northerly districts it would not be so attractive and probably too tender to be worth growing except under glass. It is widely available.

JASMINUM (Oleaceae)
Excluding the climbers there are several shrubby members of merit.

J. humile cv 'Revolutum' (E) China, 1814. Evergreen with good leaflets and slightly fragrant, rather hard yellow flowers in mid-summer. It is reasonably hardy in milder regions.

J. nudiflorum WINTER JASMINE (D) China, 1844. Not a climber, but is usually trained against a wall where it produces many flowers of a bright yellow during winter months, as it will in open ground after a hot summer. The best scheme of training is to use a fan system of bamboos, tying them to horizontal wires on the wall. Laterals from the leading shoots which are tied to the bamboos hang down and, immediately after flowering, are cut back almost to their origin. New shoots appear in spring and flower the next winter. This cycle has to be repeated each year. Good feeding of the plant after pruning is important.

JUGLANS (Juglandaceae) (D)

J. nigra BLACK WALNUT. Eastern and central USA, early seventeenth century. One of the greatest park trees: in Britain almost all the largest recorded in the last thirty years are in the southern half of England, but two in Scotland (Ross and Cromarty). It is very fine when quite young. A most valuable timber tree, it is not easy to rear. Planted small it quickly forms a tap root and then resents interference, so that it may have to be transplanted several times and root-pruned whilst still on the nursery. However *J. nigra* does keep a leader well, and it is possible to remove lower branches to give a clear trunk to 4.5m (15ft), not forgetting that pruning should not be delayed after Christmas as bleeding does occur once the growing season begins.

J. regia COMMON WALNUT has been in Britain for many centuries. When young it is subject to frost damage and may lose the leader. A replacement must be trained and kept under observation, rivals being cut away as soon as possible. Bleeding is to be avoided here also. If you have a spare acre, consider an orchard.

KALMIA (Ericaceae)

They must have acid soil and moisture and are slow-growing even in good conditions. Full sun is needed for good flowering.

K. angustifolia (E) Eastern N America, 1736. SHEEP LAUREL is evergreen and grows to 0.9m (3ft) high, and spreads. Flowers deep rosy red, late spring.

K. latifolia (E) Eastern N America, 1734. 3m (10ft) high and 4.5m (15ft) across. Flowers white or blush to deep rose. Pruning is not necessary if the plants have been correctly sited.

KALOPANAX PICTUS (Araliaceae) (D)

Japan, 1874. A small tree resembling a maple. The branches carry stout prickles. The palmate leaves on young plants are over 0.3m (1ft) long, deeply five or seven-lobed. An elegant tree, quite hardy. There are or were fine specimens at Hergest Croft, Herefordshire and Endsleigh, Devon.

KERRIA JAPONICA (Rosaceae) (D)

A hardy deciduous shrub to 2.4m (8ft) in woodland conditions. Leaves light green, flowers yellow each on a short leafy twig. The green stems look well in winter. The cultivar 'Pleniflora' is much more common and much less attractive. In both suckers abound, and lead to a thicket if not controlled by removing some and cutting some of the old shoots to the ground. This is best done after the flowers fade.

KOELREUTERIA (Sapindaceae)

PRIDE OF INDIA (D) China, 1763. A hardy tree up to 18m (60ft) (not often) with attractive pinnate leaves of light green. Flowers in panicles up to 0.3m (1ft) long, bright yellow, followed by brown capsules containing seeds like a pea. The leaves have a good yellow autumn colour but they are subject to coral spot.

Pruning not needed except in the early years in order to maintain a central leader.

KOLKWITZIA AMABILIS
(Caprifoliaceae)

A large shrub up to 3.6m (12ft) high, growing well in average soil and tolerating chalk well. It needs sun. The leaves are nondescript but the abelia-like flowers in late spring of soft pink, more definite in the clones 'Rosea' and 'Pink Cloud', are splendid.

Advice on pruning ranges from 'can be left to develop naturally' to 'prune after flowering, cutting back to new young growth'. No doubt in the early years pruning is not essential, but eventually the plant's performance deteriorates and it becomes necessary to cut out whole lengths of old wood on which there are no new shoots, which suggests that good feeding every year might have saved the day. When this valuable plant is in its prime its performance for six weeks or even more in early summer merits a deal of thought and effort.

LABURNOCYTISUS (Leguminosae) (D)

Graft hybrids between *Laburnum* and *Cytisus*.
L. adamii Of botanical interest but an impossible challenge to the pruner as each of the parents tends to appear in branches, particularly if they are pruned. Fortunately the broom, the laburnum and the hybrid all flower at the same time.

LABURNUM (Leguminosae) (D)

They grow well in any soil not waterlogged, though not often exceeding 7.6m (25ft).
L. alpinum SCOTCH LABURNUM. About 6m (20ft).

OPPOSITE:
Lavandula angustifolia 'Jean Davies'.
All lavenders benefit from being clipped back immediately after flowering is over. They are good edging plants, decorative and architectural

BELOW:
Itea ilicifolia is a superb evergreen shrub, but needs some shelter and is not suitable for cold districts

Leaves trifoliolate, dark green. Golden yellow flowers on pendulous racemes, 0.3m (12in) or more long. Summer.

These specimens are easily trained to a tree form with a 1.8m (6ft) leg and after that need little pruning. The branches are quite often misdirected and those which are crossing and rubbing should be removed entire. _L. anagyroides_ may be spur-pruned, cutting back the young growth to two buds in early winter, and this is the method used for covering arches, pergolas or tunnels.

LAURUS NOBILIS (Lauraceae)
BAY LAUREL (E)

Mediterranean, since sixteenth century, probably earlier. Not related to the COMMON LAUREL _(Prunus laurocerasus)_ or ALEXANDRIAN LAUREL _(Danae racemosa)_. It is tender in inland areas often scorched by frost and in such places is cut to the ground every few years, but always revives and gets away quickly. In maritime sites it stands the weather well. The fragrant leaves are tough, dark shining green and make a fine bush, tree or hedge. When crushed they have a spicy fragrance and are an excellent addition to stews or casseroles. The flowers are inconspicuous.

The bay responds well to pruning in spring and can be trimmed to shape in summer. It is often grown in tubs, where it requires little attention apart from reducing the new growth to shape with secateurs every few weeks in summer.

LAVANDULA (Labiatae) (D)
L. angustifolia A sub-shrub growing to 0.9m (3ft). Flowers purple, which gives the name lavender-purple, summer to autumn. In gardens and in commerce most plants show evidence of hybrid origin. Of those which do not 'Hidcote', around 0.3m (1ft), and 'Munstead', of the same height, are familiar. **L. stoechas** FRENCH LAVENDER (E) reaches 0.6m (2ft) high and the same across. It has grey-green leaves and dark purple flowers in spikes 5cm (2in) long, with a tuft of purple bracts on each spike. A very attractive plant.

All lavenders need pruning in spring, cutting off the flowers of last year and the young growth to near its base. If this is done each year the healthy and pleasant appearance of the plant is prolonged for several years. Do not prune them after flowering because then the new growth may not ripen sufficiently before winter.

Eventually it will not be possible to overcome the tendency to sprawl and die back, and replacement cuttings should be made ready.

LAVATERA (Malvaceae) (D)
Does well in poor soil, given a sunny site.
L. maritima The best species, but is unfortunately tender. The flowers are pale lilac with purple veins and a crimson blotch at the base of the petal. Suitable for maritime places.
L. olbia 'Rosea' is a favourite plant, vigorous and reaching 1.5-1.8m (5-6ft). The flowers are profuse and reddish pink from midsummer until autumn. The cultivar 'Barnsley', which has white flowers with a pink eye, is now even more favoured. Both are hardy for practical purposes, but rather short-lived.

All lavateras should be cut back in spring to 15cm (6in) from the ground.

LEDUM (Ericaceae) (E)
They are definitely calcifuge and like damp soil.
L. glandulosum Western N America. Grows to 0.9m (3ft) high, occasionally more. The white flowers, not exciting, appear in late spring.
L. groenlandicum N America, Greenland, 1763. Very hardy and has better white flowers.

Neither needs pruning except to control spread, but dead-heading probably helps to preserve the vigour of the shrub since it prevents seeding.

LEIOPHYLLUM BUXIFOLIUM
(Ericaceae) (E)

Eastern N America, 1736. A neat shrub with small leaves on short stalks and pink flower buds opening white. Its requirements and pruning are as for *Ledum*.

LEPTOSPERMUM (Myrtaceae) (E)

Natives of Australia and New Zealand as small trees or shrubs. Not fully hardy except in the warmest areas, where they may reach 3.6m (12ft).

L. lanigerum Flowers white and is comparatively hardy; has lived for years near the southern side of a wall.

L. rodwayanum 1930. Of similar hardiness and can reach 3m (10ft). White flowers.

L. scoparium 1772. The best-known and spectacular at Tresco Abbey in the Scilly Isles. At Kew, against a wall, it is killed in severe winters. There are cultivars of great merit, notably 'Nichollsii' (crimson) and 'Ruby Glow' (deep red and double).

Leptospermums do not break readily if cut into old wood. If necessary one should prune in late spring (if grown with wall protection, don't train them on the wall).

LESPEDEZA THUNBERGII
(Leguminosae) (D)

Japan, China, 1837. BUSH CLOVER stands out. Grooved stems of 1.2-2.4m (4-8ft) rise from a woody root stock and die back in the winter, a fresh set arising in the late spring and making a mass of stems. In autumn these bear large panicles of purple pea flowers. In spring the old growths are cut to the ground. Some protection from frost in winter is wise.

LEUCOTHOE (Ericaceae) (D/E)

They need a lime-free, rich soil and are hardy.

L. fonanesiana SE USA, 1793. Evergreen and makes a shrub to 1.8m (6ft) with tapering leaves and white flowers in late spring. Unfortunately they are all on the lower side of the branches and one needs Miss Jekyll's two men with a rope to bring them all into view.

Any pruning of an unhealthy stem should remove it at ground level. New growths form from the base and flower in the first year, so pruning can be completed in early spring.

LEYCESTERIA FORMOSA
(Caprifoliaceae) (D)

Half-woody and stool-like in its growth. In one season hollow stems rise to 1.5m (5ft) or more, and flower in summer with claret-coloured bracts and a purplish corolla. It likes rich soil and a sunny site.

It really has to be pruned; if left alone it quickly becomes a mass of weak and dying growths. Thinning these out seldom is enough. Better to cut down all growth to 10 centimetres from the ground in early spring. In this case it is even more than usually necessary to apply a heavy mulch in spring and water in summer. Whether it is worth it is a matter for individual taste.

LIGUSTRUM (Oleaceae)

From China and Japan, except for the least attractive which is European and a British native.

L. japonicum (E) China, Formosa, Japan, 1845. Evergreen, glossy and almost black leaves 10cm (4in) long. Flowers white in 20cm (8in) panicles in midsummer. It needs some shelter.

L. lucidum (E) China, 1794. A sizeable evergreen tree, sometimes 12m (40ft). Leaves glossy dark green. Flowers white in erect panicles 15cm (6in) or more high.

L. ovalifolium (E) Japan, 1885. Seen most often as the cultivar 'aureum Golden Privet'. It has been very widely used in town planting and only fashion has reduced it, as it will brighten places in which hardly anything else will grow. The leaves are green in the centre with a border of golden yellow. It is semi-evergreen or, in the worst soil conditions, deciduous. Useful as a hedge (see p164).

L. quihoui (D) China, 1862. Makes quite an elegant shrub with arching stems and fragrant white flowers in late autumn.

L. sinense (D) China, 1852. Hardy. Flowers white, midsummer, in masses of panicles. Round fruits, black-purple, persisting until New Year.

L. delavayanum (E) See Hedges & Topiary.

LINDERA (Lauraceae) (D)

L. obtusiloba Japan, China 1880. Seems to be the pick of the seven or so species suitable for northerly latitudes. It is a large deciduous shrub with leaves of interesting shape and dark glossy green above, turning butter-yellow with a hint of pink in autumn, but not always in colder climates. Like all the genus it must have a lime-free soil.

LINNAEA BOREALIS (Caprifoliaceae) (E)

About 1762. TWIN FLOWER cannot be omitted but is included out of respect for Linnaeus. It is a plant of Lapland and other high places of the northern hemisphere, even in NE Scotland. A creeper, a few inches high. Flowers produced in summer in pairs, pink or white. Right for a place in the informal rock garden, where pruning would be unthinkable.

LINUM ARBOREUM (Linaceae) (E)

East Mediterranean, 1788. Needs a well-drained soil and full sun, and is a neat but spreading evergreen, with golden flowers in summer. Cut back if invasive.

LIQUIDAMBAR (Hamamelidaceae) (D)

Does not tolerate chalky soils.

L. formosana The provenance of specimens in Britain seems somewhat confused but var. *monticola* (S China, Formosa, 1908) brought in by E. H. Wilson seems to be almost hardy, with leaves which turn from purple to crimson then dull green, but are crimson again in autumn.

L. styraciflua E USA, seventeenth century. SWEET GUM likes a good acid or neutral soil, though flourishing less in the latter. It makes a fine tree with a pyramidal crown, the development of which is aided by the complete removal of lower branches as the tree grows taller. The leaves, like those of a maple, turn a striking crimson in autumn. The cultivar 'Worplesdon' has become popular.

LIRIODENDRON (Magnoliaceae) (D)

L. chinense (D) China, 1901. Hardy and needs the best deep soil to show at its best. It dislikes being transplanted and should be put in its permanent place early. At Kew it has reached 15m (50ft) in seventy years.

L. tulipifera TULIP TREE (D) N America, 1688. Grows to a greater size than the Chinese tree. The trunk is very fine and smooth. The leaves are usually cut off almost square at the apex, as on no other tree. The flowers in early summer do resemble a tulip in shape, the petals greenish-yellowish with an orange spot near the base, which is a pity.

As to pruning, *L. chinense* makes a good leader without much help. *L. tulipifera* may need some help, rival leaders being searched out regularly and removed. The trunk should be cleaned to 4.5 or 6m (15 or 20ft) from the ground by gradual shortening and removal of laterals after three or four years. This tree is rarely as tall and well-shaped in Britain as it is in Pennsylvania. Is it the hotter summer there? That must be the reason. Even under the best conditions in Britain the tulip tree never rivals those in NE America.

LITHOCARPUS (Fagaceae) (E)

Natives of China and Japan except *L. densiflorus,* from SW USA. They resemble oaks but are botanically related to *Castanea.*

L. densiflorus California, Oregon, 1874. The BARK OAK is more or less hardy in the south of Britain and perfectly so at Kew. A leader must be kept going by removal of rivals, as the foliage is very heavy and small shoots are easily damaged by storms. This tree is not readily available.

LONICERA (Caprifoliaceae)

These shrubs are hardy and tolerate most soils. The climbers, which are dealt with in that chapter, are nearly all worth growing but the bushy shrubs are disappointing. They are often damaged by spring frosts and lose their flowers, and therefore berries also.

L. chaetocarpa (D) Promising in form and foliage but the floral performance, eagerly awaited, comes to very little.

L. nitida (E) China, 1908. Still much used for hedging in the form 'Ernest Wilson' (see Hedges & Topiary) and in the form 'Baggesen's Gold', with yellow leaves, as a specimen also.

L. pileata (D) More respectable, if unexciting. A low-growing shrub, evergreen if in a sheltered place. Young leaves bright green, flowers insignificant. Berries amethyst, but do not appear often. Shoots which have flowered are cut back severely.

MAACKIA (Leguminosae) (D)

E Asia. Very hardy trees, growing well in any good soil in sun.

M. amurensis Manchuria, 1864. Usually a shrub in Britain, a tree in USA Zone 4, reaching 4.5m (15ft) very slowly. The pinnate leaves resemble those of *Cladrastis* and the flowers in midsummer are dull white. Early pruning is directed to maintaining a leader; heavy feeding may help to produce a tree.

M. chinensis China, 1908. Will make a tree up to 12m (40ft) on which the leaves are silvery and the flowers unimpressive. No pruning needed.

MACLURA POMIFERA (Moraceae) (D)

South and central USA, 1878. OSAGE ORANGE is a hardy tree of moderate size with spiny branches, long and dark green leaves, inconspicuous flowers and round fruits, 5-10cm (2-4in) across (inedible). It is widely used as a hedge in the USA and Central Europe (see Hedges & Topiary). The tree needs no routine pruning.

MAGNOLIA (Magnoliaceae)

The majority are natives of China or Japan, nearly a third from eastern N America. All are worthy of cultivation with the exception, for gardeners, of *M. acuminata* (D) (E USA, 1736) a very grand tree with negligible flowers.

Their needs in the matter of soil are not clearly established, some authorities reporting that over half the species will not tolerate alkaline or chalky conditions, more than half of these being Chinese and only four American. Bean (1973) says that 'the only difficulty in cultivating these trees is in establishing them after transplanting.' There can be little doubt that *M. campbellii* (D), *M. dawsoniana* (D), *M. denudata* (D), *M. hypoleuca* (D), *M. liliiflora* (D), *M. salicifolia* (D) and *M. sprengeri* (D) cannot be made to thrive in chalky soils. In the case of the American species the explanation of failure may be, at least in part, climate – hot summers and hard winters, which are unusual in Britain. Fortunately British gardeners can grow *M. grandiflora* (E), though not as well as could be wished. *M. kobus* (D) certainly, *M. × loebneri*, *M. × soulangiana* and × *lennei*, *M. stellata* (D) and *M. wilsonii* (D), all need rich soil, retentive of moisture, and most require some shade – as in woodland.

As to pruning, most magnolias regenerate well even from old wood, and correction of faulty growth is straightforward. Any removal of stems more than 12mm (½in) in diameter is best left until the dormant period, from early autumn until midwinter. If it is left for longer than this there is likely to be 'bleeding', as growth will already have started. From long experience it is possible to say that painting wounds has no beneficial effect. If the cut is well made, infection or dieback do not occur.

× MAHOBERBERIS (Berberidaceae) (E)

× *M. aquisargentii* Believed to be a cross – *Mahonia aquifolium* with *Berberis sargentiana*, an evergreen Chinese species. A shrub to 1.5m (5ft) in ten years, with erect stems and leaves of which some are those of the *Mahonia* others of the *Berberis*, all shining dark green. The flowers are yellow, not freely borne. A not unpleasing plant of more than purely botanical interest. As the stems differ in length some shortening of the longer ones, usually the Mahonia-like specimens, improves the shape.

MAHONIA (Berberidaceae) (E)

A genus of evergreen shrubs, closely related to *Berberis* but they are all evergreen, have simply pinnate foliage and no spines on the branches. They are mostly hardy but some are tender except in mild places, such as *M. lomariifolia*; and some are definitely tender, such as *M. fremontii*. They like a good, rich soil, but *M. aquifolium* will survive under very poor conditions though not flowering well.

M. aquifolium OREGON GRAPE. Usually a small shrub, but against a wall or hedge may rise to 0.9m (3ft). Leaves shining dark green, yellow flowers in dense racemes in early spring, followed by black berries. It is very hardy and even known to naturalise on the Yorkshire Wolds. Understandably popular, it responds well to pruning if that becomes necessary, when it is best done in spring.

M. 'Charity' A seedling of *M. lomariifolia*, the other parent being *M. japonica* (see below). Apart from its beauty it flowers in early winter, a good yellow. The racemes form in succession and only those in full flower are liable to frost damage. Two deliberate crosses of *M. lomariifolia* and *M. japonica* produced 'Buckland' and 'Lionel Fortescue' with racemes freely branched and fragrant flowers opening in early winter.

M. fremontii Has blue-green leaves with flowers in small clusters. Hardy only on a south-facing wall.

M. japonica Hardy and a robust shrub to 1.2m (4ft) high. Splendid pinnate leaves and fragrant flowers opening from autumn

through winter make it a very desirable plant.

M. lomariifolia Not fully hardy but in a sheltered, partially shaded spot it flowers well on long erect spikes.

M. pinnata Perhaps now of hybrid origin as sold. Will reach 3m (10ft) and makes a graceful shrub, flowering profusely in early spring.

M. trifoliolata var. *glauca* is upright to 1.8m (6ft) high and if against a wall, which it has to be in most areas, makes branches which arch forward. Good glaucous leaves, some nearly white, and flowers not impressive. It is beautiful all the year round. No routine pruning, though removal of flowered shoots to control spread can be performed without any ill effect once they fade.

MALUS (Rosaceae) CRAB (D)

A large genus of deciduous trees including *M. domestica*, now the domestic apple, and *M. sylvestris*, the WILD CRAB. *M. domestica*, uniform in its essential botanical characteristics, is considered to be a group of hybrids, some of great antiquity. Excluding *M. domestica*, the term CRAB APPLE refers to plants derived from orchard apples crossed with 'Siberian' crabs, ie *M. baccata* which is considered to be rare in gardens, most plants grown under that name being forms of *M. robusta*, a group of hybrids.

Having conveyed some of the problems in the identification of *Malus* species and bearing in mind that there are no problems of pruning specific to the genus, it may suffice to name a few hybrids valued especially for their fruits, though most have worthy flowers.

M. 'Dartmouth'	Fruit crimson.
M. 'Golden Hornet'	Fruit deep yellow.
M. hillieri	Fruit yellow, worthy flowers.
M. 'John Downie'	Fruit orange and scarlet, worthy flowers.
M. 'Mahaleb'	Fruit yellow, worthy flowers.

Consider also one species grown only for

autumn leaf colour, which offers hues of yellow, orange, purple and scarlet – *M. tschonskii* – and finally one species which E. H. Wilson considered the finest deciduous tree he had introduced: *M. hupehensis* (China, 1900). A hardy tree to 12m (40ft), making a fine well-shaped specimen. Flowers white tinged with pink in the bud, fragrant in spring. Fruits small, becoming dark red. Its only drawback is a short (two weeks) flowering period.

M. floribunda Japan, 1862. A dense-headed tree to 9m (30ft) high, more across. It flowers in spring with a great profusion, first of rose-coloured buds, which then open to white with a pink blush. The tree is trained as a standard and then needs no pruning.

Pruning. If a feathered plant with a good central leader is obtained, this may be trained either on a leg of 0.6-0.9m (2-3ft) to produce a low growing tree, even a bush; or on a leg of 1.8-2.4m (6-8ft), to form a wide branching tree. It is not necessary to prune the centre as a rule, allowing the natural development even if this is a little untidy. Look out for suckers on a grafted specimen (as many are).

MAYTENUS (Celastraceae) (E)
M. boaria Maiten (E) Chile and Argentina. A tree to 21m (70ft) in the wild. It is said to be elegant with an oval crown and drooping branches.

M. magellanica (E) An allied species, has grown at Tintinhull for nine years from seed collected by Mr Ian Peters in Chile. It has proved hardy but grown very slowly. The unusual mid-green foliage is dense and attractive. No question of pruning yet.

MELIOSMA (Samiaceae) (D)
The hardy members are all from China and Japan.

M. cuneifolia W China. A shrub to 3.6m (12ft) in cultivation. The main attraction is provided by the panicles of yellowish white flowers, with a fragrance like hawthorn. It is

an ungainly plant but efforts to convert it to a tree have not been successful, though it does regenerate after pruning.

M. veitchiorum A superb tree 9-15m (30-50ft) high with erect branches. The leaves are up to 17cm (7in) long with red petioles. Panicles up to 45cm (18in) long by 0.3m (1ft) wide carry creamy white flowers in late spring, followed by violet fruits.

MENZIESIA CILIICALYX (Ericaceae) (D)
Japan. A shrub to 0.9m (3ft) high with oval leaves and flowers in clusters on shoots of the previous year, in late spring. After flowering the shoots should be cut back when the blooms fade, in order to allow maximum time for the ripening of new wood and to save the energy needed to form seed.

MITRARIA COCCINEA (Gesneraceae) (E)
A low, spreading shrub with bright orange-scarlet tubular flowers in succession from late spring until summer's end. No pruning.

MOLTKIA (Boraginaceae) (D)
M. petraea (D) Dalmatia, c1840. At first a greenhouse plant, later proved itself able to survive in rock gardens with some extra care. It has been largely replaced by *M. × intermedia* (*suffruticosa × petraea*), a shrub 0.3m (1ft) high with blue flowers through summer. It needs a sandy loam and full sun, and tidying of shoots in spring.

MORUS (Moraceae) MULBERRY
See Fruit Trees & Bushes.

MYRICA GALE (Myricaceae)
SWEET GALE (D)
Uplands of northern hemisphere. In moors of northern Britain a shrub around 0.9m (3ft) high. Shoots and leaves fragrant when crushed. Flowers in short catkins in early summer on wood of the previous year. If grown in a garden an acid, moist soil is necessary, and it is best to plant a clump

which will produce suckers. Long growths become untidy and may be cut to the ground after flowering, when suckers will fill the gap.

MYRICARIA GERMANICA
(Tamaricaceae) (D)
South and Eastern Europe, W Asia, grown in Britain since 1582. A shrub to 2.4m (8ft) high with erect branches clad in glaucous foliage and bearing light pink flowers in early summer on wood of the current season. Pruning in spring prevents a disorderly appearance, most of the flowered shoots of the previous year being cut down to about 5cm (2in).

MYRTUS (Myrtaceae) MYRTLE (E)
It is tempting to accept the limit in Bean (1973) that *M. communis* may prove to be the only member of this genus, though no worldwide study has been published since that of George Bentham and Hooker (fil. *Genera Plantarium*, vol 1, 1865, pp690-725) Bentham retained the species which are briefly mentioned here in Bean (vol 2, 1973, p762).

M. bullata New Zealand. A shrub 3-4.5m (10-15ft) high, hardy only in maritime regions. Flowers white, not freely produced.

M. chequen Chile, 1847 by W. Lobb. A very leafy shrub, usually found in wet places. Moderately hardy south of London. Flowers white.

M. communis COMMON MYRTLE. Abundant in the Mediterranean region, perhaps introduced from Persia or Afghanistan. Probably an early introduction to Britain from the Levant, at least well-known here in the sixteenth century. Held sacred by the Ancients

Malus floribunda. **Probably a hybrid, and perhaps the most beautiful of all crabs in blossom. The flowers are red in bud, pink when open and very abundant**

to the Goddess of Love. Flowers white, fragrant, beautiful in midsummer. Only hardy in the mildest areas. Commonly grown against a wall, or rather 0.3-0.6m (1-2ft) from it. George Brown in his book (1877) shows a photograph (plate 47) of this plant covering the wall of a cottage in Devon. It is, or was, clipped over every year. Elsewhere little pruning is practised, other than shortening of wayward shoots.

M. lechlerana A bushy shrub which does well in the mild regions. Creamy white flowers in late spring. Subject to damage by late frosts. A hedge, perhaps unique, is 7.6m (25ft) high at Trewithen in Cornwall.

M. luma Chile and Argentina, 1844 by William Lobb. A bush to 6m (20ft) high, sometimes a tree. In mild parts it has flourished and self-seeded. Noted for its flaking cinnamon-coloured bark. White flowers.

M. ugni MURTILLO UNI. Forests of Chile, 1844 by William Lobb. A shrub less than 1.8m (6ft) high. Flowers in late spring, rose-tinted and rounded. It is hardy in mild regions.

As to pruning, if it is intended to produce a tree the normal process of training a leader and reducing side shoots progressively is required. These shrubs are mostly able to grow without support especially if near, but not touching, a wall.

NANDINA DOMESTICA
(Berberidaceae) (E)
China, Japan, India, 1804. A shrub 1.8m (6ft) high with erect unbranched stems. The large compound leaves have many leaflets and the flowers are small and white in large panicles in summer. It needs a rich soil, a sunny position and shelter, with which it is hardy except in the coldest areas. It is worth growing for its shoots and leaves, the flowers being of little account except in hot summers. If it is well fed strong growths arise from the base to replace bedraggled, weather-beaten stems, which can be cut away at ground level. Shortening them is of no avail.

NEILLIA THIBETICA (*Roseaceae*) (D)

The best species, reaching 1.8m (6ft) high with erect stems, ovate pointed leaves and white flowers on branched racemes in late spring; an elegant picture. Young canes arise from the base if the plant is well nourished and suckers may arise from roots 0.3-0.6m (1-2ft) from the main plant. Some of the old wood can be removed each year, at the same time shortening the younger growths by one half.

NEOLITSEA SERICEA (*Lauraceae*) (E)

Japan and China. A small tree only for the mildest areas with large leaves which, when young, are covered with brown hairs, later becoming dark green above and glaucous on the underside. Flowers, greenish yellow in clusters, appear in autumn. No pruning except to remove dead or unhealthy growths.

NICOTIANA GLAUCA
(*Solanaceae*) (SE/D)

Argentina, Brazil, 1827. One of the few woody tobacco plants. As seen at Tintinhull, Somerset, it is an erect branching shrub, often becoming tree-like with glaucous stems, glabrous as are the leaves on both surfaces. The terminal panicles bear yellow flowers too diminutive to be in scale with the rest of the robust plant. They appear from early summer onwards. In the hot summers of 1989 and 1990, the trees have self-seeded to an embarrassing degree. However, it is only hardy in mild winters. Unwelcome branches can be removed without damage to the rest of the tree.

NOTHOFAGUS (*Fagaceae*)
SOUTHERN BEECHES

The beeches of the southern hemisphere are mainly evergreen but the seven which are deciduous include at least two of great importance, *N. procera* (D) and *N. obliqua* (D), and all but one are from Chile and Argentina; that one, *N. gunnii*, being from Tasmania.

N. antarctica (D) S America, Cape Horn to the Andes. A tree usually less than 15m (50ft) high, often a low shrub in open places in its native area. It is perfectly hardy and grows well in the first few years but then slows down. The round leaves are dark green, set closely on the branches and sometimes fragrant. The habit of this tree is somewhat ungainly, even if the leader is carefully trained, and it is inclined to be blown over in violent storms when specimens of *N. procera* (D) and *N. obliqua* (D) in the same planting are unaffected.

N. betuloides (E) A very large tree in Chile and Argentina. In temperate regions of the northern hemisphere it is hardy though intolerant of cold winds, and grows rather slowly; 13.7m (45ft) in eighty-seven years in one case at Haslemere, Surrey.

N. dombeyi (E) Chile. Grows quickly and is comparatively hardy, often making good the loss of foliage in a severe winter. The most satisfactory of the evergreen species in temperate climates of the northern hemisphere.

N. obliqua Roblé (D) has leaves with eight or nine pairs of veins on each side and they are dark green above, pale below. The wood is rather brittle and an exposed site should be avoided.

N. procera Rauli (D) Chile. Is certainly tender in the first few years, at least in some clones, but later becomes hardy and grows away. The leaves have fourteen to eighteen veins on each side, are narrowly oval, finely toothed and pale green.

There are no specific pruning problems with this genus.

NOTOSPARTIUM CARMICHAELIAE
(*Leguminosae*) (D)

New Zealand, 1883. The PINK BROOM of New Zealand. A medium-sized shrub which is best grown in a pot with protection in winter, until a woody growth is established when it can be planted out and is almost hardy. It has the habit of a weeping willow, with slender arching branches which are wreathed in summer with pink pea flowers. Normally pruning only involves tidying up, but when a bush is old and weak the whole may be cut away to young stems which are usually present at the base of the plant.

NYSSA (Nyssaceae) (D)

Two significant trees, one from S Canada, E USA and Mexico, the other from China. Before planting either of them, one must recognise that the only specific point is autumn colour, the flowers and fruit being of no aesthetic value .

N. sinensis China. Said to reach 15m (50ft) high, but in temperate climes is smaller, sometimes a shrub. The leaves are oval, narrow and 15cm (6in) long, dark green. Their autumn colour is red and yellow. The tree is hardy but rare.

N. sylvatica Eastern N America, early eighteenth century. Slow-growing and few are more than 15m (50ft) high. In America it grows in swamps and boggy land but in Britain it does best in good ordinary soil. The leaves are variable in shape, size and colour, usually dull green. In autumn they turn red and yellow and are very handsome. A good leader should be established early and the lower branches gradually shortened and eventually removed, to give a clear trunk to 1.8m (6ft) or more. The remaining branches can be allowed to develop a pendulous habit, which is natural and displays the autumn colour well.

OLEA EUROPAEA (Oleaceae) OLIVE (E)

Perhaps from SW Asia. Cultivated in Mediterranean countries for many centuries, and in Italy the gnarled branches with grey-green foliage are a leading feature of the landscape. In Britain it is cultivated only in the mildest areas. A well-known tree grows in the Chelsea Physic Garden, London and is over 6m (20ft) high in an open site. It occasionally bears fruit.

OLEARIA (Compositae) DAISY BUSH (E)

All from Australasia and evergreen. Shrublets up to treelets, but mostly medium-sized shrubs 0.9-6m (3-20ft) high. They like a well-drained loamy soil and none object to chalk. Only *O. ×haasti* is fully hardy but many survive an average winter without protection. They are nearly all propagated quite easily from cuttings and that is an encouragement to try them out.

O. arborescens New Zealand, late nineteenth century. Only moderately hardy and best in the milder regions where it makes 3.6m (12ft) high quite soon. White flowers in corymbs in late spring.

O. avicenniifolia New Zealand, mid nineteenth century. One of the hardiest, also with white flowers in corymbs, but in late summer.

O. cheesemanii New Zealand. As hardy as the last, and the flowers are more abundant.

O. ×haastii (*O. avicenniifolia* × *O. moschata*) Fully hardy, a rounded shrub up to 2.7m (9ft) high with leaves jostling on the branches, thick dark green above, white felted beneath. Flowers during mid to late summer in corymbose clusters, white, fragrant. This shrub stands Atlantic weather well and makes a good shrub under those conditions. It is propagated with the greatest of ease from cuttings taken in early autumn. Pruning, a shortening of stems, may be carried out in spring.

O. macrodonta New Zealand. *The* olearia for the weekend gardener – almost hardy, robust, usually to 3m (10ft), but sometimes 6m (20ft) high. Leaves sage-green above, white felted below. Flowers in branched clusters. In a sandy soil it presents a splendid picture and asks only for a modest weed-free area in return. No pruning, please.

O. phlogopappa Tasmania, Victoria and New South Wales, c1848. Exciting as represented by the 'Splendens' group, especially in its blue-flowered form. Unfortunately it is not hardy and if grown in the open should be propagated by a cutting in midsummer lest the worst should befall.

Pruning of olearias may be undertaken when new growth appears after winter damage, or in order to reduce any overgrown plants.

ORIXA JAPONICA (Rutaceae) (D)
Japan, China, Korea, 1870. A graceful shrub, spreading, with long branches 1.8m (6ft) high. Leaves scented dark green and glabrous, turning pale yellow and white in autumn, aromatic when crushed. Flowers inconspicuous, fruits brown. The long shoots may hang to ground level and take root; this is how the bush gradually spreads. If necessary the shoots can be pruned before they root.

OSMANTHUS (Oleaceae) (E)
China, Japan. Elegant evergreen shrubs, some resembling hollies. They grow well in good ordinary soil and tolerate chalk.
O. armatus China, 1902. A shrub to 3, occasionally 4.5m (10-15ft), high. Leaves dark green, leathery, coarsely toothed. Flowers in clusters, creamy during autumn, fragrant but very small.
O. ×burkwoodii Formerly *osmarea*. A shrub to 2.7m (9ft) high, rather dense with shining dark green leaves. Fragrant white flowers, not abundant, in spring. It lacks the elegance of *O. delavayi*.
O. delavayi China, c1900 from France. A spreading shrub usually about 3m (10ft) high, with dark green leaves, spotted beneath. The flowers are fragrant, white, in terminal clusters which almost hide the foliage and appear without fail. No pruning.
O. heterophyllus Japan, 1836. An interesting shrub which grows well in shade without much flowering (autumn) but has glossy dark green leaves which compensate for that. It is useful as a formal hedge plant (see Hedges & Topiary). Osmanthus may be distinguished from holly by its opposite leaves.

OSMARONIA now OEMLERIA (Rosaceae) (D)
O. cerasiformis California, 1848. A suckering shrub making a thicket several feet in diameter. Leaves lanceolate, sea-green. Flowers white, fragrant in pendent racemes in spring. Fruits brown, then purple, very bitter. This is a very hardy plant and grows well in any good soil, but dislikes chalk. Before the thicket becomes really large it is possible to prune by cutting down the shoots which have flowered as soon as they have done so.

OSTEOMELES SUBROTUNDA (Rosaceae) (D)
China, 1892. A shrub of moderate size in the open but not hardy and needs to be trained on a wall facing south, fan-wise and close to the surface. Grown thus the foliage is elegant and the white flowers, in branching corymbs appearing in early summer, stand out well. Pruning, once the framework is established, is directed to removing a few of the older branches after flowering. Rare in commerce.

OSTRYA (Carpinaceae) (D)
The northern hemisphere.
O. carpinifolia S Europe, Asia Minor, early eighteenth century. HOP HORNBEAM has the character of the hornbeam, with several botanical differences. The fruits, 5cm (2in) long, are attractive in autumn, as are the male catkins in spring. It readily forms a leader and makes a fine tree 15m (50ft) high.
O. virginiana Eastern N America, 1692. IRONWOOD is very like *O. carpinifolia*, but not as large. It does well in Britain under ordinary conditions. No routine pruning.

OXYDENDRUM ARBOREUM (Ericaceae)
SORREL TREE (D)
Eastern N America, 1752. A tree 18m (60ft) tall in the wild but about 9m (30ft) in northern temperate zones and, more shrub-like. Leaves lanceolate, 15cm (6in) long. Flowers

small, white, very like those of *Pieris* in late summer or autumn. This plant is definitely calcifuge and is not worth attempting except where the soil is acid, preferably pH less than 6.0. Under the right conditions the leaves turn scarlet after flowering is over. No pruning needed as a rule.

Pæonia suffruticosa 'Rock's Variety' is famous for its beauty – but also because it has been difficult, and often impossible, to grow from seed and has to be propagated by grafting. It is not freely availabe from nurseries, but meristem culture may change that. Whether such plants will prove as healthy as those grown from seed is uncertain. The picture shows 'Rock's Variety' flowering in spring

OZOTHAMNUS See *Helichrysum*.

PACHYSANDRA (Buxaceae) (E/SE/D)
Useful ground cover in shade. Though flourishing at Kew and in the rhododendron-growing areas of Surrey they fail in any alkaline soil and only survive narrowly in that which is neutral .
P. procumbens ALLEGHENY SPURGE (D)
SE USA, 1800. A splendid plant in its native region and quite good in the suitable areas of Britain. The leaves are 5-7.5cm (2-3in) long, nearly as wide, and appear at the top of stems up to 0.3m (1ft) long, which come

without branching from a root stock. The flowers are borne in spikes at the base of the stem, a rather untidy arrangement.
P. terminalis (E) Japan, 1882. Not unlike the former, but the flowers arise at the end of the previous year's shoot (even more untidy).
Pruning not normally required.

PAEONIA (Paeoniaceae) PAEONY (D)
Mainly herbaceous, but there are a few woody species which comprise the section Moutan which comes only from W China and SE Tibet.
P. delavayi China, introduced by Wilson

about 1908. Ignoring the plants found in the wild by Forrest, which may be hybrids because their colour is between red and yellow, this species has in early summer a fine blood-red flower with golden anthers in a cluster which enhances the effect. It likes a rich soil, tolerating chalk and is hardy.

P. lutea var. *ludlowii* is mentioned because it has larger flowers and is a larger shrub – up to 2.4m (8ft) – than the type. It flowers in late spring rather than early summer, as the latter does. The foliage is fine and densely deployed but the flowers are sometimes few. As the fruits ripen their shoot dies back to the terminal bud on the new shoot and may be cut off for appearances sake. This work can be left until spring when the developing buds can easily be identified.

P. suffruticosa China. Moutan section. Has been in cultivation in Chinese gardens since the Tang dynasty in the seventh century AD. It was introduced to Britain for Sir Joseph Banks in 1787 but the type of *P. suffruticosa* introduced in 1795 was a double pink variety, 'Roseaplena'. A further introduction by Fortune in 1845 seems to have died out. In Victorian times tree paeonies were never common in Britain and even now few are available commercially, not including one which is thought to be so near to *P. suffruticosa* that 'it could reasonably be placed under *P. suffruticosa* var. *papaveracea* (Andrews) 'L. H. Bailey' (Bean, 1976). This is a plant collected by Dr Joseph Rock in SW Kansu in about 1925, and introduced to Britain in 1936. A plant answering to his description is 1.5m (5ft) high and flowers regularly at Tintinhull. It is extremely difficult to propagate by conventional methods and is not recorded as available commercially (*Plant Finder*, 1990). This plant does not suffer from the spring frosts which are so damaging to many other plants. It occupies south-facing sites with some protection from the north and east.

Pruning of the paeonies is largely cosmetic. The flowered stalks die back to the terminal bud of the new growth and can be cut away just above it, but there is no urgency for this unless the appearance of these stalks is offensive. It is done in early spring, along with the removal of any dead wood. The paeony blight *Botrytis paeoniae* must be taken seriously and infected shoots should be removed at once. Fungicides are effective but run the risk of producing tolerant strains of the fungus.

PALIURUS SPINA-CHRISTI
(Rhamnaceae) CHRIST'S THORN (D)
Southern Europe, to W Asia, c1597. A shrub varying in height from 0.9 to, occasionally, 6m (3-20ft). The long stems have at each joint a pair of spines pointing in opposite directions. Leaves ovate. Flowers small, greenish-yellow in late summer. The fruits are circular and hat-like. A curious plant. It is far from common, yet perfectly hardy and undemanding as to soil. It is an untidy shrub with many crossing branches which do not encourage pruning. If it grows unhealthy or too large it can be cut right down and will regenerate.

PARAHEBE (Scrophulariaceae)
New Zealand. Shrubs or sub-shrubs forming spreading mounds. Not particular as to soil but needing sun.

P. catarractae Makes shoots up to 0.6m (2ft) and has dark green leaves and white flowers with a central area of crimson in racemes, appearing from late summer to early autumn.

P. lyallii 1870. A smaller version. Both are hardy. Some species are barely woody enough to be considered here.

Pruning is not needed.

PARASYRINGA (Oleaceae) (E)
China, 1913. A genus with one species related to *Ligustrum* and *Syringa*, closer to the former. It is a shrub up to 3m (10ft) high with dark green, rounded leaves. Creamy white,

fragrant flowers in panicles in late summer. It grows well in any good soil and is hardy, though doing better in the milder areas. It is still uncommon and not widely available in commerce. Pruning, if any, is that applied to *Ligustrum*.

PARROTIA PERSICA
(Hamamelidaceae) (D)

N Iran to the Caucasus, 1841 from St Petersburg. A genus with one species which is usually seen as a wide, spreading shrub, even when reaching a height of 12m (40ft). The smooth grey bark flakes in an attractive way. The ovate leaves, up to 12cm (5in) long, turn to gold and crimson in autumn. The flowers appear in early spring in clusters, with numerous red stamens which make a fine picture on the leafless branches.

It is questionable whether one should attempt to train a leader with a clean stem of 3m (10ft). *Parrotia* rarely looks ugly as a shrub, the branches tending to grow strongly outwards without overcrowding. If grown as a single specimen in grass, which suits it well, a problem will arise in time as the lower branches may lie almost at ground level and mowing may easily damage them. Miss Jekyll thought this difficulty was easily solved by having two men stretching a rope to lift the branches while a third did the mowing. Not many of us have access to this method.

PARROTIOPSIS JACQUEMONTIANA
(Hamamelidaceae) (D)

W Himalayas. A large shrub or tree with a smooth grey trunk and bushy head, the twigs being covered with stellate hairs. Leaves rounded, usually but by no means always turning yellow in autumn. The flowers have bracts in conspicuous clusters in mid-spring. The most obvious feature of this plant is the dense branching, forming a bushy head. With its overcrowded branches, it lacks the charm of *Parrotia*.

Pruning should be withheld if possible.

PAULOWNIA (Scrophulariaceae) (D)

A small genus of trees, all from China. *P. lilacina*, otherwise *P. fargesii Hort* (c1896), is notable as a tree more suited to temperate climates than the better-known *P. tomentosa*, from which it differs physically by having unlobed leaves and flowers of pale lilac.

P. tomentosa China, from Japan 1834. A tree to 15m (50ft) with a rounded crown. The foxglove-like flowers are in erect panicles which are formed in autumn but do not open until the following spring, and are vulnerable to the changeable British winter and spring weather.

Paulownias like a rich soil and grow fast, being especially tender when young and needing protection while a leader is being formed (often at the second or third attempt). In the end they need exposure to sun. An alternative treatment is to set out a group of young plants and in spring cut back the stems to 2.5 or 5cm (1 or 2in). Young growths then emerge and the best two are selected, the rest removed. If well fed and watered the two stems will grow to 3.6m (12ft) and will produce handsome leaves up to 0.9m (3ft) across.

PENSTEMON (Scrophulariaceae) (D)

A few half-woody shrubs in this large genus, most needing the shelter of a sunny wall or a place in a rock garden in full sun.

P. heterophyllus (D) California. Tender, but the cultivar 'Blue Gem' justifies taking a risk and 'Hidcote Pink' is equally desirable.

P. newberryi W USA. A dwarf evergreen for the rock garden and bears scarlet flowers abundantly. Hardy.

P. pinifolius (E) SW USA, New Mexico. 0.3m (1ft) high and spreading. The flowers are scarlet in midsummer. Placed in full sun it is perfectly hardy.

PERNETTYA MUCRONATA
(Ericaceae) (E)

Chile, Argentina, 1828. A shrub, usually 0.9m

(3ft) high, suckering. Leaves dark green, densely displayed. Many small white flowers in early summer are followed by clusters of berries, each about 12mm (½in) across, coloured white, pink to purple. A lime-free soil is essential for good results and full sun is desirable. There are several good forms including 'Edward Balls' (erect) and 'Thymifolia' (dwarf) with white flowers. Pruning is confined to removal of dying stems and of unwanted sucker extensions.

PEROVSKIA ATRIPLICIFOLIA
(Labiatae) (D)
Central Asia, Himalayas, N Iran, c1904. A semi-woody shrub to 0.9 or 1.2m (3 or 4 ft), with stiff, erect stems and grey leaves. The

Perovskia atriplicifolia 'Blue Spire' should be cut to one or two buds in early spring. It has grey leaves with complementary slate blue flowers

panicles of lavender-blue flowers in late summer compliment the leaves admirably. The shoots die down in winter nearly to the base and pruning is best delayed until early spring, when they are cut back to one or two buds from the base.

PETTERIA RAMENTACEA
(Leguminosae) (D)
A shrub to 1.2m (4ft) nine years after planting in optimum conditions. Trifoliate leaves. It is said to bear fragrant yellow, laburnum-like flowers in early summer. It seldom does so though hardy and apparently healthy.

PHELLODENDRON AMURENSE
(Rutaceae) (D)
Japan, China, Amur, 1885. The AMUR CORK TREE needs a rich soil and does not tolerate drought conditions well. It makes a tree about 9m (30ft) high with corky bark and wide-spreading branches. Bright green pinnate

leaves. The winter buds are silver-hairy. Flowers small, yellow. It is not easy to maintain a leader after the tree is 3m (10ft) high. The branches are vigorous. Unfortunately they are often injured by spring frosts, but the tree is almost winter-hardy.

P. sachalinense Hardy and probably better suited to northerly climates.

Philadelphus coronarius flowering from behind a 1.8m (6ft) high wall. This plant had not been pruned for at least ten years. It calls in question the statement often made that *philadelphus* flowers on wood of the previous year. It does – but also on wood of earlier years

PHILADELPHUS (Philadelphaceae)
MOCK ORANGE (D)

A genus of deciduous shrubs with opposite leaves of no great character, flowers mostly white, many scented. The species hybridise freely in nurseries or collections so that many plants sold as species are in fact hybrids, sometimes of considerable merit. If the species are a platoon, the cultivars are a battalion. *Philadelphus* owes its expansion to the French breeder Victor Lemoine of Nancy, and his successors. The development started in 1883 with a plant of *P. microphyllus* from USA, which was crossed with *P. coronarius* and produced 'Lemoinei', 'Erectus', 'Avalanche' and 'Manteau d'Hermine', all worthy plants still flourishing and obtainable.

All plants of the genus and their hybrids like a rich soil and tolerate, even enjoy, chalk, but can perform remarkably well under poor conditions. They appreciate full sun and flower best on young wood.

Pruning is generally advised to follow a regular annual routine. This comprises cutting away shoots which have flowered to a point at which a new shoot is developing and removing some of them, the oldest, to ground level, hoping that enough new growths will have formed to retain a good flowering form in the shrub. It must be said that flowering is not confined to the growth of the previous year and many large bushes of *P. coronarius* flower abundantly for years with no pruning. One has to decide the policy from experience of the individual plant, but give it adequate feeding every spring. The photograph on p99 shows an elderly example flowering very freely – local residents have known it for forty years, and are certain it has never been pruned.

If the plant becomes ugly with lengths of bare wood, cut everything nearly to the ground after flowering. There will be no flowers the next year, but after that it may be possible to restore good behaviour. Better than this is to take a half-ripe cutting and put it under a mist propagator, or to take a hardwood cutting and place it out-of-doors in a sandy medium. You may wonder that you did not do that years ago.

Of the plants in cultivation, this is a selection guided by affection based on long experience.

P. coronarius A shrub to 3.6m (12ft) with creamy white, heavily fragrant flowers in early summer.

P. insignis Flowering until midsummer and good all round.

P. microphyllus A small-leaved species to 0.9m (3ft) high. Stylish and with a fragrance of pineapple.

Cultivars 'Belle Etoile', a dense shrub to 1.2m (4ft). Single white flowers with maroon spot, very fragrant. 'Erectus' grows to 1.2m (4ft), with single flowers, well displayed and fragrant. Extremely tolerant of dry conditions. 'Innocence' wins first prize with ease. It is a vigorous shrub to 3m (10ft) with discreet creamy variegation of leaves 5-7.5cm (2-3in) long. Fragrant single flowers, most abundant in midsummer.

PHILESIA MAGELLANICA (Philesiaceae) (E)

Chile, 1847. A suckering shrub making wide thickets of stems up to 1.2m (4ft) high, with narrow rigid leaves. The crimson flowers are tubular in summer and autumn. It needs a moist and acid soil in partial shade, with some shelter, but is hardy except in the coldest places. USA zone 7. In moist, maritime areas it can climb trees or rocks for 6m (20ft). No regular pruning.

PHILLYREA LATIFOLIA (Oleaceae) (E)

S Europe, N Africa, Asia Minor, c1597. A shrub to 4.5m (15ft), occasionally a tree twice as high. Glossy dark green leaves densely disposed make an impressive shape which can be modified by light pruning after the inconspicuous white flowers, produced in spring, have faded. If this all sounds rather boring, the shrub has that elusive quality – charm. Note changes of name of *P. decora* to *Osmanthus decorus*.

PHLOMIS (Labiatae) (E)

Herbs, shrubs and sub-shrubs with worthwhile flowers in axillary whorls. They need full sun and good ordinary soil.

P. chrysophylla Lebanon. A small sub-shrub with yellowish sage-like foliage. The flowers, borne in early summer, are golden.

P. fruticosa Malta, Sicily, Sardinia, sixteenth century. JERUSALEM SAGE has grey-green foliage, yellow flowers, and grows to 0.9m (3ft) high and wider.

P. italica Balearic Isles, Portugal, Spain, seventeeth century. Oblong leaves, very woolly, flowers pink or pink lilac.

All these soon become untidy if not pruned. This should be done in spring after an inspection for signs of winter damage. If the old wood is healthy new growth quickly breaks. Any weak stems, or those with long and ugly woody shoots, can be removed at this time. Half-ripe cuttings taken in early summer root easily. *Phlomis* is not long-lived.

PHOTINIA (Rosaceae) (D/E)
Mostly evergreen shrubs and trees which like a light soil and do well with chalk. The deciduous group needs an acid soil.
P. serrulata China, 1804. An evergreen shrub to 9m (30ft), occasionally more. Leaves leathery, often red when young, later dark green. White flowers, small, in panicles in late spring. While frost-hardy in all milder districts it does not flourish except in maritime areas.

Hybrids between *P. glabra* and *P. serrulata* have been raised and named by the Fraser Nurseries, Birmingham, Alabama. The first was 'Birmingham' (E) and 'Red Robin'(E) came later. The young growths are fairly hardy and the plants are tolerant of chalk.

If frost-damaged branches are cut back regeneration soon occurs. *P. serrulata* is apt to produce shoots from the base, growing up the centre, and these should be removed. Any pruning to restrict projecting growths should be done in mid-spring.

PHYGELIUS (Scrophulariaceae) (E)
S Africa.
P. capensis CAPE FIGWORT (E) 1855. A shrub to 1.2m (4ft). Leaves 12cm (5in) long, 5cm (2in) wide. Flowers well displayed on erect panicles, scarlet with yellow throat. Often cut to the ground in winter but revives and, when that is obvious, the dead growth can be removed.
P. aequalis (E) is a sub-shrub to 0.9m (3ft) with pendulous flowers on panicles 15cm (6in) long or more. Salmon-pink outside, orange-yellow at the mouth in late summer. The cultivar 'Yellow Trumpet' has soft yellow flowers and is relatively hardy.

PHYLLODOCE (Ericaceae) (E)
Dwarf shrubs from moist uplands of western USA and Japan. They are difficult to grow in England because the summers are too hot (a rare complaint) but do well in Scotland. They must have acid soil and plenty

of moisture.
P. × intermedia (*empetriformis × glandulifera*) is the most satisfactory, with solitary flowers on slender stalks during mid-spring, bright purple.
P. nipponica (E) Japan, c1900. A neat shrub 10cm (4in) high with white or pinkish flowers in umbels in late spring. These plants produce strong growths from the base every year. Any that die are cut back to the base. No other pruning.

× PHYLLOTHAMNUS ERECTUS (Ericaceae) (E)
One of a series of intergeneric hybrids between *Phyllodoce* and *Rhodothamnus*, in this case thought to be *Phyllodoce empetriformis* and *Rhodothamnus chaemaecistus*. A dwarf shrub less than 0.3m (1ft) high. Solitary flowers of delicate rose in mid-spring. It needs a moist, lime-free soil and summer heat makes it flag. No pruning.

PHYSOCARPUS OPULIFOLIUS (Rosaceae) (D)
Eastern N America, 1687. A shrub to 3m (10ft) high. Flowers in clusters, white tinged pink in early summer. Not a distinguished plant, often relegated to neglected areas of the garden. The cultivar 'Luteus' has leaves of a good golden yellow when they emerge but all too soon they become green, as the type. Pruning consists of removing some of the older wood after flowering, as young shoots are freely formed at ground level.

PIERIS (Ericaceae) (E)
Shrubs which require a lime-free soil and ample moisture. They are of dense habit. The flower panicles form in autumn while some have reddish buds through the winter, eventually opening during mid-spring to reveal white pitcher-shaped flowers. Some plants have leaves which open red, passing through cream to plain green.
P. formosa SE USA, 1800. Hardy and slow-

growing. Flowers abundant in late spring. Young growths coppery. Var. *forrestii* (China, Burma) grows to 3m (10ft) high and has produced the cultivar 'Wakehurst'. It has vivid red foliage at first in early spring, with white flowers opening two to three weeks later.

P. taiwanensis Formosa, 1918. More hardy than the former and is not often damaged by spring frost. The young growths are bronze-red and the white flowers in mid-spring are very fine.

PIPTANTHUS LABURNIFOLIUS
(Leguminosae) (E)

Himalayas, 1821. A shrub to 2.4m (8ft) often grown against a wall, where it is hardy in most years. Foliage very like that of laburnum, hence the name. Flowers likewise, bright yellow. Somehow it lacks character. Pruning confined to the removal of dead or damaged shoots.

PITTOSPORUM (Pittosporaceae) (E)

A genus of shrubs and trees which are undemanding as to soil but not hardy enough for most temperate areas.

P. dallii New Zealand, 1913. One of the hardiest and makes a handsome shrub with coarsely toothed, dark green leaves. Flowers, white and fragrant, are never seen in Britain and rarely in New Zealand. Worth growing in a sheltered position all the same.

P. eugenioides Tarata, New Zealand. Makes an evergreen tree to 9m (30ft) in mild areas, with narrow leaves 12cm (5in) long and fragrant small flowers in mid-spring.

P. tenuifoliumn Most often seen as a hedge in seaside towns (see Hedges & Topiary). It responds to hard pruning in spring.

P. tobira China, Japan, 1804. A good wall shrub with bright, glossy leaves and creamy scented flowers. It is much used for hedging in southern Europe but is not hardy enough for that purpose in Britain or USA. Nevertheless, its foliage merits a sheltered place.

PLAGIANTHUS (Malvaceae)

The worthwhile members of this genus have been transferred to Hoheria (see p77).

PLATANUS (Platanaceae) (D)

A genus of a few species, all natives of N America or Mexico except *P. orientalis*, of SE Europe and SW Asia. In the main they are noble trees and have survived attempts to show that they cause allergic irritation of the bronchii, eyes, and even ears, first hinted at by Dioscorides in c50AD. Recently these trees were attacked in print by nature-lovers on the grounds that they do not give a house to birds and other fauna, and should therefore not be planted any more in London, one of their favourite haunts.

P. × acerifolia LONDON PLANE. Since the nineteenth century generally believed to be a hybrid-*orientalis × occidentalis*. The history of this hybrid is obscure but it may have originated in southern Europe. It seems certain that it was in Britain by the middle of the eighteenth century. It is a tree of the largest size with mottled, flaking bark and a very big crown of curved branches and large, palmate leaves, variable in shape and size. The fruit clusters are at first bristly, later becoming smoother. In the nursery a leader can be established without much difficulty and a clean stem of 2.4m (8ft) attained. Later this may be increased to 4.5m (15ft), as the character of the bark is a feature. It is evident that the plant regenerates with exceptional vigour after any lopping, as shown by the regular pollarding of some street trees.

P. orientalis Produces laterals very readily and large branches form at a low level, which has to be accepted and is attractive. The leaves are palmate with five large lobes and

Phygelius capensis **is a sub-shrub – the picture shows it flowering well in an open situation in late summer. It will probably be cut to the ground in winter but revives reliably in spring, even if the evergreen leaves have been ruined**

little variation in shape. Otherwise it is like *P. acerifolia*. Trees grow to a great age in good health and notable specimens are at Corsham Court, Wiltshire and Jesus College, Cambridge.

P. occidentalis N America. A fine tree in its native land, it is a total failure in Britain, succumbing when a sapling to spring frost and/or the fungus *gnomonia veneta* – to which *P. orientalis* seems to be immune and *P. acerifolia* almost.

POLIOTHYRSIS SINENSIS
(Flacourtiaceae) (D)
Hupeh, 1908. A tree to 9m (30ft) or more, with fragrant flowers in late summer. The leaves slender and pointed. An attempt should be made to establish a leader, but it is not easy as branching is strong.

POLYGALA CHAMAEBUXUS
(Polygalaceae) MILKWORT (E)
Central Europe, c1658. A dwarf creeper 15-30cm (6-12in) high with flowers pea-like, creamy tipped yellow through spring. It likes cool, moist, lime-free soil. No pruning.

PONCIRUS TRIFOLIATA (Rutaceae) (D)
N China, Korea, 1850. A shrub notable for the spines 2.5-5cm (1-2in) long, and fierce, which arm the stems. Leaves with three or five leaflets. Flowers fragrant (do not get too close) and pure white in late spring. The fruits are seen in mild gardens and look like small oranges. It is sometimes advocated as a hedge but after many years none has been seen. It is a slow-growing plant and would need much patience to grow to an effective size, as well as being a peril to children and pets. It can be trained by a well-gloved pruner and responds well, but grows slowly and should not need attention often.

POPULUS (Salicaceae) POPLAR (D)
There are so many species that they are here classified into four groups (as by Bean, 1976),

with one or two examples in each. All are deciduous.

1 **Leuce** ASPENS. White and grey poplars. Includes *P. alba* and *P. canescens* – *P. tremula*. *P. alba* Eurasia – *Abele* is a tree seldom more than 9m (30ft) high, and is short-lived. The young shoots and lower surfaces of the leaves are covered with white wool.
   P. canescens (tremula × alba) – a hybrid. Europe to Siberia and W Asia. A superb tree when well grown and suckers all too readily. It responds well to pruning but almost invariably forms a leader without any assistance. In forty years of cultivating it the author has never seen any sign of disease.
   P. tremula ASPEN Britain, temperate Old World. Noted for quivering leaves, even on some still days. It makes a large crown with a fine display of autumn yellow leaves. It resembles *P. tremuloides* (Canada, all USA, 1812).

2 **Leucoides**
   P. lasiocarpa China, 1900. Slow-growing to 12m (40ft), rarely more, with a rough trunk and very large leaves up to 25cm (10in) long and half as wide on a red petiole. The best poplar for gardens. Seldom recognised as a poplar. Pruning not needed. *P. wilsonii* (China, 1907) similar.

3 **Tacamahaca** BALSAM POPLARS Includes *P. balsamifera, candicans* and *trichocarpa*. Most trees supposed to be *balsamifera* are *candicans*, 1773.
   P. trichocarpa Alaska, Canada, W USA, 1892. BLACK COTTONWOOD enjoys the British climate and grows very rapidly. The leaves give off the balsam scent and colour well (yellow) in autumn. A tendency to canker has been almost overcome in recent clones. Suckering may cause trouble.

4 **Aegiros** BLACK POPLARS. *P. × canadensis* forms an important group of hybrids. Among the best are *P. × eugenii* and *P. × robusta*, both handsome in leaf and shape.

P.nigra BLACK POPLAR. West Eurasia. Seldom planted now, replaced by hybrids.

P. var. *italica* LOMBARDY POPLAR. 1758. Still holds its own. It is usually planted in rows, which is unfortunate as a single specimen has a better landscape effect. It is easily propagated from hardwood cuttings.

The pruning of poplars is straightforward and they readily form a leader. If a clean trunk is made by pruning lateral shoots it should not exceed 4.5-6m (15-20ft), so that ladder work is sufficiently safe. Such pruning is often followed by the formation of epicormic growth which will need to be cut away every winter. Mistletoe often colonises the tree but does no harm.

POTENTILLA (Rosaceae) CINQUEFOIL (D)

It seems prudent to confine discussion of this genus to the garden varieties and hybrids from *P. fruticosa*, since the other species have been treated by some botanists as varieties of that. The shrubby potentillas do well in any average garden soil and flower for several weeks from late spring to midsummer. 'Beesii' is a dwarf shrub with golden flowers on silvery foliage. 'Elizabeth', bushy and about 0.9m (3ft) high, and has flowers of soft yellow. One of the best, 'Katherine Dykes' is up to 1.2m (4ft) high and desirable, with profuse yellow flowers. 'Longacre' is a lower version of 'Elizabeth'. 'Tilford-Cream' grows to 0.9m (3ft) high and the flowers are cream. 'William Purdom' (China, 1911) is a large shrub to 1.2m (4ft) high, with canary-yellow flowers in dense cymes. Prune all these, not severely, in spring, reducing shoots by one third.

PRUNUS (Rosaceae)

A genus which includes plums, apricots, cherries, bird cherries and the cherry laurels. The leaves are alternate, the flowers white, pink or occasionally yellowish-white. There are five subgenera with botanical features which distinguish them. Generally speaking, they all enjoy a loamy soil and tolerate lime completely. They are hardy, with a few exceptions, and those that are deciduous need a southerly exposure with some shelter from north and east. Examples from the subgenera are given below.

1 *Prunus* Plums and Apricots - *P. cerasifera* CHERRY PLUM (D). Myrobalan, Balkans, W Asia, sixteenth century. Round-headed, small tree, white flowers in early spring. Good for hedging.

   P. cerasus American plums – *P. subcordata* OREGON PLUM (D). A small tree. Flowers white. Few American plums succeed in Britain.

2 *Armeniaea* Apricots – *P. mume* JAPANESE APRICOT (D). China, Korea, 1844. Small tree. Double form with pink flowers in late winter is good.

3 *Dwarf shrubs* Axillary buds in threes – *P. incana*, WILLOW CHERRY (D). Asia Minor, SE Europe, 1815. Shrub to 1.8m (6ft). Flowers red, spring.

4 *Trees or shrubs* Buds solitary in leaf axil – *P. avium* GEAN, MAZZARD (D). Europe. A big tree. Flowers white. A stock for orchard cherries.

   Leaves conduplicate (folded together) in bud – *P. padus* BIRD CHERRY (D). Old World, Britain to Japan.

   Flowers in terminal racemes – fragrant, white on racemes 15cm (6in) long.

5 *Laurocerasus* CHERRY LAURELS – *P. lusitanica* PORTUGAL LAUREL (E). Spain, Portugal, 1648. A wide shrub 3m (10ft) or more high. Leaves shining dark green, petioles red. Flowers small, white, scented, early summer. Hardier than *P. laurocerasus*.

Most *Prunus* only need regular pruning during the nursery stage but before that comes the choice of a site and of the appropriate sort of tree. This is such a large genus that it should be possible to find one even for a really small garden, eg _Prunus × cistena_ growing to 1.8m (6ft) with pointed leaves, crimson at first, later bronze, and white flowers in mid-spring.

Assuming that a need to prune has arisen, for example due to damage to a branch or unwanted spread, there are some indications of the best time of year for the task. The winter is the time for the fungus _Chondrostereum purpureum_, silverleaf, to attack pruning or other wounds, especially on plums, but all species of _Prunus_ are susceptible. Any major pruning should, if possible, be planned for midsummer. A further advantage of this choice is that 'bleeding' (see p12) will not occur, as the rise of sap has ceased by then.

PSEUDO-WINTERA COLORATA (Winteraceae) (E)

New Zealand. Related to _Drimys_ and a shrub to 0.9m (3ft) high. Bark almost black. Aromatic oval leathery leaves, pale yellowish green above, flushed pink, edged and blotched with purple, glaucous beneath. It is for the milder areas only. Best in woodland conditions.

PTELEA TRIFOLIATA (Rutaceae) (D)

Canada and E USA, 1704. HOP TREE is a low, wide shrub or tree whose leaves are trifoliate; flowers in corymbs, yellowish in early summer, very fragrant as are the clustered fruits, which are winged and persistent. Once fallen they often lie on the ground through the winter. A background of deciduous shrubs or trees will enhance the autumn display. A clear trunk of 0.9m (3ft) with staking suits the poorly developed root system, which allows the plant to lean over if unsupported. The cultivar 'Aurea' has leaves of soft yellow

which later become lime-green. A fine tree in the USA, but often poor in Britain. No routine pruning once established.

PTEROCARYA (Juglandaceae)
WING NUT (D)

Three species and one hybrid are available in Britain; all are very desirable and adapt well to local conditions. The emerging foliage is

The shrubby pyracanthas can be trained to make formal patterns against walls or fences. With handsome fruit in autumn, they are a valuable garden addition

liable to be ruined by spring frost but is soon replaced.

P. fraxinifolia CAUCASIAN WING NUT. Caucasus, 1782. There was a large tree, over 30m (100ft) tall, at Melbury, Dorset. Trunk with furrowed bark. Leaves around 45cm (18 in) long, and up to thirteen pairs of leaflets. Flowers greenish, pendulous catkins, the females 38cm (15 in) long and attractive.

× rehderiana *(fraxinifolia × stenoptera)* Raised at the Arnold Arboretum, USA. A large wide tree, often surrounded by a grove of suckers, as at Westonbirt, Gloucestershire, UK. It seems to be more vigorous than either of its parents, and hardier. At the nursery stage it readily forms a leader and maintains it. It can be propagated from cuttings with the greatest ease. Very fine.

P. rhoifolia Japan, 1888. Like *P. fraxinifolia*.
P. stenoptera China, c1860. A fine tree to 23m (80ft). Very like *P.×rehderiana*, one of its parents.

There are no pruning requirements specific for this genus.

PTEROSTYRAX HISPIDA
(Styracaceae) (D)
China, Japan, 1875. A shrub to 6m (20ft) high, occasionally a tree. The oval or obovate leaves are fresh green, the white flowers small on pendulous panicles in early summer. It seems preferable to allow this plant to make a shrub rather than to train it as a tree. No regular pruning needed.

PUNICA GRANATUM (Punicaceae)
POMEGRANATE (D)
S Europe, N Africa, Persia, Afghanistan. Cultivated for many centuries. Even in milder regions it needs a summery south-facing wall, and then bears scarlet funnel-shaped flowers – but not always fruit, and never any that can be eaten with enjoyment. Some of the older shoots may be cut back in summer; not in winter, as living wood cannot easily be distinguished from dead at that time. Var. 'Nana' is hardier than the type and suitable for a rock garden. It flowers well but only sets fruit occasionally. If the climate continues to warm up, it will succeed in the twentyfirst century.

PYRACANTHA (Rosaceae) (E)
Shrubs with alternate leaves and white flowers. The fruits are yellow, orange or scarlet. The shrubs do well in any average soil and are nearly all hardy.

Grown in the open they are usually left alone without pruning and, if any is needed to restrict the size of the shrub, it is best to remove shoots entire as the cut ends are unsightly. The flowering performance is better with wall-training, for which pyracanthas would be ideal if the colour of the berries were more civilised, less blatantly orange and red. Fan-training with plenty of room between the shoots allows the formation of spurs which will fill the space completely. After flowering a light pruning removes wood which is protruding forward, but take care not to damage faded flowers or berries already forming. In autumn another pruning session removes part of any shoots which are concealing berries and allows the maximum colour display.

Good species are:

P. atalantioides	Fruits scarlet, prone to fireblight.
P. coccinea cv 'Lalandei'.	Fruits orange-red.
P. crenato-serrata	Fruits red.
P. rogersiana cv 'Flava'.	Fruits yellow.

PYRUS (Rosaceae) PEARS (D)
The true pears are all natives of the Old World and include some of the largest trees in this family. The flowers are mostly beautiful, if rather fleeting, but the fruits – if one excludes those which are grown in the kitchen garden – are of little merit (however, see Fruit Trees & Bushes).

P. communis COMMON PEAR. All Europe. A tree as far as any description defines a plant with such indeterminate origins, up to 18m (60ft) high, with splendid tessellated bark and branches with short spurs which bear white flowers in mid-spring, abundantly enough to make a picture rivalling that of the apple. The fruit is often brownish and small but until recently was good enough to make perry in Worcestershire, where in Elizabeth I's reign nearly every lane was lined by these very long-lived trees. Removal of dead or diseased limbs is arduous, the timber being dense and hard.

P. nivalis SNOW PEAR. S Europe, 1800. A small tree with ascending branches. White woolly leaves, which appear in mid-spring along with the pure white flowers. Fruits small, round, yellowish.

P. salicifolia CAUCASUS WILLOW-LEAVED PEAR. 1780. A small tree to 7.6m (25ft) high, the younger branches pendulous. It resembles *Elaeagnus*. Leaves narrow and lanceolate, covered with a silvery-grey down when young. Flowers pure white in mid-spring, in corymbs. This pear is mostly grown as the cultivar 'Pendula', with branches more drooping than on the type. Pruning, if any, should be timed for midsummer when the risk of fireblight is slight and there is time for small wounds to heal before winter.

QUERCUS (Fagaceae) OAKS

There are almost 450 species but only about seventy are in cultivation. Two of these are British natives – *Q. petraea* and *Q. robur*, the latter the best-known and best-loved of large British trees. Oaks in general must have a deep rich soil to thrive and do best of all in one which is rather acid; at least we assume so, when considering the wonderful oaks of the eastern USA in their native areas, and compare them with their failure in many areas of Britain, some on alkaline soils. There follows a list of species which are satisfactory in the British Isles and are commercially available at most times.

Q. acutissima (D) Japan, China, 1862. A tree of medium size with bright green leaves, slender and pointed. It gets away well from seed and makes a leader readily, needing little attention.

Q. canariensis (D) N Africa, S Portugal, Spain, c1845. A splendid tree to 27m (90ft), notable for its dark green, lobed, obovate leaves which do not fall until Christmas. It is perfectly hardy and easily cultivated but when grown from seed it is very likely to produce the hybrid *canariensis × robur*. In my experience of seed collected in 1976, the result in each of six which germinated was an upright tree more suggestive of *canariensis*, with foliage more like that of *robur*.

Q. castaneifolia (D) Caucasus, Iran, 1846. Very vigorous and erect, reaches 30m (100ft).

It has oval, shining, dark green leaves and no problems requiring pruning.

Q. cerris (D) S and Central Europe, Asia Minor, 1735. TURKEY OAK is very hardy and grows rapidly when young. The foliage is dark and rather rough to the touch but the appearance of the tree is handsome.

Q. coccinea (D) SCARLET OAK. Eastern N America, Canada, 1691. Never very common and probably requires acid soil to flourish. It is noted for brilliant red autumnal leaves, which persist for several weeks, but this colouring is very variable among trees raised from seed. Early training is straightforward.

Q. frainetto (D) S Italy, Balkans and Hungary, 1838. HUNGARIAN OAK is more tolerant of sandy, neutral soils than most oaks and one of the best-looking of the genus, with large leaves up to 20cm (8in) long and deeply lobed. It easily makes a leader.

Q. × hispanica (*Q. cerris × Q. suber*) A group of hybrids, the best-known being cv 'Lucombeana', the LUCOMBE OAK raised by Mr. Lucombe, an Exeter nurseryman, about 1763. The original clone is seen mainly in SW England and makes a noble tree up to 30m (100ft), with branches turning up somewhat at their ends. More often seen now is a clone derived from a seedling of 1792, with dark green leaves which normally persist until spring except in the hardest winter.

Q. ilex HOLM OAK (E). Mediterranean region, sixteenth century. A superb tree which thrives in rather light soil and makes a very dense mass of foliage. It is hardy in milder regions and tolerates the sea-front. It has only two faults: leaves are shed every day during early summer, and often later, and it is quite difficult to raise the tree from acorns, which need to be grown in pots for two or three years before planting out. Pruning becomes necessary when lower branches spread too widely. It is straightforward though often requiring professional help.

Q. palustris SE Canada, E USA, 1800, (D). PIN

OAK is a large tree with a dense but graceful crown. Leaves are dark, shining green, with good red autumn colour in acid or neutral soil. Does not thrive on chalk. Best with a trunk clear to 3m (10ft) at least, as long branches droop gracefully.

Q. petraea W Central and S Europe including Britain. DURMAST OAK (D). Replaces _Q. robur_ in some areas, particularly the west, and is distinguished from it by the long stalked leaves and sessile fruits; though foresters do not find the differentiation easy to make with certainty.

Q. robur ENGLISH OR COMMON OAK (D). Europe, Caucasus, Asia Minor, N Africa. A large, fast growing tree with a broad crown. Leaves sessile, fruits on slender stalks, shorter than those of _Q. petraea_. The early training is usually easy and very little pruning is called for until maturity, when die-back is apt to occur at the top of the tree, causing a 'stag-headed' appearance. The greater part of the tree is often unaffected and the cause is not obvious, though a fall in the watertable is suspected. Removal of the 'stag heads' is eminently worthwhile and may retain the tree in fair health for many years. It is a job for professionals.

Q. rubra RED OAK (D) Eastern N America, 1724. Quickly makes a sturdy tree with a broad crown. Early training aims at a clear trunk to 2.4m (8ft) or a little more. Autumn colour is variable, often a striking red lasting two to three weeks.

Q. variabilis (D) China, Korea, Taiwan, Japan, 1861. Capable of 24m (80ft) in height,

OPPOSITE:
Quercus ilex HOLM OAK. **Here this noble tree has been trained into cylinders at Arley Hall, Cheshire, a surprising feat**
BELOW:
This picture shows it growing freely to maturity at Fonmon Castle, Glamorgan, Wales

but usually less. The bark becomes corky in time, perhaps ten years. The leaves are oblong, up to 17cm (7in) in length, with bristly teeth. The upper surface is dark green, glabrous, the lower felted grey. The tree is slender but has an elegant habit, needing little pruning. To display the corky bark one should remove low branches to give a clean trunk to 1.8m (6ft).

RHAMNUS (Rhamnaceae) BUCKTHORN
About 160 species of trees and shrubs grown mainly for their foliage. They grow in any average soil, tolerate drought quite well, and are mostly hardy.

R. alaternus Mediterranean, Portugal, c1600. A bushy shrub 2.4-3.6m (8-12ft) high. Leaves small, dark green. Not hardy in cold areas. Cv *Argenteo-variegata*. Leaves green, marbled grey with a creamy white margin. Vigorous and hardy except in unusually severe winters, and even then recovers. One of the best variegated shrubs. No routine pruning.

R. cathartica COMMON BUCKTHORN (D). Europe, W and N Asia. Doubtful native of Britain, but exceptionally common on chalky soils. Carries shining black berries in autumn.

R. imeretina (D) Caucasus, 1879. A large shrub with big oblong leaves up to 35cm (14in) long, with parallel veins in fifteen to twenty-nine pairs, dark green above, turning bronzy purple in autumn.

R. purshiana (D) Western N America, c1870. Included only as the source of the laxative 'Cascara Sagrada', as is the native *R. cathartica*. Its use, torture to generations of children whose mothers insisted on regular bowel habits, has now been largely abandoned.

Generally the buckthorns can be allowed to develop without interference and *R. alaternus* in particular makes a shrub with a very neat, informal surface.

RHAPHIOLEPIS (Rosaceae) (E)
R. indica China, c1806. Tender but against a warm wall in mild, maritime zones it may grow well and flower freely.

R. umbellata Japan, Korea, c1862. A good deal hardier, and carries pure white scented flowers.

R. × delacourii (indica × umbellata) Leathery leaves and charming rose-pink flowers in spring, continuing into summer. It is hardy in milder areas and very desirable. No pruning needed for twenty years at least.

RHODODENDRON including
AZALEA (Ericaceae)
This huge genus, of which over 500 species are in cultivation in Britain, presents a formidable assignment for any writer, let alone one who has not lived in a garden which included rhododendrons as a feature since the age of ten.

Fortunately it is agreed among experts in this field that regular pruning is not needed, and then most often to correct a miscalculation in the choice of site and the distance from neighbouring shrubs and trees. Add to this the fact that rhododendrons like best a soil with pH 5, and will not tolerate any amount of lime in the soil, and the size of the problem diminishes further as it is not worth attempting their culture in a garden with limey soil when there are many calcicole lime-lovers ready to give no such trouble. On neutral earth the deciduous *R. luteum (azalea pontica)* will perform admirably, given a rich soil.

Heavy clay soils do not suit any of the genus and need improving before any planting is considered. Peat was no doubt the best additive to improve the texture and ability to conserve moisture, but had to be used repeatedly, having a way of disappearing in clay (recent work has produced substitutes for peat that are claimed to be superior to it in making composts). Manure and spent hops are effective, but mushroom compost may have been treated with lime (make a friend of the grower to find the answer). Homemade compost is excellent if really well matured. Leaves, grass cuttings, the tops of herbaceous plants, and some wood shoots up to 5cm (2 in) in diameter, put through a shredder, should make it possible to keep three compost heaps going, so that one is mature at the end of three years without any fertiliser or watering. It is mature when it achieves the texture of a good madeira cake.

Pruning is needed for plants that are deprived of adequate light, which may suffer from die-back. Dead wood should be cut away. Any plants that have become drawn up by the lack of light may be cut back hard and will soon produce new shoots. Those that have smooth peeling bark, such as *R. thomsonii*, seem to peel off their dormant growth buds or at any rate lose them for no obvious reason. The hardy hybrids such as 'Pink Pearl' like to grow in full sun and have no need of the pruner. Dead-heading is advised after flowering, a period as busy as any in the gardening calendar, using finger and thumb, and taking care not to damage the young growth or any buds which are about to open. If you find this task tedious you may take heart from the fact that there is no hard evidence that it makes the plant flower more abundantly than if it is left alone.

If you have room for only one rhododendron in a common-or-garden garden, choose *R. yakushimanum*, Japan, or one of its hybrids. Christopher Lloyd tells you to plant three for foliage and flowers.

RHODOTYPOS SCANDENS
(Rosaceae) (D)
China, 1866. A shrub to about 1.8m (6ft). Leaves ovate with long points, margins deeply toothed. Flowers appear in late spring until midsummer and are pure white, resembling a rose. Fruits black. It flowers on shoots thrown up from the base in the previous year. Prune after flowering, cutting the oldest shoots to their origin, others by half their length.

RHUS (Anacardiaceae) SUMACH (D)
A large genus with few species worthy of the garden, and some of these are disappointing as the autumn colour of the foliage is apt to be spoiled by the untidy appearance of the leaves. The toxic properties of the sap are known, especially in *R. vernix*, POISON SUMACH, a small tree about 3m (10ft) high, noted for the orange and scarlet fall colours (eastern USA, early eighteenth century). *R. vernix* should not be grown; its sap is extremely toxic. It is wise to assume that the sap of any sumach is poisonous and to wear rubber gloves for any pruning.

R. typhina Eastern N America, c1610. Withstands pollution and was formerly much planted in cities for that reason. It will form a small tree if trained with a 1.2m (4ft) clear stem. The flower panicles are not to everyone's taste but if the cultivar 'Dissecta' is planted, and cut back in spring to the ground, the foliage is handsome and reaches 1.8m (6ft) high with leaves 0.9m (3ft) long.

R. verniciflua Himalayas, China, before 1862. VARNISH TREE is a very handsome specimen, with smooth pale brown bark when young, pinnate leaves to 0.6m (2ft) long and large leaflets. Flowers and fruit negligible. It becomes more beautiful with age.

R. potaninii China. Trained with a little difficulty because is it very vigorous, but can be made to form a clear stem to 1.5m (5ft) and then a good crown. Flowers and fruit are seldom seen. It is remorseless in producing suckers but these can be used to make new plants. No general pruning necessary.

RIBES (Grossulariaceae)
A numerous genus. The species are mostly deciduous, a few evergreen. They can be divided into two groups, distinguished by differences of botanical characteristics – currants and gooseberries. The latter have spines at the joints, of some interest when starting to prune. Here some of the better garden plants are listed alphabetically.

R. alpinum MOUNTAIN CURRANT (D). N and C Europe. A shrub of dense habit, 1.8-2.7m (6-9ft) high. Unarmed, dioecious in flowering. Fruits red, not recommended for eating. It is hardy, tolerates shade well and maintains its good outline in poor soils. It could be a useful hedge plant and seems to have been used for that purpose at Troutbeck Hall in Cumbria, as tall plants exist there in an old hedge. Pruning is hardly needed except for a hedge, when overlong shoots should be reduced.

R × gordonianum (*odoratum × sanguineum*) (D) Vigorous and hardy, growing only to 0.9m (3ft) high, sharing the characteristics of its parents. The flowers are bronze red on the outside, yellow within; an acquired taste perhaps.

R. laurifolium (E) China, 1908. Unarmed and dioecious. The flowers in late winter are greenish yellow, the males more ornamental than the females. The shrub makes a pleasant picture when in flower. No pruning.

R. odoratum (D) Central USA, 1812. BUFFALO CURRANT is a medium-sized shrub of loose growth. Leaves shining green.

R. sanguineum (D)Western N America, 1817. An unarmed shrub to 2.4m (8ft) high. Leaves unremarkable, flowers red in mid-spring. The cultivar 'King Edward VII' (1904) remains as good as any, with flowers of splendid crimson two weeks later than 'Pulborough Scarlet' (1959), said to have flowers of Bengal rose. One could grow both. Pruning is of some importance. The species and its cultivars are best pruned immediately after flowering. Cut the older shoots, perhaps one quarter of the whole plant, to 2.5-5cm (1-2in) from the ground with secateurs. After that a good mulch, including manure, is indicated. Neglected shrubs may be hard pruned, removing all top growth in the dormant season and foregoing a year of flowering. Better still, take 0.3m (12in) cuttings of the current year's growth in late autumn and insert them in the open ground; or, an even better option, persuade the owner of a healthy plant a few years old to let you have a cutting – or three.

R. speciosum (D) California, 1828. A shrub, the most beautiful of the gooseberries. It is very early into leaf, in late winter. The flowers are rich red in pendulous clusters. It is worth growing against a south-facing wall, though fully hardy, as it is possible to train young shoots which come from the base to replace the oldest ones. Tie them in to produce a fan form. Flowers are borne on one-year-old wood so this training can be carried out after flowering. Feeding in spring is necessary.

ROBINIA (*Leguminosae*) (D)

Named after Jean Robin, herbalist to Henri Quatre of France (died 1629). Deciduous trees and shrubs with pinnate leaves and pea-type flowers. All do well in ordinary, not rich soil. Rich earth makes them grow coarse and unshapely, and their branches brittle. They are hardy and, if on their own roots, can be propagated from suckers which are readily produced. If grafted, as they usually are, on roots or stems of *R. pseudacacia*, any suckers will be of the latter.

R. hispida ROSE ACACIA (D). SE USA, 1743. Unarmed. In the wild suckers freely, but for some reason in nurseries it is grafted as a standard on *R. pseudoacacia* to form a small tree which is very liable to storm damage, the wood being naturally brittle. Perhaps in thin soil they would do better. The flowers are held on short racemes in late spring and are deep rose in colour.

R. kelseyi (D) S. Allegheny Mountains, USA, 1901. Unarmed. A shrub or small tree, with rose-coloured flowers in early summer and red pods. A handsome shrub but too brittle for culture as a tree.

R. pseudacacia (D) Eastern USA, after 1601. FALSE ACACIA is a tree to 24m (80ft) with deeply furrowed bark, the twigs with spines 2.5cm (1in) long. The white flowers appear in long racemes in early summer. It thrives in any soil that is not too moist and makes very hard trunks. When young it grows rapidly and may lose branches in a storm. It should have a leader so that a more or less straight trunk is formed, and no laterals should be allowed to make rival growth. All this involves regular inspection and prompt action if necessary, preferably in winter. Cultivars in some instances avoid the brittleness which prevents *R. pseudacacia* from living to old age. 'Bessoniana' is one with a rounded crown, and considered the best street tree, but is shy flowering. 'Frisia' has no obvious faults and carries golden leaves which do not fade in summer. Cultivar *umbraculifera*, the MOP-HEADED ACACIA, is not suitable for exposed sites but is now used in borders, associated with herbaceous plants. It is grafted to make a small standard and rarely flowers, but has a good rounded crown.

ROMNEYA (Papuveraceae) (D)

Would be thought of by most non-botanical gardeners as a herbaceous plant and Graham Stuart Thomas, the most scrupulous of authors, does include it in his book *Perennial Garden Plants* into which no other shrubby plant gained admission. The austere Alfred Rehder excludes it from the *Manual of Trees and Shrubs*. Never mind. One should not miss a chance to refer to this wonderful plant.

R. coulteri CALIFORNIA TREE POPPY. S California, 1875. A semi-shrubby plant with succulent herbaceous stems 1.2-2.4m (4-8ft) high (Bean, 1980). It spreads by suckers in a mild setting. The leaves are glaucous and lobed, the flowers fragrant, solitary or in pairs 10-12cm (4-5in) across, the petals like 'crumpled silk' (Arnold Forster, 1948) with a mass of golden yellow stamens. The soil should be deep, rich and well drained. Chalk is acceptable.

R. trichocalyx S California extending into Mexico, c1900. Less tall and has more finely divided leaves. Other botanical differences entitle it to rank as a species. An earlier edition of Bean (1938) described it as 'a better plant for colder situated gardens, being of hardier constitution, not too gross in habit and cultivated with less trouble.' In California *R. Coulteri* is preferred.

Though *Romneya* is hardy, at least in milder areas, it is best to grow it against or near to a south or south-west-facing wall. The stems are cut back in a hard winter but the root stock survives and will usually produce new shoots and flowers in the next summer. Leave the old growth until spring when it can be removed with a little of the live shoot. This can safely be done every year.

ROSA See Roses.

ROSMARINUS (Labiatae)

Mediterranean, N Africa, Portugal, Spain. In Britain at least 400 years.

R. officinalis ROSEMARY (E)

A shrub of dense habit, at times 1.8m (6ft) high or even more. The only species, but there are forms and cultivars. The leaves are glossy green above, white below, fragrant when crushed. Flowers blue in late spring. The following cultivars are of note: 'Benenden Blue' and 'Miss Jessopp's Upright', hardier than most with broad leaves; 'Prostratus', tender trailing; and 'Severn Sea' with arching branches and a good blue flower, but rather tender.

It is strange that no standard text refers to the gilded rosemary, which was in Britain in the reign of Elizabeth I. It is the type plant, except for splashes of gold on the leaves, and just as hardy. Some do not like it.

Rosemaries may be pruned immediately after flowering, the shoots being reduced by up to one half, that which remains becoming more compact. If there is winter damage or shoots have become leggy, a quite drastic pruning into living wood will produce regeneration. Propagation from cuttings is easy and, if in doubt, it is better to be able to introduce a new plant.

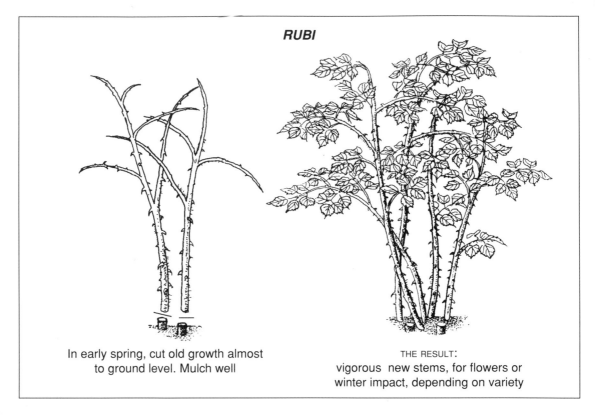

RUBI

In early spring, cut old growth almost to ground level. Mulch well

THE RESULT:
vigorous new stems, for flowers or winter impact, depending on variety

RUBUS

There are numerous species but few qualify for admission to the garden. Those few do so by virtue of their attractive habit of growth, their foliage, or the covering of white or purple bloom on the stems. Those with edible fruits, and grown specifically for them, are considered in Fruit Trees and Bushes. That group includes blackberries, dewberries, loganberries and raspberries. All the _Rubi_ prefer a rich soil and none objects to lime.

R. cockburnianus (D) China, 1907. A vigorous deciduous shrub to 3m (10ft) high with purple, arching stems covered by a white bloom. The fern-like leaves are attractive but the flowers are not. Fruits black. Perhaps not as good as _R. thibetanus_ (see below).

R. deliciosus Colorado, 1870. Has been largely replaced by _R. tridel_ (see below).

R. lineatus (D) SW China, Malaysia, 1905. Valued for its fine foliolate leaves, dark green above and covered with a silvery down below. The leaves alone call for no other quality. It is not entirely hardy and merits a sheltered position.

R. thibetanus (D) W China, 1904. An erect shrub with purplish stems covered with blue-white bloom. The pinnate leaves are up to 23cm (9in) long with seven to thirteen leaflets, making quite a dense head to the stems; the flowers are of little account. It is hardy and undemanding.

R. tricolor (S/E) W China, 1908. A semi-evergreen ground-covering shrub with pleasant shining, dark green leaves. The flowers are white, 2.5cm (1in) across, but are seldom seen in the shady sites for which the plant is used. Given a good soil and enough moisture the shoots, which are covered in brown bristles, extend rapidly and root on contact with the soil. Altogether a desirable ground cover.

R. 'Tridel' (_R. trilobus_ × _R. deliciosus_) (E) Raised by Collingwood Ingram in his garden at Benenden, Kent. Of these clones the best was named 'Benenden', a vigorous shrub producing annual stems 2.4m (8ft) or more high, which in late spring or early summer bear pure white flowers 5-7.5cm (2-3in) wide. It seems to do best in full sun and is a faultless plant.

Pruning of the *Rubi* is guided by the knowledge that they flower on growth of the previous year, though some retain their canes for several years, flowering less well. New shoots appear each year and stems which have flowered are cut to the ground if these replacements are adequate. In large clumps the young shoots may be thinned out.

RUSCUS (Liliaceae) (E)

These are not really shrubs or even sub-shrubs, as they have no woody base or stems. However, they are welcome here as only two species call for attention. They survive in any soil but certainly benefit from feeding with manure or compost.

Ruscus are usually doomed to live in very shady places. Whether they would perform to better effect if afforded the lifestyle of a sunny border does not seem to have been recorded.

R. aculeatus BUTCHER'S BROOM. Europe, N Africa, Near East. An erect native shrub to 0.9m (3ft) high, with cladodes which are not leaves but flattened stems, spine-tipped, borne on the upper branches of the ascending stems. The flowers are very small, dull white. Fruit a round red berry, not often seen in cooler climes, partly because female plants are rare and this is a dioecious plant.

R. hypoglossum S Europe, c1600. Not very different but perhaps even more tolerant of shade and dry conditions from the competition of tree roots.

Pruning of both species is confined to the cutting down of dead or unhealthy stems in early spring. There is no need to thin out the stems.

RUTA (Rutaceae) (E)

Canary Islands, Mediterranean, Caucasus, S. Europe, early seventeenth century.

R. graveolens RUE is a sub-shrub with a little wood at the base and in the branches. Grows to 0.9m (3ft). Leaves glaucous, flowers in terminal corymbs, dull yellow (but it goes well with the leaves). When well grown in good soil with lime, and cut back throughout to the last season's origin in spring, it is a very handsome plant. It has very irritant effects on the skin of some people, who should wear gloves to handle it or – better – keep away if a ready slave is at hand. Its former use for colic, hysteria and the vapours seems to have disappeared even in the most rustic areas. The cultivar 'Jackman's Blue' is often supplied and is smaller than the type, with blue-grey foliage.

SALIX (Salicaceae) WILLOW (D)

A large genus varying in size from tiny shrubs hugging the ground to very large forest trees. Many like a damp site and all need a good loam, but few flourish on chalk.

S. aegyptiaca S Russia, mountains of Asia, c1820. A large bush or small tree with a dense head and grey felted shoots. In late winter it bears bright yellow catkins.

S. alba 'Chermesina' SCARLET WILLOW. Narrowly upright with pale leaves. The young shoots in winter are bright orange-scarlet, this being more striking if hard pruning is carried out in early spring every year or other year.

S. caprea GOAT WILLOW. Europe, W Asia. Noticeable in early spring (but not at other times) for the large yellow male catkins. The female's silver catkins are pussy willow. A large shrub or small tree, of sentimental interest. If pruned it regenerates freely but becomes untidy.

S. daphnoides VIOLET WILLOW. N Europe, C Asia, c1928. An erect tree to 12m (40ft). Very rapid-growing at first, with purple-violet shoots overlaid with a plum-coloured bloom.

Catkins appear in early spring. The best regime for the maximum effect from the shoots is to prune in the first few years to produce a framework of branches and, when this is achieved, to prune hard in early spring, but every other year.

S. elaeagnos S and C Europe, Asia Minor, c1928. A dense shrub with linear leaves, the catkins appearing with them in mid-spring. It has no special attraction of colour but its form is very charming. Its only drawback is its size – 3.6m (12ft) high and across, little altered by pruning in spring, and difficult to place in a smallish garden.

S. exigua COYOTE WILLOW. Western N America, 1921. A shrub or small tree to 3.6m (12ft) with slender leaves, silvery silky. Best without pruning.

S. helvetica European Alps, c1872. A small shrub with orange buds and grey-green pubescent stems and leaves. It has been grafted on a 1.5m (5ft) standard and produces a rounded head which needs no pruning. Very effective in formal designs.

S. hookeriana Western N America, c1891. A shrub or small tree with stout, red-brown branches, leaves glossy green above, white felted beneath. A handsome tree only to be pruned to make space.

S. lanata WOOLLY WILLOW. Highlands in Europe and Asia. A bush to 1.2m (4ft) high with ovate, silver-downy leaves and stout yellow-grey catkins in spring. A good combination. No pruning.

S. magnifica W China. A small tree with large oval leaves, which suggested magnolia to E. H. Wilson. A very handsome plant, but not fully hardy.

S. purpurea PURPLE OSIER. Europe. The cultivar _eugenei_ is an erect-branched small tree with narrow, oblong, light green leaves and many grey-pink male catkins. Well worth a place in a wild garden or a paddock without horses.

S. repens var. _argentea_ Atlantic coasts of Europe to the North Sea and Baltic. A shrub to 1.8m (6ft) in cultivation. Spreading by un-derground stems. Leaves silvery-silky.

S. sachalinensis Sakhalin, Japan, E Russia and Siberia, 1905. The clone 'Sekka' is noted for the fasciated growths in some of the stems, which are brownish-red on plants grown in sunlight. It is very vigorous and needs plenty of space even if regularly pruned in spring.

S. viminalis COMMON OSIER. Most of Europe except the Mediterranean. Should not be ignored, though cultivated mainly for basketwork. The tapering leaves, dark green and glabrous above and covered with a silvery grey down beneath, are agreeable, especially when the catkins appear in spring.

SALVIA (Labiatae)

Most are herbaceous or so little woody that they are not included.

S. guaranitica (alias _Coerulea ambigens_) S America, 1925. A shrub with erect stems to 1.2m (4ft). Leaves ovate and long racemes of deep blue flowers from late summer into autumn. An excellent hardy plant.

S. fulgens Mexico, 1829. CARDINAL SAGE has heart-shaped leaves and long racemes to 0.9m (3ft) of brilliant, almost strident, scarlet flowers in late summer.

S. involucrata Mexico, 1824. The cultivar 'Bethellii' is most often grown and the bright crimson flowers are borne on racemes from midsummer into autumn.

S. microphylla (E) Mexico, 1829. Probably identical with _S. grahami_. A shrub to 1.2m (4ft) high. Leaves ovate, dull green. Flowers on terminal racemes, bright red at first, later magenta. Not entirely hardy in most temperate regions unless in a sheltered spot. None of the above salvias is repeat-flowering but are worth dead-heading for tidiness' sake.

S. officinalis Spain and W Yugoslavia. Intro-

Salix alba ' Chermesina' has bright red-orange stems in the first year of growth, less so in the second year. For the best winter effect it should be cut to the ground each year in late winter and well manured after that and at every annual pruning

duced in medieval times as a medical and culinary herb. An almost evergreen shrub 0.3-0.6m (1-2ft) high. Covered in a down which gives it a grey appearance. Leaves wrinkled, aromatic. Flowers in whorls on terminal racemes, purple from early summer. Good cultivars are 'Icterina', leaves variegated yellow and pale green; and 'Purpurascens', with leaves purple when young.

All the sages like full sun and a light soil. Pruning is cosmetic only, but *S. officinalis* benefits from being cut well back in early spring.

SAMBUCUS (Caprifoliaceae) ELDER (D)

About nine of these, all shrubby, are hardy in temperate zones. They have pinnate leaves which always have an odd (three to thirteen) number of toothed leaflets. Elders like good soil, not dry, and not too much shade.

S. nigra Europe, N Africa, SW Asia. COMMON ELDER is a British native shrub, too easily dismissed as a weed since the seeds are distributed by birds and germinate profusely. That is certainly a nuisance but is forgiven as one drives on a summer day down a quiet country road and sees on each side, and admires, numerous large bushes in full creamy flower arising from the hedges. This shrub grows to 6m (20ft), with pinnate leaves and flowers which have an odour not too agreeable. The berries are round and black. The form 'Laciniata', PARSLEY-LEAVED ELDER, is a good cut-leaved variety.

S. cultivar 'Guincho Purple' has leaves coloured bronze-purple and came from the gardens of Mrs Mackie in Ulster. Excellent.

S. racemosa Europe, Asia Minor, Siberia, W Asia, sixteenth century. Not a native of Britain. RED-BERRIED ELDER is not as vigorous as *nigra*. It bears yellowish white flowers in mid-spring and seldom the red berries, which are abundant in France and Switzerland. The cultivar 'Plumosa Aurea' has deeply cut golden leaves, very handsome.

All the desirable elders require feeding in early spring after pruning, which is usually needed. The older growths are cut to near ground level while one-year shoots are cut by about a third. If the shrub longs to be a tree it is quite manageable, but growths from low down, up to 1.2m (4ft) from the ground, have to be removed and some above that cut back moderately.

SANTOLINA (Compositae)
LAVENDER COTTON (E)

Low-growing evergreen sub-shrubs with dense foliage and button-like flower heads on long stalks in midsummer. They need a sunny position.

S. chamecyparissus S France, Pyrenees, sixteenth century. A dwarf species under 0.6m (2ft) high. Leaves crowded on the shoots, the whole covered by a white felt. The flowers are bright yellow. *S. neapolitana* and *pinnata* are probably varieties of *S. chamaecyparissus*.

S. rosmarinifolia (formerly *S. virens*) S.France, Spain, Portugal, early eighteenth century. An evergreen bush to 0.6m (2ft) high with bright green leaves and bright yellow flowers in midsummer. The plant, if enclosed, has a very agreeable scent.

Pruning is carried out in the autumn, cutting off old flower heads and stalks. If this is neglected dead stems and leaves collect and may kill the plant. If deterioration continues, hard pruning may restore the vitality of this shrub. If that fails, a new plant is the solution.

SARCOCOCCA (Buxaceae) SWEET BOX (E)

The cultivated species from China and the Himalayas. All are worthwhile but the following are the most highly regarded. They are all hardy plants.

S. confusa Origin unknown, 1916. A densely branched shrub to 1.8m (6ft) high, much less in shaded conditions, though it will still remain healthy with shining foliage. The modest white flowers in midwinter are very fragrant if the weather is mild, impressive on entering the main gate at Kew Gardens. Berries black.

S. hookeriana var. digyna W China, 1908. Has smaller flowers in early spring; the berries are black.

S. humilis W China, 1907. Similar to the last, has shorter and broader leaves. Berries blue-black.

S. ruscifolia C and W China, 1901. Reaches 1.2m (4ft) high, has very dark shining leaves. Milk-white flowers in midwinter and round crimson berries.

SASSAFRAS ALBIDUM (Lauraceae) (D)

E and C USA, 1630. A large tree in its native territory, but in northern temperate climates it is normally a shrub, reported to be perfectly hardy though the unfolding leaves may be ruined by frost. It requires lime-free soil and some shelter, best provided in woodland. It has a tidy conical habit and dark green leaves which colour well (yellow) in autumn. During the early stages the trunk is gradually cleared of branches up to 2.4m (8ft) to display the furrowed bark. Suckers may appear at some distance and can be potted up.

SATUREIA MONTANA (Labiatae) (E)

S Europe, N Africa. Long used for flavouring and by herbalists as a remedy for flatulence. A bush about 0.3m (1ft) high, aromatic with narrow leaves, greyish green, flowers in midsummer, white to purplish. No pruning.

SCHIMA ARGENTEA (Theaceae) (E)

S China, 1919. An evergreen tree, in the wild 18m (60ft) high but in cultivation only 1.8m (6ft). It is evidently a handsome plant with ivory-white flowers, like those of a camellia, but only fit for a mild and wet climate, with no lime in the soil. It should be trained fan-wise on a south-facing wall.

SENECIO (Compositae)

A genus of over 1,000 species. Most of those woody enough and hardy enough to grow outdoors in temperate regions are natives of New Zealand, as are all those mentioned here. It has been suggested that they all should be included in the genus *Brachyglottis* rather than *Senecio* but this change has not yet been confirmed. Most of these shrubs do well in a light sandy soil, tolerating chalk, but only a few are really hardy.

S. Dunedin hybrids (E) Outstanding is the cultivar 'Sunshine', perhaps *S. ×compactus × laxifolius*, often misnamed as *S. greyi* or *S. laxifolius*; it has non-wavy leaves, white felted flower stalks and involucral scales. Flowers bright yellow and profuse. It is almost hardy and very reliable.

S. hectoris (E)1910. A rather gaunt shrub to 3m (10ft) high with pure white flowers in midsummer.

S. monroi (E) A small, much-branched shrub with wrinkled leaves and yellow flowers.

No regular pruning for any.

SHEPHERDIA ARGENTEA (Eleagnaceae) BUFFALO BERRY (D)

Central USA and Canada, 1818. A shrub to 3.6m (12ft) high with branchlets often spine-tipped. Leaves oblong, silvery, scaly and opposite (in *Elaeagnus* they are alternate). Flowers insignificant in early spring, the berries scarlet, edible (so it is said). It is slow-growing and should be trained to a single stem; then it may look tree-like. It is always compared unfavourably with *Elaeagnus* but it is not without charm and has no bad habits. It grows slowly and rarely needs pruning.

SINOWILSONIA HENRYI (Hamamelidaceae) (D)

C and W China, 1908. The only species in this genus, named for E. H. 'Chinese' Wilson. A small tree, as seen at Kew. Leaves 15cm (6in) long, strongly veined beneath, with stellate down. A pleasant, elegant tree. Worth training in the nursery stage to form a leader.

SKIMMIA (Rutaceae) (E)

A small genus, the species being all evergreen or small trees from the Himalayas or E Asia. They like a rich, moist soil and moderate shade. As they are dioecious, it is necessary to plant one male to every three or four females to achieve a good crop of fruits, but there is an exception to this in *S. j. reevesiana* (see below).

S. japonica Japan mainly, 1838. A small, dense shrub with obovate leaves. Flowers unobtrusive. It is dioecious and female plants need a male to achieve fertilisation. The fruits are bright red. Cultivar 'Nymans' is very free-fruiting. These shrubs are well suited to forming a clump and a mixture of forms and cultivars would work well as all are similar. Any cosmetic pruning is for the spring.

S. j. reevesiana China, 1849. Not more than 0.6m (2ft) high. Monoecious, fruits good crimson, quite abundant without a male plant being needed.

SMILAX See Climbers.

SOLANUM CRISPUM (Solanaceae) (D)
See Climbers. *S. jasminoides*, ditto.
S. laciniatum Australia, New Zealand, 1772. KANGAROO APPLE is a sub-shrub to 1.5m (5ft) high. Leaves lanceolate, deeply cut. Flowers violet-purple in mid to late summer. Fruits egg-shaped, green at first, later yellow (see note below). A tender plant, best grown as an annual from seed. It will not survive the winter in most areas.

S. valdiviense Chile, Argentina, 1927. Produces arching shoots 2.4-3m (8-10ft) high. These produce leaves which are not fully developed by late spring, when the growths of the previous year come into flower in racemes of blooms, pale mauve or lavender. Any borne on their stems are removed immediately after flowering and the plant should be well fed in early spring.

Note It is wise to assume that the fruits of all shrubby *Solana* are poisonous to man and animals. Fatal cases of children eating the fruit of *S. laciniatum* are documented.

SOPHORA (Leguminosae)
Trees, shrubs, sub-shrubs and some perennial herbs, widely scattered.

S. davidii (D) China, 1897. A shrub to 3m (10ft) high, rounded, with pinnate leaves, terminal racemes bearing blue and white flowers in early summer. It seems to like sun and a rich soil, yet in China, according to Augustine Henry, it covers large tracts of barren country, as gorse does in cooler climates. Once through the first three or four years it is perfectly hardy and does not need pruning.

S. japonica (D) China, not Japan, 1753. Grows to 24m (80ft), can be trained as a tree but will not flower for thirty to forty years. When it does it is outstandingly beautiful, its regular rounded crown carrying a dense mass of bloom, carried on panicles which stand out from the foliage. No pruning.

SORBARIA (Rosaceae) (D)
A genus found in the Himalayas and E Asia. All need a rich soil with moisture, and are hardy.

S. aitchisoni Afghanistan, Pakistan and Kashmir, 1895. Has established itself as the best species. A shrub to 3m (10ft). Leaves pinnate with eleven to twenty-three leaflets. Flowers white in midsummer on panicles.

S. arborea C and W China, 1908. Similar, but is considered the best of the genus by some. It suckers freely and these growths have to be removed unless the plant grows in a wild area.

Pruning is carried out in winter, removing some stems which have flowered, reducing the number which grow from the base and ultimately improving the display of flowers.

SORBUS (Rosaceae) (D)
A genus with about one hundred and twenty species, mostly from the Old World. They require only ordinary soil, preferring chalk and an open position; the Rowan group is intolerant of drought and prolonged heat.

Only _S. insignis_ is tender and its hardiness is too dubious for its inclusion in this book.

S. aria (section Aria) WHITEBEAM. Parts of Europe, including England and Ireland (only Galway), not in Asia. A tree to 12m (40ft), occasionally more, with a dense head. Leaves oval, greyish white, later bright green above with a white felt below, turning to gold in autumn. Flowers in corymbs, dull white. Fruits scarlet red, beautiful but soon taken by birds. Early training aims at establishing a leader with a clear trunk to 1.8m (6ft). The branches have an erect habit, making a well-shaped crown. Cultivar 'Lutescens' develops leaves covered by a creamy white down which becomes green by late summer. A very popular tree but _S. aucuparia_ is more satisfying in the long run.

S. aucuparia (section Sorbus [Aucuparia]) ROWAN, MOUNTAIN ASH. Europe and Asia. A tree to 18m (60ft), but not often. It is usually a neat grower to 10m (30ft) with pinnate leaves and white flowers, followed by bright red fruits, soon taken by birds. Cultivar 'Beissneri' has coppery brown bark of trunk and branches . Leaves colour yellow in autumn.

S. cashmiriana (section Sorbus [Aucuparia]). Himalayas and Kashmir, c1932. A small, slow-growing tree, rather open in branching. Flowers soft pink in late spring, larger than most _Sorbi_. Fruits like white gleaming marbles, which stay after the early leaf fall and persist until they decay.

S. domestica SERVICE TREE. A tree to 15m (50ft) with a broad crown. Pinnate leaves. Flowers of no account, fruits either like a pear (_pyriformis_) or an apple (_maliformis_). A beautiful tree as seen at Kew Gardens. No routine pruning.

S. hupehensis (section Aucuparia) W China, 1910. A tree to 15m (50ft), usually less. The large leaves have a blue tinge. Flowers inconspicuous. Fruits round, 5mm (¼in) wide, usually white, sometimes faintly pink. It is easily propagated from seed and its early growth is rapid, producing a leader without training.

S. 'Joseph Rock' A tree of uncertain origin, certainly in the section Aucuparia, reaching 10m (30ft) high is fine in its structure. Leaves turn red-copper or orange in autumn, and globular fruits change from green to yellow, finally to yellow by mid-autumn. An excellent tree deserving good soil and adequate moisture.

S. reducta (section Aucuparia) China. A dwarf shrub up to 0.6m (2ft), spreading by underground runners from which rise erect stems, leaves with red petioles and shining dark green leaflets, which turn reddish in autumn. Though said to be easily grown in any good moist soil, it has proved a failure on two occasions with us, in spite of every care. Perhaps it is calcifuge.

S. torminalis (section Aria), Europe, Asia Minor, N Africa. One of the best native British trees, given a chance. Of medium size, it grows quite quickly in the first few years and forms a leader with little training but opens out at 1.8m (6ft) if not stem-trained. It should be allowed ample space. The leaves are like those of a maple, sharply lobed, strikingly dark green, turning bronze-yellow in autumn. This tree self-sows in woodland but the seedlings do not develop well unless transplanted to open ground.

SPARTIUM JUNCEUM (Leguminosae) (D) S Europe, N Africa, Asia Minor, c1548. SPANISH BROOM thrives in a sunny position with rather dry soil. It has a loose habit with rush-like stems to 3m (10ft). Leaves inconspicuous. Flowers fragrant, 12mm (½in) long, in terminal racemes 0.3m (1ft) long, of a rather harsh yellow throughout summer.

It needs to be pruned in spring just before new growth appears. After the first year of planting out the growth is cut back by half. This is continued each year, taking great care not to cut into the old wood. If the plant becomes old and straggly it may be cut back nearly to the ground and will regenerate moderately, but it is time to think of a replacement. It is a good seaside shrub.

SPIRAEA (Rosaceae) (D)

A large genus from which many well-known species have been stripped, including _Holodiscus_ and, among the herbaceous, _Aruncus dioicus, Filipendula purpurea_ (Meadow Sweet) and _Filipendula rubra_ (formerly _Spiraea palmata_). There remain many good shrubs, graceful in habit and in foliage, less exciting in flower. All do well in good soil, tolerating chalk and a sunny position, though some perform adequately in partial shade eg _S. bumalda_.

The pruning regime can be separated into two distinct categories according to the flowering season of the shrub, and they are so listed here.

Those which flower on wood of the previous year are pruned back to two or three buds immediately after flowering. They include:

S. × _arguta_ Comes from a seedling of _S. × multiflora_, the other parent uncertain. It is a plant of rounded habit and medium size. The flowers are pure white in small clusters in late spring.

S. × _cinerea_ cultivar 'Grefsheim' Was the result of a self-sown seedling of uncertain parentage. It is smaller than _S. arguta_ but resembles it, flowering earlier.

S. _nipponica_ Japan, c1885. Reaches 1.5m (5ft) and carries pure white flowers in clusters, very fine, in early summer. The flowered stems can be cut right back as the shrub is very vigorous and will produce plenty of new shoots. It should be well manured.

S. × _vanhouttei_ _(trilobata ×cantoniensis)_ Liable to frost damage in low-lying places, but is otherwise very hardy. Arching stems reach 1.8m (6ft). White flowers abundant, in early summer. The older stems should be cut out after flowering.

Those which flower on the current year's shoots are pruned to two or three buds in early spring, at which time any weak or unhealthy shoots are cut away entirely. They include:

S. _japonica_ Japan, Korea, China, c1870. Known by its numerous cultivars, the best-known being 'Anthony Waterer'. Also one of the best plants, with flowers of carmine covering the surface. Though often described as a dwarf shrub it can be pruned in spring to 0.3-0.6m (1-2ft) with a good result. It is widely available.

S. _japonica bumalda_ 'Anthony Waterer', produced at the Knap Hill Nursery in Surrey c1890 and a particularly fine shrub with carmine flowers in midsummer.

S. _douglasii_ with dark rose flowers in summer is another example. It may be advisable to cut the whole plant down every few years and start again, manuring well.

STACHYURUS (Stachyuraceae) (D)

S. _chinensis_ China, 1908. Very close to _S. praecox_, which is better-known and is considered by some to be a better plant (it is commercially available). It flowers about two weeks after _S. praecox_ so you should have both.

S. _praecox_ Japan, 1864. Grows to around 1.2m (4ft) high. Flowers, twelve to twenty in drooping racemes, pale yellow, in late winter. It is hardy, but can be trained to the surface of a wall, though that might be thought wasteful. Older branches can be removed after flowering, but not every year.

STAPHYLEA (Staphyleaceae) (D)

Not regarded as a 'first team' plant, but is modestly attractive.

S. _colchica_ Caucasus, 1850. A shrub to 3m (10ft) high with erect branches. Leaves made up of five leaflets with fine teeth. Flowers in erect panicles, white. Fruit an inflated capsule 10cm (4in) long.

S. _pinnata_ Europe. Grew in the Strand, London, in 1596 according to Gerard. It is similar to *S. colchica* but has smaller capsules containing larger seeds. In a hot summer the leaves may turn an attractive foxy brown, persisting for several weeks.

These shrubs do not require regular pruning but young growth from the base may be thinned and the best shoots allowed to develop, while older growths are removed to make way. This is usually done in winter.

STEPHANANDRA (Rosaceae) (D)
S. incisa Japan, 1872. A shrub to 1.2m (4ft), notable for triangular leaves with margins cut into deep lobes, and also for the pleasant brown stems in winter.
S. tanakae Japan, 1893. Perfectly hardy and has slender arching stems with leaves less often lobed, and uninteresting flowers in early summer. The leaves turn light brown in autumn. A pleasant plant in a quiet way.

After flowering old growths are cut back almost to ground level and good mulching ensures that young stems will be produced.

STUARTIA (Theaceae)
A genus of very beautiful trees and shrubs but not easy to grow well, for reasons not always apparent. Certainly it would be rash to attempt them in chalky soil, but even in the best peaty loam they are often not robust. They need sun, and a clearing in woodland may be the most suitable site.
S. malacodendron (D) SE USA, 1740. This is among the best *Stuartia* and is a shrub or small tree to 4.5m (15ft). Leaves 5-10cm (2-4in) long. Flowers solitary, petals white, stamens purple, anthers blue, conspicuous in midsummer.
S. pseudo-camellia (D) Japan, prior to 1878. A tree to 10m (30 ft), has thick leaves turning red and yellow in autumn, flowers white, solitary, stamens white, orange anthers. These flowers are short-lived but are soon replaced through summer. Shelter from wind is necessary, as is sun but combined with shade, plus moist soil.

S. sinensis (D) C China, 1901. A large shrub or small tree with very attractive flaking bark, but undistinguished flowers which are fragrant. The trunk may be cleared of any branches below 1.8m (6ft) but otherwise pruning is not normally needed for this or any other *Stuartia*.

STYRAX (Styracaceae) (D)
A genus from America, E Asia, China, Japan and (only one) Europe. All need a lime-free soil with humus added, and a sheltered site. Not all are hardy, none absolutely.
S. hemsleyana China, 1900. A small tree with open branching, leaves broad, elliptic with deep veins. Flowers white, anthers yellow in long racemes in early summer. A leader should be trained from the start since branches develop at a low level.
S. japonica 1862. A shrub or small tree with wide-spreading branches and bell-shaped flowers, pure white, hanging from the underside of the branches. It readily makes a tree and when in flower is spectacular seen from below. This tree needs shelter and some temporary cover if spring frosts threaten. No regular pruning.
S. obassia China, Japan, 1879. Similar to *S. hemsleyana*, but slower-growing and slower to come into flower.

SYCOPSIS SINENSIS (E)
China, 1901. A bushy shrub to 2.4 or 3m (8 or 10ft). Leaves leathery, elliptic, lanceolate. Flowers small, monoecious, without petals, yellow stamens, red anthers in late winter. This shrub branches freely from the base, and should be encouraged so that the flowers can be seen at close quarters, though this is not exciting. If pruning is needed because of damage, regeneration is adequate.

SYMPHORICARPOS (Caprifoliaceae) (D)
A genus of rather commonplace species, but with some worthy hybrids and cultivars.
S. albus N America, 1879. Usually grown as

var. *laevigatus*, is a coarse shrub to 1.2m (4ft) high. Fruit globose, pure white, ripe in autumn, unattractive to birds. Much used for dark corners and unattractive areas. Makes a dense thicket.

S. × chenaultii (orbiculatus × microphyllus) is best seen as the cultivar 'Hancock' which is procumbent and layers freely. It is an excellent ground cover, as seen in London under plane trees.

Doorenbos hybrids A series of seedlings from various species and *S. × chenaultii*, the most successful being 'Mother of Pearl' and 'White Hedge'. Pruning is not easy because of the suckering habit and occasional digging out may be helpful, but why not accept defeat – and a thicket? No routine pruning for any *symphoricarpos*.

SYRINGA (Oleaceae) LILAC (D)

A genus of hardy, deciduous shrubs and small trees, flowering in late spring and early summer. They appreciate good soil, especially chalky earth, and full sun. The majority are vigorous and grow rapidly.

S. × josiflexa (josikaea × reflexa) A race of hybrids raised by Miss Isabella Preston in Ottawa. Perhaps the best clone is 'Bellicent', with very large panicles of rose-pink fragrant flowers.

S. meyeri China, 1908. The cultivar 'Palibin' is a dwarf, slow-growing shrub derived from *S. meyeri*, with violet-purple flowers in early summer in panicles up to 10cm (4in) long. A good rock garden plant.

S. × persica An ancient hybrid from Persia and India. A shrub 1.8m (8ft) or more high, bushy and rounded, with lanceolate leaves and lilac flowers which are moderately fragrant and produced in late spring. A splendid sight in the spring after a hot summer in the previous year. 'Alba' has white flowers.

S. vulgaris Mountains of E Europe, sixteenth century. COMMON LILAC is a shrub or small tree to 6m (20ft) high, with erect branches. Leaves ovate. Flowers lilac, richly scented. So common and easy to grow (without pruning) that it is often, even usually, taken for granted, but it has more charm and character than many of the bloated garden lilacs.

Garden Lilacs (Vulgaris group) Most of the

A pleached lime avenue at Chatsworth, perhaps *Tilia cordata*, beautifully maintained. It flowers in midsummer after most other limes

cultivars have been raised in the last 100 years, a large number by the company of Lemoine in Nancy, and some of the earliest remain in every list – Souvenir de Louis Spaeth (1883), single, deep wine-red; Charles Joly (1896), double, dark reddish purple; Michel Buchner (1885), double, pale rosy lilac; and Madame Lemoine (1890), double, white.

Pruning. *Vulgaris* lilacs flower from buds formed in the previous season. As they open the growth buds immediately below them begin to grow quickly and may be some inches long as the flowers fade. It helps to remove the faded blooms, but taking care not to damage the developing growths which will produce the next season's flowers. If much damage occurs there will not be suffi-

cient development in the ensuing season for flowering to occur. Overgrown or misshapen branches may call for drastic pruning to 0.6 or 0.9m (2 or 3ft) above ground level. There should be rapid regeneration if the soil is in good condition, but no flowers can be expected for two years.

TAMARIX (Tamaricaceae) (D)
Shrubs and small trees, easy to grow in any good loam in inland areas, though they are native of hot, maritime regions. Two species represent the different flowering habits of the genus.

T. parviflora Aegean and Balkans. Long cultivated in Britain, this is a shrub to 4.5m (15ft) high with arching branches, sessile leaves, flowers in racemes up to 5cm (2in) long, with petals rosy pink, borne on the old wood in late spring. It is absolutely hardy and flowers freely every year. This plant is pruned after the flowers fade and any tidying up may be done at the same time.

T. pentandra N and C Asia, c1880. Alias *T. ramosissima*, S. Russia, Asia Minor, China. Has the same general character as *T. parviflora*, growing to 4.5m (15ft) with rosy pink flowers but on wood of the current year; therefore it is pruned in spring before new growth starts. It is hardy and reliable. Any damaged branch may be cut away and regeneration should follow.

TAXUS
See Conifers; Hedges & Topiary.

TELOPEA TRUNCATA (Proteaceae) (E)
Tasmania at 610-1,219m (2,000-4,000ft),1930 by Harold Comber. TASMANIAN WARATAH is a shrub or tree to 6m (20ft) with leathery leaves and rich crimson flowers in terminal heads in early summer. 'It thrives where the rainfall is above average and the soil acid' (Bean, 1980). It needs conditions that suit the rhododendron, with sun above and shade at the root. No routine pruning.

TETRACENTRON (Tetracentraceae) (D)
China, 1901. A tree to 12m (40ft) of spreading habit. Leaves ovate or heart-shaped, pointed. Flowers tiny but numerous on a pendulous spike. It is moderately hardy and tolerates lime but grows better without it, in average loam. It should be sited in the open on a lawn or in a woodland clearing, the lower branches being encouraged so that the catkin-like spikes may be displayed in summer. No pruning.

TEUCRIUM (Labiatae) (E)
T. chamaedrys WALL GERMANDER Europe excluding Britain, N Africa, SW Asia, c1750. A semi-shrubby plant, woody at the base. It has a creeping root stock and erect stems, leaves bright green and hairy, flowers small and rosy.

This low shrub is useful for ground cover and is best cut back in spring, using shears for a large mass but secateurs if avoiding an edge to a lawn or path, with the object of presenting an informal outline.

T. fruticans Mediterranean, 1724. SHRUBBY GERMANDER is less hardy and usually grown against a wall in a light soil. It should be lightly pruned after flowering and any shoots killed in winter cut away in spring.

THYMUS (Labiatae) THYME (E)
T. serpyllum Europe, including Britain. A sub-shrub only a few centimetres high, woody at the base with trailing stems. Flowers rosy purple on upright stems from summer to autumn.

T. vulgaris S Europe. GARDEN THYME is 15-30cm (6-12in) high with a woody base, and greyish down on shoots and leaves. Flowers lilac or pale purple in whorls on a terminal spike.

T. ×citriodorus, LEMON THYME. An old garden plant making a bush to 0.3m (1ft). The lemon scent remains as strong as ever.

None of these plants requires any regular pruning beyond some gentle tidying up after flowering.

TILIA (Tiliaceae) LIME, LINDEN (E)

Noble trees which grow well in any fertile soil, are hardy and tolerate hard pruning and pleaching. They are native to Europe, including Britain, eastern N America, China, Korea and Japan. None of the American species has flourished in Britain, but the Chinese do well and are trees of character.

T. cordata Most of Europe, Caucasus, England as far north as the Lake District, Wales. A tree to 18m (60ft) high, usually smaller, but occasionally reaching 30m (100ft). The leaves are rounded, finely toothed, dark green, flowers yellowish-white in midsummer. A splendid tree, not planted often enough.

T. × euchlora Doubtful origin. Forms a large crown, the outer branches being pendulous, often sweeping the ground. The leaves are large, dark green and shiny. The flowers are yellow and attractive to bees. It is strikingly free from aphid attack but has come under a cloud in recent years, through a damaging disease of uncertain origin.

T. × europea COMMON LIME. Believed to be *cordata × platyphyllos*. Once popular for avenues and parks, it is now out of favour as it is liable to aphid attack, their excrement turning black on the leaves, making these unsightly and early to fall. This tree also produces suckers at the base, often arising from large burrs. These suckers can be removed, a tedious task, but the burrs cannot.

T. japonica Japan and E China, 1875. Has a dense leafy crown and flowers profusely in midsummer. There is a splendid specimen at Westonbirt.

T. oliveri China, 1900. A spreading tree, perhaps not more than 15m (50ft) high in cultivation. A fine specimen is close to the *T. japonica* mentioned above, at Westonbirt.

T. petiolaris Origin unknown. A very large tree up to 30m (100ft) and more occasionally. The branches are pendulous and produce a very graceful outline. The leaves are dark green above, white beneath, and the flowers in late summer are very fragrant.

T. platyphyllos Europe, probably including Britain. A very large tree, with bigger leaves than most others and an impressive outline. The cultivar 'Rubra', with twigs red in winter, is even better.

T. tomentosa The Balkans, Hungary, Russia, 1797. EUROPEAN WHITE LIME is notable for the silvery white felt on the underside of the leaves. It grows quickly and in time becomes handsome.

The pruning of limes is straightforward. Initially the object is to establish a single leader and shorten, if necessary, any laterals, removing any that are becoming upright. If damaged or badly placed limbs on mature trees need cutting back, the work should be done in midsummer to allow time for the wound to heal before winter.

TRACHYCARPUS FORTUNEI (E) China, 1830. CHUSAN PALM is woody and hardy, so cannot be ignored, but it is difficult to imagine any system of pruning which could be applied to this plant. Its stem is clothed by the disintegrated bases of the leaves, which can persist for many years. In the open air in southern England plants at least seventy years old are 3.6-4.5m (12-15ft) high, but healthy.

TROCHODENDRON ARALIOIDES
(Trochodendraceae) (E)

Japan, Taiwan, c1890. A large shrub or tree, branching freely from the base. The foliage is described as 'recalling that of a tree ivy' (Bean 1980, p621), and the flowers, in an erect terminal inflorescence, are vivid green. It needs lime-free soil and shelter from wind. It has done well in Suffolk, Hampshire, Gloucestershire and Cornwall. No pruning.

ULEX (Leguminosae) (D)

A genus allied to the brooms.

U. europaeus W and C Europe. It infests huge areas of moorland, doing best on the poorest soils and growing to 1.2m (4ft) or so. The side

This photograph of *Viburnum plicatum* 'Mariesii' shows clearly the tabular arrangement of the branches and the abundant heads of white, sterile flowers. Do not disturb the structure by unnecessary pruning

branches end in a strong sharp spine. Leaves insignificant; flowers, calyx and petals are bright yellow in late spring, when they are at their height, though they show a little in late winter on wood of the previous year. For pruning, see below. Cultivar 'Flore Pleno', DOUBLE-FLOWERED GORSE, needs the same conditions and is more compact. It bears semi-double flowers which last a long time in mid-spring, and produces no seed, which makes it suitable for gardens with thin soil. Propagation has to be by cuttings.

U. gallii W Europe, England, especially South West, notably the heaths of Dorset (those that are left). A dwarf shrub under 0.6m (2ft). It flowers from late summer to autumn.

U. minor W Europe. Flowering in early autumn, and very welcome then.

Pruning of gorse depends on the season of flowering. If it is spring (*europaeus* and 'Flore Pleno'), prune immediately the flowers are past, giving time for ripening new wood. If flowering is in autumn (*gallii* and *minor*) prune, not too hard, in early spring.

ULMUS (Ulmaceae) (D)

To the English up to the latest generation the word elm suggests *U. procera*, the ENGLISH ELM. Few, however, would have recognised the distinction between that and *U. carpinifolia*, the SMOOTH ELM, a native seen only in eastern England and almost certainly the tree celebrated by John Constable in his Suffolk landscapes; or *U. plottii* or *U. coritana*, both seen only in the Midlands. To a Scot or a Welshman *U. glabra*, the WYCH ELM, would be *the* elm and it is native of both those countries whereas *U. procera* is not English, though nobody knows quite where it came from.

As described below, the arrival in the late 1960s of the aggressive strain of 'Dutch' elm disease has altered the appearance of a large part of the country and, by 1977, about 50 per cent of the 23 million elms existing previously had been killed. It seems likely that no species escaped entirely and exact information is hard to gather, hence the descriptions that follow may not be up-to-date.

U. americana AMERICAN or WHITE ELM. E and central N America, 1752. The best-known type is vase-shaped, the trunk separating into large branches which eventually sweep outwards in wide arches, the height being up to 36m (120ft). This is, or was, the best-loved

tree in eastern America but in England there were few, widely separated plantations and none lived more than fifty years. Regrettably the trees have suffered from elm disease as severely in America as in Britain.

U. carpinifolia SMOOTH ELM. Europe, N Africa, SW Asia. Related species take the place of it in the British Midlands – *U. plottii*, and *U. coritana*.

U. glabra WYCH ELM. Europe, Spain to W Russia to Britain. A large tree with arching branches, very handsome. Good for exposed coastal situations. Self-seeds.

U. procera ENGLISH ELM. Origin uncertain. To watch its disappearance was an extremely painful experience. Nothing can replace this superb tree, stout yet graceful, densely leafy, the leaves turning a fine yellow in autumn. The leafless tree is impressive and beautiful in a modest way when the first flowers appear in late winter.

U. pumila C Asia, Siberia, N China, 1770. A small tree to 7.6m (25ft), related to *U. carpinifolia* but smaller in all features. It is probably immune to elm disease.

Dutch elm disease is now known to be due

to the fungus *Ceratocystus ulmi*, transmitted from infected trees by the elm bark beetles *Scolytus scolytus* and *Scolytus multistriatus*. It is considered possible that the disease has been present in a relatively mild form for several centuries, but was definitely identified in 1927 in Hertfordshire. In the mid-1930s there was increased severity of the disease in many areas. Certainly in Worcestershire many trees were killed, and others disfigured but left alive as the attack receded. By the late 1940s the disease was quite mild and the onset of the aggressive form began acutely just before 1970, later traced to elms imported from Canada with the bark still intact. By 1979 about half the total elm population of 23 million, reckoned to exist at the onset of this outbreak, had died. Around 1980 there was evidence that regenerated elms were growing to 3m (10ft) or more, and by 1990 specimens 9m (30ft) tall and in good health were recorded in Hertfordshire. The author grew *V. americana* and *U. procera* from cuttings of dying trees in 1972 and these plants are healthy, but only 6m (20ft) high.

UMBELLULARIA (Lauraceae) (E)
Oregon, California, 1929. CALIFORNIA LAUREL is a tree to 30m (100ft) in California, less than 18m (60ft) in more northerly and temperate climates. It makes a dense head of leafy branches. Leaves leathery, pungent when crushed, and said to cause headache if inhaled for more than a few minutes. This tree needs a warm position in good soil, or otherwise it may suffer spring frost-damage. In early life it should be trained to a single stem with a stake. The laterals are usually well formed and need no pruning.

VACCINIUM (Ericaceae)
A genus of shrubs requiring an acid soil, not rich. They tolerate some shade. Their flowers are pleasant but not remarkable. All are hardy in the west of Britain.

V. floribundum (E) N and C Andes, c1840. A shrub to 1.2m (4ft) high, leaves dark green, rosy pink flowers in early summer on lower side of shoots. Tiny red berries. Young growths red-tinted.

V. ovatum BOX BLUEBERRY (E) Western N America, 1826. A shrub to 3.6m (12ft) in temperate regions. Flowers in short racemes, white. Berries black, round. The leaves emerge coppery red and later become shining green.

V. vitis-idaea COWBERRY (E). Northern N America, Europe, Asia. A dwarf, creeping shrub, native in north and west Britain. Leaves small, like those of box, dark green above, pale beneath. Flowers white, tinged pink in short racemes, borne all through summer; berries red, edible but bitter. A good ground cover in shade.

The smaller plants of this genus need no pruning, except for the removal of poor growths in spring, but some larger deciduous shrubs tend to retain weak elderly shoots which should be cut away in winter.

VIBURNUM (Caprifoliaceae)
A large genus with many species worthy of culture. Most are grown for their flowers, but the fruits are fine in a few, limited by self-incompatibility which requires pollination from a plant of a different clone and the presence of an active insect to carry it out. Corrugated foliage is a feature of *V. rhytidophyllum* (E) China, 1900, and some hybrids of it, notably *V.* × 'Pragense' (E) where the leaves are dark green and shining. Some give a good display of autumn colour, especially *V. opulus* (D), sadly often thought too coarse for the garden. If so it is the garden which needs modifying. Here is a selection of worthy, reliable plants, a few omitted because they favour an acid soil or are doubtfully hardy.

V. betulifolium (D) China, 1901. A tall erect plant with corymbs of white flowers, not impressive, in early summer. In autumn the long branches are weighed down by bunches of red fruits, which last until winter, but the self-incompatibility mentioned above must be allowed for. Splendid at Abbotsbury, Dorset.

V. × bodnantense (farreri × grandiflorum) (D). A rather gaunt, upright shrub producing from late autumn clusters of aromatic rose-tinted white flowers, which may be damaged by severe frost.

V. × burkwoodii (carlesii × utile) (E). A vigorous, easily grown tall shrub with fragrant white flowers from late winter to late spring.

V. × carlcephalum (carlesii × macrocephalum) (D). A good medium-sized shrub whose leaves often colour well in autumn and which has very fragrant, large flower heads in late spring (though beginning in early spring in the mild regions).

V. cinnamomifolium (E) China, 1904. Has the most handsome leaves of the evergreens. The flowers are uninteresting. A splendid specimen clothes the wall of the kitchen garden at Borde Hill, Sussex.

V. odoratissimum (E) China, c1818. Very similar but rather tender. Fragrant white flowers on large panicles arrive in late summer and the older leaves colour in winter.

V. opulus GUELDER ROSE (D). Europe, NW Africa, Asia Minor, part of central Asia. A large shrub with long shoots which spread widely, and maple-like leaves which colour splendidly in autumn. The flowers, produced in early summer, are of no account but the fruits are red and translucent, lasting into the winter. It chooses boggy sites.

V. plicatum (D) China, Japan, 1844. The cultivar _mariesii_ has strikingly tabular branches on which the white flowers are crowded on the upper side. A splendid plant.

V. 'Pragense' (rhytidophyllum × utile) (E) has shining dark green corrugated leaves. The flowers are creamy white, not bad; the plant is elegant.

V. rhytidophyllum (E) A large shrub with corrugated leaves, dark green above, grey hairy beneath. Creamy flowers in cymes appear in late spring. Single specimens do not fruit readily (see above). It should be in rich soil (chalk is tolerated) and given shelter from storms.

V. sargentii f. **'Onondaga'** Has young leaves coloured deep bronze and red flower buds. Stylish is the word.

V. tinus (E) Mediterranean, S Europe, c1850. Now represented by several cultivars of great merit including 'Eve Price', compact with smaller leaves than the type and flower buds bright pink; and 'Lucidum', a vigorous shrub with large leaves. Unfortunately it is only really successful in the milder regions.

Pruning. If shrubs are healthy there is no need for regular pruning in most cases. _V. betulifolum_ has negligible flowers but the flowered heads will not be cut back as you will be hoping for a crop of fruits. _V. × bodnantense_ produces stems from the base freely, which permits removal of old and unproductive wood. This is best carried out in early spring, at the end of flowering, and that applies to the other winter and spring-flowering shrubs, including _V. × burkwoodii_, _V. carlecephalum_ and _V. juddii_. _V. cinnamomifolium_ and _odoratissimum_ will need only a mild tidying in early spring. Any pruning of _V. opulus_, rarely needed, is done in early spring. _V. plicatum_ should be approached with great care as nothing must be done which will disturb the tabular structure of the stems. Only dead or diseased wood should be cut away. _V. rhytidophyllum_ produces shoots from the base and these have to be removed unless some of the older growth needs to be cut off. In general it is grown from a central main stem and laterals may be shortened if they seem to be failing. _V. sargentii_ f. _onondaga_ needs no pruning. It develops slowly in an elegant way. _V. tinus_ only needs pruning if it is outgrowing the space allotted to it. As it ages or is damaged by frost, some hard pruning in spring is indicated and it will regenerate vigorously.

VINCA (Apocyanaceae) (E)

A genus of sub-shrubs and herbaceous perennials from Europe, N Africa, and SW and C Asia. Those described here are evergreen shrubs, trailing and carpeting.

V. difformis (E, but often dying back in winter) SW Europe. In our Somerset garden in the shade of *Quercus ilex* it does not die back, but flowers are rather scanty from autumn to spring and are pale violet-white. The plants are trimmed in spring.

V. major GREATER PERIWINKLE. W and C Mediterranean region, wild in Britain. A shrub with flowering stems erect up to 0.6m (2ft) high. Flowers bright blue, appearing in late spring and continuing until autumn.

V. minor Europe, W Asia, wild in Britain, perhaps a garden escape. The long trailing stems root readily. Flowers bright blue, from late spring to summer and intermittently until autumn. The cultivar 'Azurea Flore Pleno' has flowers of a lovely sky-blue, and double. Like all the vincas it flowers much more freely in full sun.

VITEX (Verbenaceae) AGNUS CASTUS (D).

Mediterranean region, SW and C Asia, by sixteenth century. A shrub of spreading habit with leaves narrow and dark green, flowers fragrant, produced in late summer and early autumn in large panicles. It is only hardy in the open in mild areas but does fairly well in maritime places. No doubt it needs more sun than England offers. Arnold-Forster (1948), writing from Cornwall, thought it would be worth trying in a hot place, planted in quantity with *Caryopteris clandonensis* and some warm contrasting colours such as those of red hot pokers.

Flowers are produced on wood of the current season: annual pruning in spring is indicated, cutting back all growth to 2.5-5cm (1-2in) from the framework of branches.

WEIGELA (Caprifoliaceae) (D)

Hardy shrubs related to honeysuckle.

W. florida Japan, N China, 1845. A shrub to 2.7m (9ft) high with arching branches. Leaves oval to 10cm (4in) long. Flowers in clusters, reddish on the outside, paler within. It has produced many successful hybrids and cultivars: for example 'Folis Purpureis' with purple flushed leaves and 'Variegata', more compact with leaves edged creamy white and pink flowers.

W. middendorfiana Japan, N China, 1850. A fine shrub to about 1.5m (5ft) with sulphur-yellow flowers in cymose clusters during late spring. It may be damaged by spring frost. Among the hybrids are some of the oldest: the still-popular Abel Carrière, deep carmine flowers (1876); Eva Rathke (about 1880), flowers crimson red; and *Looymansii aurea*, leaves golden, flowers pink.

Pruning. As a rule it pays to prune these plants immediately after flowering to allow time for new growths to ripen before autumn. If the stool from which new shoots develop becomes weak it may be cut right back and new growth will soon appear, but this may be so thick that the weakest members may be removed. This is left until midsummer, otherwise a fresh crop of weak stems may appear. Be on the lookout for reversion of growth on variegated forms and cut it out at once. Good feeding is essential in spring for all weigelas, whether or not this system of pruning is adopted.

WISTERIA – See Climbers.

XANTHOCERAS SORBIFOLIUM (Sapindaceae) (D)

N China, 1866. A large shrub or small tree to 6m (20ft) high. Erect in growth. White flowers in late spring in erect panicles, reminiscent of horse chestnut. It grows well in any good soil, tolerating chalk. In the open it needs summer heat to perform really well. It is subject to coral spot disease and affected branches should be cut back. Otherwise no pruning is needed.

XANTHORHIZA SIMPLICISSIMA (Ranunculaceae) (D)

E USA, 1776. A shrub with creeping roots and erect stems to 0.6m (2ft) high. The pinnate leaves with three or five leaflets are handsome and the flowers, in panicles, appear in early spring. It does well in semishade but dense shade is too much for it. It needs adequate moisture. Use it as ground cover. No pruning is needed.

YUCCA (Liliaceae) (E)

It is difficult to think of this genus as shrubby and Graham Stuart Thomas reasonably excuses his inclusion of it in his *Perennial Garden Plants* as it 'resembles a shrub so little and so little has been written about it'. As pruning is the excuse for this book and plays virtually no part in the culture of *Yucca*, little will be written about it here either.

ZANTHOXYLUM (Rutaceae) (D)

A genus of trees and shrubs, little-known though not without merit, characterised by the strong, usually disagreeable odour of the crushed leaves and the spines on young branches and leaf-stalks. The leaves are pinnate and the most handsome feature.

Z. americanum TOOTHACHE TREE, E USA, c1740. The popular name was given because the bark and seed capsules were chewed to ease toothache. A shrub to 3m (10ft) with leaves pinnate, up to 15cm (6in) long, leaflets in five to eleven pairs. Flowers inconspicuous. Fruits black. This plant needs rich soil to flourish. It has an upright habit and a single leader should be established without difficulty.

Z. piperitum China, Japan, c1875. JAPAN PEPPER has a tidy bushy habit, and the eleven to twenty-three leaflets are conspicuous. It should not need pruning.

Z. planispinum Japan, China, c1870. It has leaves with a winged petiole and three or five leaflets, and the spines are broad and flattened. After a hot summer there are small red fruits. Should not need pruning.

ZELKOVA (Ulmaceae)(D)

Four species are in cultivation: all have smooth trunks and coarsely toothed leaves, rough to the touch. They should have a deep rich soil and some shelter. Two of the species are rare in Britain:

Z. abelicea Crete, 1929. A late introduction though it was described in a letter of 1594 to Clusius. There are healthy specimens at Kew and the RHS garden, Wisley.

Z. sinica C and E China, 1920. A plant from this is thriving at Kew. Very rare.

The other two species are more familiar.

Z. carpinifolia Russia, Iran, c1760. A large tree which divides not more than 0.3m (1ft) above ground into many erect branches, which seem to suffer no ill-effect from this crowding and present a remarkable picture. There are large specimens at Kew and one at the Natural Botanic Garden, Glasnevin, Dublin. The trees are exceptionally healthy, which is just as well because the removal of single limbs would be extremely difficult. This is a rare tree and hard to find.

Z. serrata Japan, Taiwan, 1861. Comparatively common. It can be trained to have a clean stem of 1.8-2.4m (6-8ft), the branches being almost erect, but the outer ones are spreading and pendulous at their extremities. It is a slow-growing tree and has been convicted of developing elm disease, but is still much the most easily obtainable.

ZENOBIA PULVERULENTA (Ericaceae) (D)

USA, SE Virginia to S Carolina, c1800. A shrub, rather untidy to 1.2-1.8m (4-6ft). Young shoots and leaves covered by glaucous bloom. White, bell-shaped flowers in clusters in early summer. Perfectly hardy, and must have a lime-free soil with a little shade. It does not tolerate drought. Pruning consists of removing the dead flowers and a little of the stem on which they form. If the plant is elderly and failing, it may respond to hard pruning, with a rich lime-free mulch.

CLIMBERS

All Climbers have the urge to grow upwards, sooner or later needing the support of walls, pergolas, arbours, frames, pillars, trees or hedges. They differ, however, in *how* they climb:

1 By means of **aerial roots** which adhere to a surface – wall, timber, tree trunk branches and so on. Ivies are the most obvious example.
2 By means of **tendrils** which branch and end in small suckers, adhering as in Group 1. The prime example is *Parthenocissus* (Virginia Creeper, Boston Ivy).
3 By means of **twining stems**. Examples are wisteria and honeysuckle.
4 By means of **twining petioles**. Clematis is a notable example.
5 By means of tendrils which are **modified branch stems**, arising opposite leaves and ending in spring-like coils which waft freely until they touch another object, which they then coil around. In this way, when repeated, the plant may reach a height of 1.8m (6ft). Examples are vines and garden peas, and among the weeds White Bryony (*Bryonia dioica*).

All of these groups are true climbers. One more category is less convincing – the scrambler. This has long sinuous shoots often armed with thorns, which are able to attach the shoots firmly to other plants or to wires and trellis. Such are many of the roses and brambles. One plant which does no more than scramble is *Clematis × jouiniana*. If cut back in winter it makes vigorous shoots, which spread along the ground unless given encouragement by being 'attached' to a neighbouring shrub, perhaps a climber such as one of the loniceras. Then it will rise to 1.8-2.4m (6-8ft). This plant is a hybrid, *C. vitalba × C.heracleifolia* var. *davidiana*, and does not have the characteristics of a climber but it will spread over a stump and make ground cover. The flowers are white with blue shading.

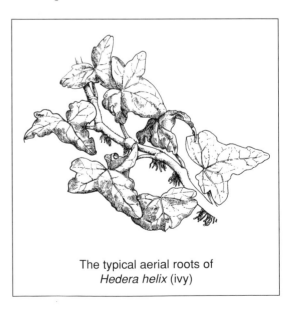

The typical aerial roots of
Hedera helix (ivy)

Supports

For wall climbers use coated wire stretched horizontally at 0.6m (2ft) intervals and held by vine eyes driven into the wall, with straining bolts at one end to maintain tension. An alternative is trellis work held 5-7.5cm (2-3in) from the wall surface. An expensive system is the use of square-headed nails with lead tags which lightly hold the plant stems.

Planting

Most climbers should be planted at least 0.3m (1ft) from a wall, as the soil close to it dries out easily.

CLIMBERS AS GROUND COVER

Some climbers trail on the ground as readily as they hoist themselves upwards, but others may be too rampant to be used in this way. The common ivy, *Hedera helix,* would need frequent trimming at busy times of the year. Its cultivar 'Sagittifolia' is neat and relatively slow-growing, and will need only annual clipping in spring. *Hedera colchica* is rather more vigorous and has leaves 20cm (8in) long, dark green and sombre in a well-planned garden with trees which will slow the ivy's growth. In a more open position between shrubs *Schizophragma hydrangeoides*

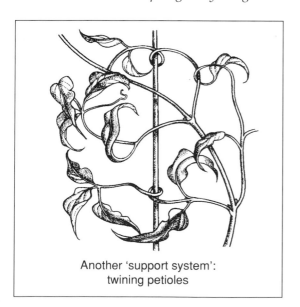

Another 'support system':
twining petioles

or the larger *S. integrifolium* makes a dense carpet of good green foliage with flower heads of creamy white in early summer. Extension growths can be cut back in the dormant period, avoiding the buds of the coming year's flowers. *Clematis × jouiniana,* already mentioned as a scrambling climber, will grow freely on the flat and the bluish-white flowers are borne in partial shade from late summer for several weeks.

ACTINIDIA (Actinidiaceae) (D)

A. chinensis Very vigorous to 7.5m (25ft), the shoots being covered with red hairs as are the veins and stalks of the leaves. Flowers white becoming buff. Hardy but best (most orderly) against a wall. Old shoots can be replaced by young growth from low down in winter, though not after midwinter as the sap rises early and there is a risk of bleeding. The fruits, which are only rarely edible in Britain, are available from New Zealand as kiwi fruit.

A. kolomikta appeals to many but few have the conditions to suit it: wall space 4.5m (15ft) high by 6m (20ft) long. The foliage starts more or less purple, then develops a variegation, white on pink with some green. This lasts from late midspring until midsummer, when the leaves become dull green. Train it to cover the space. Later just cut back shoots which come forward.

AKEBIA QUINATA (Lardizabalaceae) (D)

A very vigorous twiner, evergreen in sheltered places. Flowers purple, fruit rare in Britain. Often recommended for scrambling into a tree, but can be a nuisance as the long shoots multiply and disfigure the tree if it is alive, and hardly conceal it if it is dead. A wall can provide a sound support and the shoots can be allowed to fall forward from a coated wire at 1.8m (6ft) above ground. This also makes pruning simple, for it involves shortening the sound growth and removing that which is weak.

As this picture suggests, *Ampelopsis brevipedunculata* is a very vigorous climber, making a dense mat of lobed foliage. The main attraction is the colour of the fruits which is deep blue, but these only make a display if the plant is exposed to full sun and the summer is hot. Long untidy shoots have to be removed throughout the summer and in early winter the whole plant is cut back to two or three buds on the strongest stems

AMPELOPSIS (Vitaceae) (D)

A. brevipedunculata NE Asia, 1870, climbs by tendrils. It is valued for its blue fruits and handsome leaves and should be planted on a south-facing wall. Growth is rapid and extensive, covering a large area. A sufficient number of shoots is tied in, the rest being sacrificed and cut back to two buds in winter (not after midwinter as the sap rises early).
A. megalophylla has leaves 0.6m (2ft) by 0.45m (1½ft) and needs a post at least 4.5m (15ft) high.

ARISTOLOCHIA MACROPHYLLA (Aristolochiaceae) (D)

Eastern USA. Sent by John Bartram in 1783. A vigorous deciduous climber. Needs a warm site but is suited to wall, pergola or pillar. Leaves 12.5-25cm (5-10in) long, almost as wide. The early summer flowers are solitary, tubular, bent in the lower half like a syphon, yellowish-green, with the mouth purple. After flowering, thin out shoots and remove any that are wayward.

BERBERIDOPSIS CORALLINA (Flacourtiaceae) (E)

Chile, 1862. An evergreen climber twining to 6m (20ft). Leaves ovate with spiny teeth, dark green above, glaucous. Flowers in a terminal raceme, deep crimson, in midsummer continuing for two months. It is not an easy plant to grow: it is not very hardy, needs a rich, moist loam and is intolerant of alkaline soil. It is best sited on the north side of a 1.8m (6ft) wall, protected from north and east winds. Pruning is seldom necessary beyond shortening weak shoots. In spite of this gloomy picture this plant is widely available in commerce. Perhaps most of the customers have decided to give it just one more chance.

BILDERDYKIA BALDSCHUANICA

(formerly *Polygonum baldschuanicum*)
(Polygonaceae) (D)

Russia. A very vigorous climber, hoisting itself by twining. Leaves ovate, pale green, flowers white tinged pink, in crowded panicles from late summer and through the autumn. Its twining habit makes it more suitable for covering an unsightly object or an old tree than a wall, on which it will be at least untidy and dead wood will accumulate quickly. It would also be effective growing up a bank. Under these conditions pruning is not indicated except for cosmetic reasons or the removal of dead wood, which is difficult without damage to the living.

CAMPSIS RADICANS (Bignoniaceae) (D)

TRUMPET VINE. SE USA. Climbs by aerial roots to 12m (40ft). Leaves pinnate, up to 38cm (15in) long. Flowers in midsummer in a cluster, corolla scarlet and orange, trumpet-shaped. The lateral growths should be cut to two or three buds. This will encourage flowering.

CELASTRUS ORBICULATUS
(Celastraceae) (D)

NE Asia, 1860. One of a small number of species which climb by twining and are grown for their long-persistent capsules containing brightly coloured seeds. It is vigorous and able to reach 9m (30ft) high. Leaves obovate to orbicular, up to 12.5cm (5in) long, turning clear yellow in autumn. Flowers inconspicuous. Capsules split open in autumn to show the bright red seeds. A tree is considered the best host for a climber such as this. Old trunks of _Robinia pseudoacacia_ have been suggested since their wood is so durable. Pruning is limited to cutting back some of the longest shoots and, of course, any dead wood. This is done in summer as it is not easy to distinguish dead from living tissue when the plant is dormant.

CLEMATIS (Ranunculaceae) (D)

A large genus including a few worthy herbaceous plants. The majority are climbers which raise themselves by twining leaf stalks (petioles) which attach themselves to stems or shrubs or trees; failing such support, they simply twine round each other. In some respects a wall provides the simplest background for the pruner, as the upward progress of the shoots can be observed often and they can be directed if a structure of wire or trellis work is installed. Pergolas, trellises and arbours are effective but rather more trouble. Training over a shrub of little importance can produce a spectacular result, as was achieved inadvertently at Tintinhull by planting _Clematis_ 'Etoile Violette' 0.9m (3ft) from an aged honeysuckle, which was a tangle of stems. The clematis is pruned to 0.45m (18in) at the end of winter and in spring, having worked its way through the tangle, spreads itself in a flat mass 1.5m (5ft) in diameter from midsummer until mid autumn. This way of growing clematis was used by William Robinson at Gravetye in Sussex with success, and at Kew early in this century. Untrained branches of oak stuck in the ground, three to a bed, tied together at the top were equally effective. Most clematis like plenty of sun on their flower-bearing part, but the blooms may fade if sunshine is

Clematis 'Comtesse de Bouchaud' is vigorous but not tall. It begins to flower in early summer, the colour being 'pinky-mauve' (C. Lloyd) with each flower from 10-15cm (4-6in) across, later becoming smaller, always abundant

prolonged. The lower part should be sheltered by a 0.6m (2ft) plant to avoid drying out.

The difficult part of clematis pruning is concerned entirely with a group which flowers in early summer on shoots arising from the wood of the previous year, but meanwhile the new growth of this year is preparing to produce flowers in late summer and early autumn. To produce the best of both worlds, you must cut back some of the stems from last year which have just flowered and they will set about providing growth which will carry flowers in early summer next year. The remainder will be left until the next early spring and then be cut to the lowest buds, to provide growths for flowering in the next late summer and autumn. The problem is that you may achieve a mediocre result in both early and late summer. The least troublesome conclusion is to leave all pruning until late winter, and achieve an excellent flowering of 'The President', 'Duchess of Edinburgh', × _jackmanii_ and others.

Of the 'late flowering' group, some flower as early as midsummer, eg 'Perle d'Azur', followed by 'Royal Velours', _C. orientalis_, × _jackmanii_ and _C. viticella_. All these should be cut down to 30cm (1ft), or even less, in late winter. To encourage earlier flowering, a few stems may be cut to 45cm (18in).

The third group starts with _C. cirrhosa balearica_, an evergreen often in flower by late winter. _C. alpina_ starts to flower in early spring and includes 'Frances Rivis', deep blue, and 'Pamela Jackman', azure. Both are very good. The evergreen _C. armandii_, flowering in mid-spring, benefits from a wall on its north side. It has big leaves, brownish when young, white flowers with good scent, and is certainly best pruned back by half of all growth when flowering has finished. This group also includes _C. montana_, very vigorous, as are its cultivars, except 'Picton's Variety'. 'Elizabeth' (pink flowers with a good scent) is desirable. All this group benefit from pruning as for

C. armandii above, after which the plants can set about producing new growth to flower next year.

Christopher Lloyd, who knows all there is to know about clematis, calls this third group A. The difficult group that flowers first on old and later on younger growth is group B, and the late summer flowering group is C. If you need more details follow his guidance.

ECCREMOCARPUS SCABER
(Bignoniaceae) (D)

Chile, 1824. A sub-shrub, semi-woody and almost evergreen under sheltered conditions. Leaves doubly pinnate, light green. Petioles end in a branching tendril which twists round any object in its path. It flowers from early summer, orange or red or in between, and tolerates poor soil, thriving at the foot of a yew hedge on which it will climb to 3.6m (12ft), making seed freely and self-seeding. It is perennial and survives for several years in southern England. The seed pods are subject to invasion by a pest – the light-fingered visitor.

HEDERA (Araliaceae) (E)

IVY. A small genus of evergreen climbers. All ivies climb by means of aerial roots, which attach themselves firmly to any surface while the leaves arrange themselves in one plane. Eventually the plant produces bushy growths and flowers, but ceases forming aerial roots. The genus ranges from the Canary Islands and Madeira through Europe, including Britain, Asia Minor to China and Japan. It is not native of the USA but 'English Ivy' is a noted weed there.

H. canariensis Canary Islands, Madeira, Portugal, is now mainly represented by the cultivar 'Gloire de Marengo', with large leaves margined with creamy white and irregular splashes of green along the main veins. It is often used as a house plant, but is reasonably hardy.

H. colchica Caucasus. PERSIAN IVY has large

leaves to 46cm (18in) long, dark green, handsome. It is said to be a huge plant in the forest of the Caucaus, but in Britain it is not spectacular, though it makes a good dense cover for a wall. The plant responds to clipping in spring and needs a nutritious soil, unlike H. helix Cv 'Paddy's Pride' has leaves with an irregular central splash of yellow merging into pale and finally deep green.

H. helix Europe, Asia Minor to Northern Iran. COMMON IVY is the toughest and hardiest of the ivies, a plant which will grow well where few others will – a virtue in rough parts of the garden – and to some extent against buildings or trees, but a considerable nuisance in a hedge bottom or among valued trees. It is often said that ivy does no harm to brickwork, but when this is old the mortar may easily come away when the stems are pulled off or when stems in the arborescent stage are disturbed by strong winds. One disadvantage of ivy on a house wall arises when the stems encroach on windows and encourage the entry of earwigs and other insects. The number of cultivars is legion, among them 'Conglomerata' with erect stems and leaves with a wavy margin. It needs some support. 'Hibernica', IRISH IVY, has bright green leaves, turning to copper in winter. It is useful for ground cover, rooting readily. 'Sagittifolia' has five-lobed leaves, the central one large and triangular. It has the virtue of growing slowly.

Pruning of ivies usually consists of clipping over the surface of the plant in late spring. This leaves a bare stem for three or four weeks. An alternative is to pull off the growth, having hooked it from the wall, leaving a few feet of the plant only from ground level. Avoid this if there is old mortar. With ivy up a tree it is the best system.

HOLBOELLIA CORIACEA
(Lardizabalaceae) (E)
Hupeh, China, 1907. A vigorous species to 5.4m (18ft). Leaves with three glossy green leaflets. Flowers in midspring, male purple in terminal clusters, female greenish-white in axillary clusters. The fruit is a pod 7.5cm (3in) long. It is hardy, useful for a wall or up a tree, scrambling. In spring the weaker growths may be cut out and in summer long growths shortened.

HYDRANGEA (Hydrangeaceae)
Two climbing species call for attention.
H. petiolaris (D) Japan, Korea, Taiwan, 1878. Will climb to 18m (60ft) on a tree by means of aerial roots and does well on a north-facing wall. It is better still on a mound 0.9m (3ft) high, which it will soon cover and then need only light pruning to restrict erratic growth. Leaves ovate, dark green. Corymbs up to 25cm (10in) across expand in early summer, with white sterile flowers at the margin and small, dull white flowers filling the centre. When grown on a wall, extension growths which are not needed are cut back as they emerge in summer. Some of the spurs are cut to two or three buds in spring each year. This plant is not to be confused with *Schizophragma hydrangeoides* (see p144).
H. senatifolia (E) is evergreen with tough, obovate leaves. Flowers small, white in crowded panicles in late summer. Best against a wall, south - or west-facing. Prune in spring, only one third of the plant each year.

JASMINUM (Oleaceae)
JASMINE, JESSAMINE. Twining and scandent shrubs, easily grown in fertile soils. Most are fragrant.
J. beesianum (D) China. Vigorous with leaves dark green above, flowers rose to carmine in early summer. Fruit like a pea but black, shiny. No regular pruning, but shoots may need thinning in spring every few years.
J. mesnyi China, 1900. PRIMROSE JASMINE, evergreen, is quite widely available but is regarded by most experts as only suitable for the mildest areas. Perhaps it is most often grown in a pot from spring till autumn and

Hedera colchica makes a fine covering for a wall with its large, dark green leaves. It is one of the best ivies and an ideal companion plant to other climbers

then put under cover for the winter. The most handsome jasmine.

J. nudiflorum (D) China. Not a true climber, but can be trained on wires against a wall and bears yellow flowers throughout winter. Old shoots are replaced by young growth, a few each year. No hard pruning.

J. officinale (D) Caucasus, Iran, China. A classic plant of English gardens, now mainly of cottages, even when commuterised. In the open it forms a bush without any support if pruned back every spring. It flowers mainly on wood of the previous year, and to a lesser extent on the new growth. Some of the former may be removed immediately after flowering (compare Clematis Group B, p140).

LONICERA (Caprifoliaceae)

HONEYSUCKLE. All like a good loamy soil with a cool site for the roots, and in some cases partial or even complete shade.

L. × americana (*caprifolium × etrusca*) (D) has fragrant flowers in whorls, Corolla yellow, tinged purple outside in early summer. It is a very fine plant.

L. brownii (D) is usually seen as 'Dropmore Scarlet' with flowers orange and scarlet. It is best on a wall.

L. giraldii (E) China. Makes a dense mound of hairy stems with a velvet surface of leaves. Small purple flowers, but the leaves are enough to make it worthwhile. Clip back in spring.

L. japonica (E) has very fragrant flowers, white turning to yellow in the cultivar 'Halliana', perhaps the finest of all climbing honeysuckles. At Tintinhull the National Trust installed metal tree guards 1.8m (6ft) high, on each of which three plants have been trained. In spring, early growths escaping from the guard are cut back and later shoots which protrude at ground level are removed. The head of shoots at the top of the guard is lightly trimmed in early spring.

L. japonica 'Aureoreticulata' is often grown against a wall but is disappointing, the leaves being scanty and shabby. It is better clipped hard from late spring as a mound about 0.6m (2ft) high without flowers, but with healthy leaves showing the gold variegation well.

L. periclymenum WOODBINE, HONEYSUCKLE (D) Europe, including Britain, Asia Minor, Asia. One of the best known and best of our native plants, a twining shrub with stems up to 6m (20ft) long. The flowers are yellowish white, turning orange-brown after pollination, extremely fragrant especially in the early morning or evening, continue from midsummer for two months. Prune lightly after flowering. The cultivar 'Belgica' is more bushy; 'Serotina' is said to have a longer flowering period.

L. sempervirens (E) E and S USA A splendid evergreen with flowers of rich orange-scarlet in whorls throughout summer. Needs sun.

L. × tellmanniana (*tragophylla × sempervirens*, cv 'Superba') (D) has unscented flowers, 5cm (2in) long, yellow tipped with red in profuse clusters from early summer. The lower half should be shaded if possible by a shrub of modest size such as *Daphne burkwoodii*.

L. tragophylla China. Bears bright yellow flowers and prefers shade.

PARTHENOCISSUS (Vitaceae) (D)

A small genus of climbers, all those of garden interest being deciduous. They climb by leaf tendrils, which either twine or carry adhesive pads on their extremities.

P. henryana C China, has digitate leaves variegated with silvery-white along the midrib and main veins. It is best on a low wall where the leaves can be admired. The long shoots may need to be shortened two or three times a season.

P. quinquefolia VIRGINIA CREEPER. E and C North America, before 1629. Once very common, but in the late nineteenth century was largely replaced by the Japanese *P. tricuspidata*. Now *P. quinquefolia* is widely available, but it is rivalled mainly by the cultivar 'Veitchii'. *P. quinquefolia* has compound leaves, that is leaves which are formed of similar leaflets, whereas *P. tricuspidata* has very variable leaves of three kinds. It is also even more vigorous and colours in autumn just as strongly. Both may be grown on pergolas, the annual growths being cut back to just above the lowest bud. December is the right time in Britain as there is then no risk of bleeding. Early in the New Year the sap begins to rise.

PASSIFLORA CAERULEA
(Passifloraceae) (S/E)

PASSION FLOWER. S Brazil. A vigorous climber more or less evergreen in southern Britain if grown against a wall. The leaves are palmate. Flowers 7.5-10cm (3-4in) across, white, blue and purple, beginning in early summer and continuing until autumn. The plant attaches itself by twining tendrils to wires or wooden supports, the main stems trained to uprights, the laterals hanging down with the flowers on the current year's growth. They are pruned to a single bud at the base in spring. 'Constance Elliott' is a fine cultivar.

PILEOSTEGIA VIBURNOIDES (E)

India, China, Taiwan, 1908. A plant with very few problems, accepting any fertile soil, and climbing by aerial roots. It is hardy. Leaves leathery, flowers crowded in a terminal panicle, creamy white, in late summer and autumn. In spring any protruding branches can be shortened. In summer any extension growths which go beyond the allotted space can be cut back.

ROSA - See Roses

RUBUS (Rosaceae) (E)

The climbers are grown for their handsome foliage and some for an elegant form.

R. flagelliflorus China, 1901, has long scandent stems to 1.8m (6ft) in a season, white felted when young. Leaves ovate, shallowly lobed and finely toothed, the lower surface covered by a yellow-white felt. The black fruits in autumn are edible. An elegant plant when trained up a post or tripod. The shoots should be cut to the ground after the fruits are gathered.

R. henryi China, 1900, is similar and needs the same management.

SCHISANDRA RUBRIFLORA (D)

China, 1908. Climbs 3-6m (10-20ft). Flowers in the leaf axils of new shoots, deep crimson, on pendulous stalks, late spring. Berries scarlet. The best species. It is hardy and may be trained fanwise on a wall to 1.5-1.8m (5-6ft) and then allowed to hang down, but is reduced by cutting out the weakest shoots. The oldest wood is cut away in winter.

SCHIZOPHRAGMA (Hydrangeaceae) (D)

Two climbers closely allied to *Hydrangea*, needing a good loamy soil which does not dry out, and a wall or tree trunk to which they can fasten themselves by their aerial roots.

S. hydrangeoides Japan, about 1900, has broadly ovate leaves 10-15cm (4-6in) long which are coarsely toothed. Flowers small, yellowish-white in a broad cymose inflorescence with pale yellow bracts in midsummer.

S. integrifolia China, 1901, is larger in every way, with flower heads up to 0.3m (1ft) across, freely borne in midsummer. It may be grown against a wall, not necessarily south-facing, and may need the help of a wire system as the main growths enlarge. From the framework produced by early pruning, long and self-clinging extension growths are formed and may reach several feet in a sea-son, with short laterals at their base. In addition, branched laterals grow from the main framework and are the flowering growths on which the buds can be seen in winter at the end of the spurs. During the dormant season many extension growths may be removed, only those useful for filling space being retained.

SENECIO SCANDENS (Compositae) (S/E)

China, Japan, Taiwan, Philippines, India, 1895. A half-evergreen, semi-woody climber, the only climbing *Senecio* grown in Britain. it makes scandent stems up to 1.8m (6ft) long and bears small, bright yellow groundsel-like flowers in panicles during autumn. It is best planted to scramble over something which is not precious, as it is not a first-class plant though pretty in the way that groundsel is. Fairly hard pruning in spring will get rid of dead stems, but an eye should be kept on the soft new growths which may need some tying to enable them to climb.

SOLANUM (Solanaceae) (D)

Two climbers of this large genus are good garden plants.

S. crispum Chile, c1830. A vigorous shrub with scrambling stems to 1.8m (6ft) long. The flowers are 2.5-4cm (1½) inches across, rich purple-blue borne in loose clusters through midsummer, sometimes into autumn. It likes chalk but also needs a south- or west-facing wall. 'Glasnevin' is an improved cultivar.

S. jasminoides needs one even more, as it is less hardy but faster growing. Flowers pale slate-blue in clusters. Pruning of these plants in spring is directed to cutting out weak wood and any damaged by frost.

STAUNTONIA HEXAPHYLLA
(Lardizabalaceae) (E)

S Korea, Japan, 1874. A strong-growing plant, capable of reaching 9m (30ft) by twining. It is best grown against a south-facing wall with a wire system, so that the stems may hang down from the top strand and display the fragrant violet-tinged white flowers, male and female on separate racemes. Once this position is achieved, weaker growths are completely removed each winter. It is related to and very like *Holboellia*, which has rather better leaves but less good flowers. Fruits are occasionally seen. Cut back to 60cm (2ft) in early spring.

TRACHELOSPERMUM (Apocynaceae) (E)

Two species are in gardens in Britain. They need wall protection and a good soil, and climb by twining. The leaves are oval and a dark, glossy green.

T. asiaticum Japan, Korea, climbs by twining, to 6m (20ft) if allowed. The fragrant flowers are 2.5cm (1in) across, creamy white.

T. jasminoides China, Japan, 1844, is less hardy, has pure white, very fragrant flowers produced on small laterals from the old wood. Pruning for both these plants consists of removing some weak growths and cutting back extension growths above the wall or coming forward from it, to a point just above a flowering stem.

VITIS (Vitaceae) (D)

A large genus of climbers, most of them vigorous, using twining tendrils. Can be used to cover walls, pergolas, fences and hedges. The flowers are insignificant but in a good season will be followed by bunches of small grapes, not for dessert. The majority of species come from North America, or rather stay there, as they have proved very successful as rootstocks for grapes to make wine. After 1853 the Concord Grape was studied intensively, except in California where *Vitis vinifera*, the European grape, was dominant. It would hardly be seemly for a British author to give a critique of American viticulture.

In gardens, the vines of China and Japan are valued for their handsome leaves and fine autumn colour. The common grape vine of Europe, which probably originated in Asia Minor, has produced some fine ornamental cultivars, but it is a species which is rightly the most famed.

V. coignetiae Japan, about 1880. A very vigorous plant climbing by twining tendrils to the tops of large trees. The ovate leaves can be 0.3m (1ft) long and 0.5m (20in) across, dark green above, covered by rust-coloured tomentum below. The berries are black with a purple bloom. In autumn the leaves turn brilliant crimson and scarlet. It is without a rival among vines.

Pruning depends on the way in which the plant is trained. If over a stump or a disused rock garden, it may be left to cover the whole area before it needs any cutting back. On a pergola some shortening of the long shoots is necessary, as they are too untidy and liable to get in the way. The cut is made to leave five or six leaves. These shortened stems are hard pruned in the dormant season before the New Year, when 'bleeding' can occur.

WISTERIA (Leguminosae) (D)

A small genus of climbers from Eastern USA and NE Asia. Leaves are alternate, unequally pinnate, deciduous; flowers in axillary or terminal racemes. They are hardy in the southern half of Britain and are not particular about soil, but must have a sunny position.

W. floribunda Japan, 1830, climbs by twining clockwise to 9m (30ft). Leaves up to 38cm (15in) long with eleven to nineteen leaflets. Flowers fragrant, violet-blue in slender racemes 12.5-25cm (5-10in) long. The cultivar 'Alba', has white flowers, tinged lilac on the keel. 'Multijuga' has pale flowers violet with a yellow mark at the base, in racemes about 0.6m (2ft) long.

W. sinensis China, 1816, has pinnate leaves, 25-30cm (10-12in) long with, usually, eleven leaflets. Flowers in late spring, mauve or lilac in racemes 20-30cm (8-12in) long. The cultivar 'Alba' has white flowers.

All the Wisterias have the same pruning system, whatever the type of training adopted

– wall, pillar, pergola, as a tree or as a bush. For the first three of these the main growths are tied to supports, keeping them 0.3m (1ft) apart and making sure that they do not twine together or, if they do, cutting one away. In midsummer the laterals, which by then are long trailing growths, are reduced to three buds, except for any that may be required to fill the allotted space. In the following winter cut back the leader to 0.9m (3ft) from the highest laterals, which are cut back at this time to two buds. Each summer the shortening of laterals, and of the leader if it is necessary because of space, takes place in midsummer, later rather than earlier. It can be spread over several weeks and the winter pruning follows as before. Wall training makes it possible to train the main laterals horizontally, and this ensures maximum flowering. Feeding is desirable in spring, though mature plants manage without it in good soil.   _(see illustrations overleaf)_

OPPOSITE:

Wisteria sinesis **is a superb wall climber with few problems once established. Here is an old plant in flower, encouraged by the previous hot summer. There are two periods for pruning [1] In midsummer the long (up to 6m) (20ft), extension growths are cut back to 15cm (6in) [2] In winter these shortened growths are cut back to two buds. Look out for any branches which are twisting together and remove one of them**

BELOW:

Vitis **arch in the lower garden at Powys Castle. Each pillar supports a different vine, notably _V. coignetiæ_ with leaves which turn crimson in autumn. Each requires individual attention (see p145)**

WISTERIA

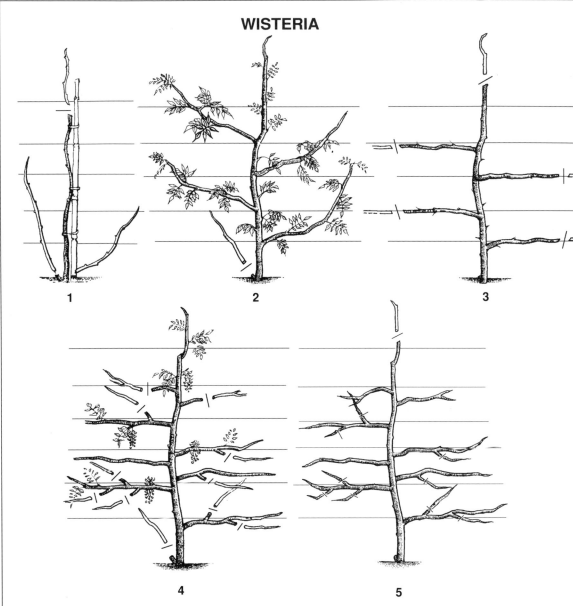

1 At planting in winter. Cut back the most
   promising shoot to 1m (3ft) from the ground

2 In summer train that shoot to be the
   vertical leader. Train four laterals to 45° and tie
   them in. Cut away any shoots from the base

3 The following winter cut back the leader to
   45cm (18in) from the highest lateral. Bring
   down the laterals to the horizontal

4 In summer tie in any new laterals horizontally.
   In late summer cut back sublaterals to about
   15cm (6in)

5 In winter cut back the leader to 1m (3ft) from the highest lateral.
   Cut back sublaterals to 2-3 buds

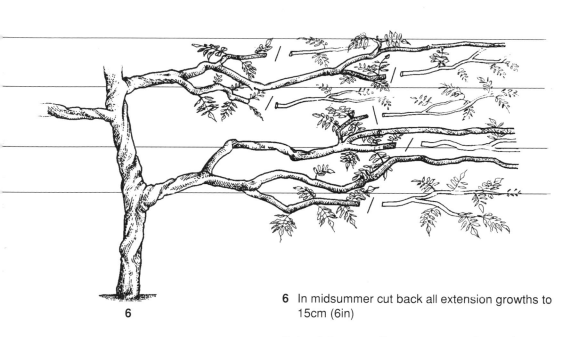

6

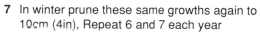

6 In midsummer cut back all extension growths to
15cm (6in)

7 In winter prune these same growths again to
10cm (4in), Repeat 6 and 7 each year

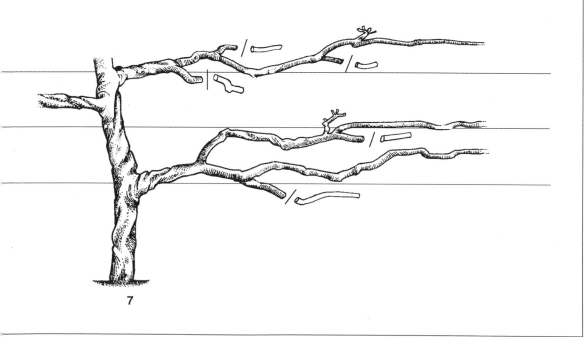

7

CONIFERS

Conifer is, naturally enough, a name for a tree which bears cones, and is used loosely as if it implied 'belonging to the conifers'. However, that was the name for a group now consisting of eight families, some of which do not produce cones, such as *Ginkgo*, the Maidenhair Tree and *Taxus*, the yew. All conifers belong to the large family of gymnosperms whose ovules are not enclosed, in fact 'naked' as the name indicates. Such are the oddities on which botanists thrive. There are only three species of conifer native of Britain, *Juniperus communis, Pinus sylvestris* and *Taxus baccata*, but owing to the activities of British collectors and those from other countries, especially the USA, from the seventeenth century to the present day this country accumulated a rich variety of conifers, though their actual number is not large.

A CHOICE OF CONIFERS

The great majority of the conifers which can be grown in the open in Britain are considered to be suitable only for gardens of at least 0.4ha (1acre). Even so there is a place in a smaller garden for one or two sizeable trees, if the owner is unable or unwilling to develop the garden in the conventional way. If you are that owner you may choose a grand tree which will grow slowly to 15m (50ft) or more in fifty years, and it is unlikely that you will have to decide its future when that time is reached (the average duration of occupancy of a family house is something under seven years). *Picea brewerana* might seem a good choice. At Exbury near Southampton it put on 9m (30ft) between 1931 and 1968. Its most striking feature is the arrangement of the smallest branches, which hang down perpendicularly with leaves projecting all around the shoot. However, it is twenty-five years or so before this feature appears, so a Leyland cypress × *cupressocyparis leylandii* – which will make a handsome tree 18m (60ft) high in twenty-five years – might be preferred. It is now commonplace, and for something more exciting try *Athrotaxis laxifolia (Taxodiaceae)* from the mountains of Tasmania (1857), the best of the genus, quite hardy and growing well in the mild areas of western Britain. It is both interesting and beautiful with scale-like, convex leaves, curving out and then in to a point. No pruning is needed.

Now to the dwarfs, not exceeding 1.8m (6ft) except occasionally, and suitable for a garden of modest size. You must interpret 'modest' for yourself. The majority of such conifers are cultivars of well-known large species, valued for their slow growth and low stature when mature. They are regarded as alpines and are often planted as features, sometimes as exclamation marks in the rockery (a Victorian term now unfairly derided along with the 'shrubbery'). It is no doubt effective planting but needs something to set it off, which as a rule turns out to be heather – and that often fails to produce either the intended natural effect or a semi-formal appearance.

PRUNING CONIFERS

When conifers are raised from seed or cuttings they tend to develop a single leader naturally, but any rivals should be removed and this process should be continued after planting out, spring being the best time for it. Laterals are retained, except for those low on the trunk; they will, in any case, die naturally but there is no harm done if they are cut off. As the tree grows larger, extra leaders may develop and grow close to the main leader without being noticed: this is most common in the *Chamaecyparis* species and cultivars. In time they will be troublesome as they begin to grow outwards and are best removed, perhaps not an easy task. In the case of slender fastigiate trees such as *Cupressus sempervirens* the problem does not arise, a leader being naturally retained, but the Irish Yew, *Taxus baccata* 'Fastigiata' (see p157) has upright growths which often need to be tied together.

The best time for pruning conifers, if that becomes necessary because of irregular or excessive spread, is autumn or early winter. For dieback, see Glossary.

DWARF CONIFERS

For all the dwarf conifers pruning is only needed to control spread or improve the outline. It can be carried out at any time, apart from a prolonged frosty spell.

ABIES NORDMANNIANA

Caucasus, 1840. A large and grand tree, but it has a cultivar 'Golden Spreader' which is almost prostrate and has the dense foliage of its parent but coloured gold, reliably keeping a low profile. Not widely available.

CEDRUS LIBANI

A massive tree, reaching 300 years of age or more. However, it has a dwarf cultivar 'Comte de Dijon' which in many years can reach 2.7m (9ft) high and 1.8m (6ft) across, but keeps a dwarf character with the dark green leaves of the species. Rare in commerce.

CRYPTOMERIA JAPONICA

'Elegans' Forms a bushy tree with soft juvenile foliage which persists throughout its life and becomes red-bronze during autumn and winter, in spring returning to grey-blue. 'Nana' is truly dwarf with the same foliage as the parent, very handsome at all times.

JUNIPERUS

J. chinensis Has spawned innumerable cultivars but none in the ordinary literature seems to be a genuine dwarf.

J. communis COMMON JUNIPER, on the other hand, is a British native that can claim one cultivar which is truly dwarf, even prostrate: 'Hornibrookii', collected in County Galway, Eire, where it follows the contours of the rocks as a net a metre across and 10-12cm (4-5in) high.

J. horizontalis A native of N America, including the coasts of New England, it has produced the cultivar 'Bar Harbor', found wild on the north-east side of Mount Desert Island, Maine, growing in crevices on the rocky coast. The leaves are glaucous, almost steel-blue. Widely available.

J. × media The cultivar 'Pfitzerana' is the most favoured of all junipers, and understandably so. It is a shrub reaching rather more than 1.8m (6ft) high and spreading widely with a flat top. The height can be restricted by pruning of the main stem but the cultivar 'Pfitzerana Compacta', with mainly juvenile awl-shaped leaves (an awl is a tool tapered to a sharp point, a bodkin), would be a better choice.

J. sabina COMMON SAVIN. C and S Europe, Russia, early sixteenth century. Too large for our purpose but the variety *tamariscifolia* is a low shrub of less than 1.8m (6ft), with leaves mostly juvenile, awl-shaped. It is used for clothing dry banks and can extend for several metres. It is sometimes suggested as an edging for lawns but this would certainly involve trimming it back and so produce an unnatural effect.

TAXUS BACCATA

The cultivar 'Adpressa' is a fine shrub of spreading habit with small, dark green leaves 12mm (½in) long. Bought from a caravan at Membury Service Station on the M4 motorway it has reached 1.5m (5ft) in ten years and is in perfect health. In the absence of a suitable caravan the *Plant Finder* (1990) produces only two nurseries to offer it.

THUJA PLICATA

Cultivar 'Hillieri' is a slow-growing dense bush with leaves in irregular whorls, certainly interesting. The original plant occurred in Hillier's nursery before 1900 and had reached 2.3m (7ft 6in) when sold in about 1925 (what was the price?).

LARGE CONIFERS

For a larger garden the choice of a big conifer needs plenty of thought and a visit – or several – to some arboretum in which labels are used even for the most commonplace specimens.

ABIES (Pinaceae)

Europe, N Africa, temperate Asia, America from Canada to Guatemala.

A. grandis Western N America, 1832. GIANT FIR would have to exceed 45m (150ft) to excite comment. Moderately lime-tolerant, it does best with heavy rainfall but good drainage. Growth is very rapid and if checked it is usually by damage at the top, which is quickly made good by new leaders.

A. nordmanniana CAUCASIAN FIR. Caucasus, Asia Minor, 1842. A very handsome and robust tree, often exceeding 30m (100ft). It needs high rainfall but is lime-tolerant.

A. pinsapo SPANISH FIR. SE Spain, 1839. Leaves dark green and rigid, radiating all round the branchlets. A very good-looking tree, it succeeds in dry areas and tolerates lime. Trees over 24m (80ft) are not rare.

A. procera W USA, 1830. A great tree which does well in moist chalk-free soils. The cones are up to 25cm (10in) long, rich brown-purple in colour.

CALOCEDRUS DECURRENS

(Cupressaceae) INCENSE CEDAR

SW USA, 1853. Most cultivated specimens belong to the form 'Columnaris', which really is columnar. With adequate light it retains its foliage down to ground level. It should therefore be placed in isolation and grows quite rapidly without any training after the initial leader has been formed. It was unable to tolerate the pollution of large towns.

CEDRUS (Pinaceae)

A genus of four species of evergreen trees of the grandest style.

C. atlantica Atlas Mountains in Algeria and Morocco, c1840. The branches are ascending at first but the uppermost are level in the mature state. There is, regrettably, the cultivar 'Glauca' which is the most planted of any conifer, and when it becomes 'Glauca Pendula' regret is increased. However, *C. atlantica pendula* (non-'Glauca') is something different. The photograph on p155 shows the remarkable tree in the National Botanic Garden, Glasnevin, planted around 1875. It needs no description.

C. deodara Himalayas, 1831. The foliage is usually grey or glaucous green, ending dark green in the mature tree. It is particularly charming when only a metre or two high, with drooping shoots, but is always graceful. Growth is quite rapid, 0.3m (1ft) a year in good conditions until around seventy years. Then growth slows down progressively.

C. libani CEDAR OF LEBANON. Lebanon, where it is now rare, c1670. It is now common in Europe, including Britain where its lateral spread predominates and specimens over 30m (100ft) high are very uncommon. Perhaps it does not get enough sunlight. It is apt to lose large branches in a gale and regeneration is very unlikely. Its large roots are superficial and undoubtedly suffer from the patter of large feet. If grown on a frequented lawn there is a case for roping off specimens at 10-12m (30-40ft).

CEPHALOTAXUS (Cephalotaxaceae)
A small genus of shrubs growing well in shade. They differ from yews in their longer leaves, which have two broad white bands beneath, and in their large olive-like fruits.
C. harringtonia Probably China, 1829. A spreading shrub or small tree, leaves dark green above, densely disposed along the branchlets in two ranks. The cultivar 'Fastigiata' is in habit like the Irish Yew (*Taxus baccata* 'Fastigiata'). The branches become heavy and may pull the bush out of shape. Tying in may be tried but hard pruning may have to be used and regeneration will be slow.

CHAMAECYPARIS (Cupressaceae)
A small genus of evergreen trees with a large number of cultivars.
C. lawsoniana Oregon and California, 1854. Usually a broad pyramid with fern-like sprays of foliage reaching to the ground if there is sufficient space and light (see Hedges & Topiary). The forms and cultivars are too numerous to make a selection here.
C. nootkatensis Western N America, c1853. One of the best of this genus, very hardy, healthy and not demanding of soil. Like *C. lawsonia*, it too spoils the gardener for choice through the number of its forms and cultivars.

CRYPTOMERIA JAPONICA
'Elegans' Japan, 1861, is a more satisfactory and more beautiful tree than the type. The juvenile foliage is retained permanently and the leaves are larger, slenderer and softer. Their glaucous summer colour changes in winter to a foxy red. This tree is apt to be ruined by heavy rain or snow and may be bent down to the ground. If staking is not possible the main trunk can be cut to within a few feet of the ground and may regenerate, but not to perfection (see also Hedges & Topiary).

× CUPRESSOCYPARIS (Cupressaceae)
Bigeneric hybrids – *Cupressus* × *chamaecyparis* – all of which have arisen in cultivation. They are extremely and sometimes unfortunately vigorous.
× *C. leylandii* Leighton Hall, Montgomeryshire, 1888; subsequently there again and at Haggerston Hall, Northumberland, 1892. The LEYLAND CYPRESS will produce a good specimen 15-18m (50-60ft) high in twenty-five years. It is perfectly hardy and not affected by sea winds. Where space is adequate it makes a fine conventional conifer specimen, furnished to the base with good dark green foliage on upswept stems. Its use for hedging (see p162) shows its reaction to drastic pruning, to which it responds admirably. Its capacity to grow anywhere vigorously has got it a bad name among those who were unaware of that ability, but it does not deserve this poor reputation.
Cupressus macrocarpa California, c1838. MONTEREY CYPRESS, on the other hand, has earned bad marks for its tendency to become bare in its lower part, especially when used as a hedge. As a tree it does admirably in the warmer areas, being somewhat tender when young.
C. sempervirens Near East, Greece, Italy, sixteenth century at the latest. ITALIAN CYPRESS is seen as a cultivated tree in the Mediterranean region. It has a fastigiate habit and gives a special character to the Italian landscape, especially in Tuscany. In Britain there

are fine trees in the south and south-west but their survival is unpredictable in most areas, and hardly justifies the risk of planting one.

FITZROYA CUPRESSOIDES
(Cupressaceae)
Chile, Argentina, 1849. Named after Commander Fitzroy Captain of the *Beagle*. An evergreen tree which grows slowly in northern temperate regions and there is more often a shrub. Few are as much as 15m (50ft) after 80 to 100 years. It is a very handsome bushy tree with leaves in whorls of three. Young trees, 0.3m (1ft) high begin to form competing leaders, one of which should be selected and tied to a stake until well established, competitors being reduced to one. It is quite hardy in the south and south-west of Britain and is easily propagated by cuttings taken in late summer. Quite widely available.

GINKGO BILOBA
See end of this section.

JUNIPERUS *(Cupressaceae)*
A large genus of trees and shrubs from prostrate alpines to tall columnar trees. The dwarf forms are considered on p151.
J. recurva E Himalayas, c1822. Seems to be unsatisfactory in temperate zones. Suitable for burning for incense, as in Buddhist temples in its native region.
J. recurva coxii Upper Myanmar, 1920. An elegant small tree, with drooping branchlets, sage-green.
J. virginiana E and central N America, c1664. Hardy and makes a medium to large conical tree. It does well on chalk and needs sufficient space to develop. Into maturity it is well furnished with foliage almost to ground level. Pruning is not indicated.

LARIX *(Pinaceae)*
L. decidua EUROPEAN LARCH. European Alps and Carpathians, c1620. This must serve as the most satisfactory if not the most beautiful

larch. It starts with a conical shape, later with branches drooping. Leaves light green, especially on emerging in spring. It is best as a single specimen with ample space to develop its shoots, otherwise the lower branches die off and cannot be replaced. Shortening branches does not help.

METASEQUOIA GLYPTOSTROBOIDES
(Taxodiaceae)
DAWN REDWOOD. Central China, 1948. A vigorous deciduous tree with shaggy grey bark, peeling eventually. Leaves opposite in two ranks, blue-green above, light green below, on opposite branches. The tree is hardy apart from susceptibility to damage by late spring frosts, thriving in moist but well-drained soil. It readily forms new leaders – too readily – but those that are superfluous make excellent cutting material. It has not been a success for hedging because hard pruning leads to abundant top growth.

PICEA
P. abies NORWAY SPRUCE. N Europe, c1500. The Christmas Tree has produced many forms, none of outstanding merit for gardens except the following.
P. breweriana See p150.
P. omorika SERBIAN SPRUCE. Jugoslavia, 1889. A tall graceful tree with drooping branches which curve upwards at the tips. It does well in any decent soil and tolerates chalk. It readily forms a leader and needs no pruning. Why is it not used more often in developments and streets?
P. smithiana W Himalayas, 1818. Another splendid large tree with drooping branches, long leaves and long cylindrical cones.

PINUS *(Pinaceae)*
A large genus in temperate regions of the northern hemisphere and in subtropical regions of both hemispheres. Some tolerate very poor soils but those with fine needles dislike shallow chalk soil.

P. armandii W China, Formosa, 1895. A tree of medium size, leaves in fives, cones in clusters of two or three, becoming pendulous. Does well where there is no chalk.

P. jeffreyi SW USA, 1852. A large conical tree. Leaves in threes, long, bluish green, cones 20cm (8in) long. Very handsome, but is short-lived.

P. nigra AUSTRIAN PINE. Europe, Austria to Italy, Greece, Yugoslavia, 1835. A large tree with dark brown bark and a dense head. Leaves in pairs, dark green. Good in chalky soil and in bleak exposure. Var. *maritima*, or CORSICAN PINE (Corsica, Sicily, S Italy,1759) is very common in Britain, especially on heaths and sandy soils in southern England where it is replacing Scots Pine. Bark in old trees heavily ridged, dark grey. Narrowly columnar with a conical top, ultimately flat. Leaves in pairs, light green, dark on old trees.

P. pinaster MARITIME PINE. W Mediterranean, sixteenth century. A sparsely branched tree of medium size. Leaves in pairs. Cones solitary or in clusters, often persisting intact on the branches for several years.

P. pinea UMBRELLA PINE. Mediterranean, sixteenth century. A tree of short or medium height with a characteristic umbrella-shaped head of spreading branches. Leaves in pairs, cones up to 30cm (12in) long.

P. sylvestris Europe to the Caucasus. A common tree of great beauty at its best, ie when seen as a large tall-stemmed specimen.

Cedrus atlantica 'Pendula'. Examples of this remarkable form of the majestic Atlas cedar occur in the wild, but it is not known how it appeared in cultivation. This fine specimen in the National Botanic Garden in Dublin, Eire, was planted around 1875. The grey-glaucous foliage remains fresh. The steeply pendulous growth inhibits branches on the inner plant and makes pruning unnecessary

Young bark reddish. Leaves in pairs. Does best in good average soil, neither damp nor dry, nor more than a little chalky.

P. wallichiana HIMALAYAN PINE. Himalayas, 1823. A rapidly growing tree, leaves in fives, 12-17cm (5-7in) long, often pendulous. Cones 15-25cm (6-10 in) long. An unusual-looking pine, said to be short-lived and declining at 100 years. Do not let that deter you, but note that it will not tolerate chalk.

PODOCARPUS (Podocarpaceae)

The majority are distinctly tender, but some suitable for the milder areas.

P. nivalis New Zealand, early twentieth century. ALPINE TOTARA is a low shrub, rarely upright to 3m (10ft), of dense habit. Foliage dull green. Quite pleasant ground cover, tolerating shade and not needing pruning.

P. nubigenus Chile. Has foliage of rich green, rather similar to *nivalis* but more handsome and hardy. It seems to need a moist soil to grow beyond a low shrub.

PSEUDOLARIX AMABILIS (Pinaceae)

China, 1852. It is slow-growing and dislikes lime but is perfectly hardy. At first sight it looks just like a larch, but it has clustered male catkins and large woody scales on the cone. Good training is essential, with care to establish a leader. The horizontal branches should not be shortened as they weep nearly to ground level, often laden with cones. After transplanting to its final position the tree must be fed and watered regularly. Most of the notable trees in Britain are in the south and south-west. It has been much admired but is rare, in both cultivation and commerce.

PSEUDOTSUGA MENZIESII (Pinaceae)

Western N America, 1827. OREGON DOUGLAS FIR is a great tree of the largest size, but is useless on poor, dry soils and hates chalk. It cannot be regarded as a garden tree but there are many fine examples in England and especially in Scotland (Perthshire).

SCIADOPITYS VERTICILLATA
(Taxodiaceae) UMBRELLA PINE

Japan, 1861. A slow-growing tree of medium size. Bark exfoliates to reveal the reddish brown inner bark. The best form has a single leader and makes a very shapely small conical tree, with horizontal branches bearing clusters of rich, glossy green foliage. The fused pairs of leaves are arranged in whorls like the spokes of an umbrella. If your appetite is whetted and you garden on chalky soil, be assured that this is a plant you cannot raise.

SEQUOIA SEMPERVIRENS

California, Oregon, 1843. A massive evergreen for country estates or large parks.

SEQUOIADENDRON GIGANTEUM

California, 1853. WELLINGTONIA is another gigantic evergreen for parks or estates. It can live to 3,000 years of age in California but in England seems to be failing at a little over 100 years.

TAXODIUM DISTICHUM (Taxodiaceae)

SWAMP or BALD CYPRESS. Southern USA, 1640. A large tree with reddish brown bark, buttressed at the base. Leaves flattened, arranged alternately in two opposite ranks, spirally on the persistent branchlets. Though they grow quite well in average soils, they belong to bogs and marshes and there develop 'knees' projecting from the roots above the ground. It has been shown that the knees serve no necessary function. Pruning is not indicated.

TAXUS (Taxaceae)

The type of a small genus which is thought to constitute a distinct order *Taxales*.

T. baccata COMMON YEW. N Africa, W Asia, Europe. An evergreen tree, very large but seldom over 15m (50ft) high. Bark brown-red. A rounded or spreading head of branches bearing glossy, dark green leaves. Fruits with an aril. Familiar to most people in England, seldom identified by visiting Americans.

There are many cultivars. Cv 'Adpressa' has been described on p152. *T. b. f. aurea* was first identified in the seventeenth century. William Barron (1800-1890) gardener to the Earl of Harrington at Elvaston Castle, Derbyshire, collected such plants for his employer with great energy and by 1849 there were a thousand Golden Yews there. The best was named *Taxus b.f. barroni*. Strangely *Taxus b.f. aurea* is now listed by only four nurseries in the *Plant Finder* (1990), whereas ten nurseries offer *Dovastoniana Aurea*. The latter is certainly a handsome tree, as is the plain *Dovastoniana*, Westfelton Yew.

T. baccata fastigiata IRISH YEW. A columnar tree of great merit found on a rock above Florence Court in County Fermanagh, N Ireland. All true Irish Yews are descended from this specimen by vegetative propagation. The leaves start out all round the branchlets and are dark, dull green. The cultivar *Fastigiata Aureo-marginata* is even more popular but lacks the gravitas of the plain tree, which is a rather rustic version of *Cupressus sempervirens*. No pruning. For the use of yew for hedging see p165.

THUJA (Cupressaceae)

A genus of a few evergreen trees which favour a good moist soil.

T. plicata Coastal western N America, 1853. WESTERN RED CEDAR is the best for ornament and timber but not remarkable (see Hedges & Topiary).

THUJOPSIS DOLOBRATA
(Cupressaceae)

Japan, 1853. A small evergreen tree or shrub of dense conical habit. Large sprays of silver-backed leaves make it an attractive plant.

Reasonably widely available.

TORREYA CALIFORNICA (Taxaceae)

CALIFORNIAN NUTMEG. California, 1851. A small evergreen tree, its conical form well furnished to ground level with shining dark green leaves. A lead should be trained in the nursery stage, when the tree should have protection from frost. If this leader is killed numerous laterals take over and the shape is lost.

TSUGA (Pinaceae)

A small group of evergreen trees which, in areas of high rainfall, make very handsome specimens.

T. canadensis Eastern N America; Nova Scotia to the Great Lakes and south to Alabama and Georgia, 1736. EASTERN or CANADA HEMLOCK does well in western England and in eastern Scotland, Perthshire. It tends to branch low down and form a rounded head. It is lime-tolerant. Cultivars are legion, including 'Jeddeloh' with light green foliage and a semi-prostrate habit spreading 0.75m (2ft 6in).

GINKGO BILOBA

This tree cuts a lone figure in this company being deciduous and having no cones. It is of ancient family, in Britain about 160 million years ago. Introduced from Japan via Europe c1758, the fan-shaped entire leaves make it easy to recognise and are very fine in their yellow autumn colours. It is perfectly hardy and tolerant of most soils, but grows slowly – very slowly if the earth is not rich and loamy. The famous tree at Kew was planted in 1762, and was 17m (56ft) tall in 1888 and 22m (72ft) in 1970.

HEDGES & TOPIARY

HEDGES

The original function of the hedge was to keep out intruders, men or animals, and this usage seems to persist in Hamlet's 'there's such divinity doth hedge a king that treason can but peep to what it would'. In Britain hedges were familiar in Anglo-Saxon times and increased through the Middle Ages. It has been shown that the count of species of shrub in a 9m (30yd) length of hedge gives the approximate age of that hedge to the nearest century. Many are at least 1,000 years old and comparatively few date from the parliamentary enclosures of the eighteenth century.

The practical value of hedges was modified by the invention of barbed wire in the nineteenth century, and further reduced by the emphasis on arable farming in the Second World War and after it. Thousands of kilometres of hedge were grubbed up to create large and easily managed fields, and consequently the laborious practice of 'laying' hedges to keep them stockproof almost disappeared.

At a Worcestershire farm, however, it continued until 1970 and the owner had then practised it for fifty years. The thorn hedges (*Crataegus monogyna*) were originally grown from seed. They were 'brushed', that is clipped lightly, in autumn until 1.2m (4ft)

high and after that withy stakes (*Salix viminalis*, the Common Osier) were driven in at intervals of 1.8-2.4m (6-8ft), having first been debarked because willow will root at any time of year and soon outgrows the hedge. Selected long growths of hawthorn were split with billhooks and trained horizontally against the stakes. This was repeated every four years and in other years the hedge was brushed each autumn. Strong seedlings were not discouraged except for those of Elder (*Sambucus nigra*), which is apt to kill plants close to it.

Other uses for the hedge ensure that it survives and is an almost essential element in all but the smallest gardens. It may define the boundary of the property and keep out stock, cats, dogs, foxes, raccoons in the USA and, of course, man, who often wants to know what goes on within. The English de-

Fagus sylvatica **makes a good opening for a path. Beech grows fairly fast, but annual clipping should suffice once the spheres have been formed. On each side of the opening one upright stem is allowed to grow above the line of the hedge, and is cleared of branches for about 30cm (1ft) of its length once it has reached the required height. The branches above this are then cut back in late summer to produce the spheres**

sire for privacy calls for a hedge 1.8m (6ft) high. The suburban front garden without a boundary to divide it from neighbours can be a real success if all co-operate and are gardeners. A good example was set on the Bournville estate in Birmingham, which was originally laid out for the employees of Cadburys, the maker of chocolate. It was a success but since some houses were leased to outsiders has been rather less so. In the USA such an open plan is common, privacy not such an obsession, and readiness to accept neighbours more natural; though that may be changing.

A wall may seem the least troublesome if most expensive alternative to a hedge and offers opportunities for growing climbers, but has at least one drawback. In windy conditions air is forced upwards and, as it drops on the other side of the wall, may form a damaging vortex, a violent eddy round an axis, which is bad for any plant in its path. A

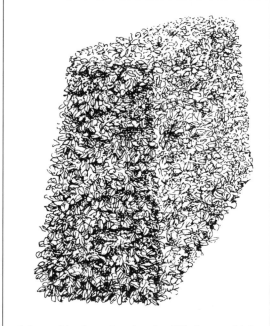

A formal hedge, showing the 'A' shape which allows maximum light to reach the base of the hedge

hedge, on the other hand, filters and slows down the airstream. Unfortunately, in order to achieve worthwhile noise abatement, a hedge must be too thick to be practical for most gardens. It seems that making the source of noise invisible does reduce the impact of the sound, on humans at least. Jonathan Swift remarked that 'Walls have tongues and hedges ears.'

One other point arises. It was discovered, or at least became well known fifty years ago, that cold air moving down a slope would be held to some extent by an obstruction, even a hedge. Making sizeable gaps in the hedge could allow the air to pass through, so reducing the danger of frost on the slope above the barrier, and thus was of great value to the cherry and other fruit orchards in valleys. Sadly the cherry orchards have mostly disappeared.

Our first consideration in planning a hedge is to decide whether it is appropriate to the site in question: whether it should be formal or informal, tall or short, and whether it should divide the garden into 'rooms', each with its own character and acting as extensions of the house. Whatever the decision such hedges will need regular and reasonably skilled pruning, with very few exceptions.

Many shrubs and some trees can be used for hedging but the list that follows contains some which are of proven merit as far as growth and response to pruning are concerned.

ACER CAMPESTRE FIELD MAPLE (D)

An excellent plant for an informal hedge if cattle are kept away. Prune with secateurs and a double-action lopper, reducing strong shoots by one third and removing any that are weak. Once a year is enough, in the dormant season, not before leaf fall as the yellow autumn colour is good. Rabbits chew the bark and can kill a large stem, close to the ground. Maple is much used on the Continent of Europe. Why not more in Britain?

AUCUBA JAPONICA (E)

The green-leaved form is much preferred by right-minded people. It makes a good evergreen hedge in poor soil and shade. If you can put a male near females you should have a fair crop of egg-shaped fruits. In that case pruning should be delayed until early winter and then comprises removal of shoots arising from ground level or slightly higher. Clipping means that some leaves are partly cut and the result is unsightly, so use of *A. japonica* for formal hedging is not advised.

BERBERIS DARWINII (E)

If well treated and fed, this is a splendid shrub for hedging. It has pleasant dark, glossy green leaves and golden or orange flowers leading to worthwhile blue fruits, taken by birds only in dry spells. If there is a good crop delay pruning until late summer, cutting back the shoots which have flowered and bringing them in line with the new shoots which are developing.

BERBERIS × STENOPHYLLA
(Darwinii × Empetrifolia) (E)

A dense mass of stems produces arching shoots to 3m (10ft) when mature. The flowers are of yellow-orange – not the best of colours – nor are the fruits remarkable, so pruning is undertaken as the flowers fade. However, the habit and healthy nature of this plant recommend it.

BUXUS SEMPERVIRENS COMMON BOX (E)

Perhaps a British native and will in time(not less than 200 years) make a tree 9m (30ft) high. For a hedge it is among the best choices and normally needs clipping only once a year. High summer is usually recommended for this but experience following the advice of James Hancock, head gardener at Powys Castle, Powys, Wales, has confirmed that early summer is better, and the fragrance of the new growth which results is pleasant. Ted Bullock at Felbrigg Hall (both these are National Trust gardens) finds that it is easier to cut box when it is wet. He has managed to renovate old box hedges by cutting back to 10cm (4in) in early spring and feeding with fertiliser when there are signs of renewed growth. The cultivar 'Suffruticosa', with a dwarf habit and small leaves, is traditionally used for edging flower beds. It often formed the pattern in the knot gardens created in the sixteenth and seventeenth centuries, and occasionally today. It needs frequent clipping to maintain the dwarf state. If left unpruned it will grow to a handsome light green bush of 1.2-1.5m (4-5ft).

CARPINUS BETULUS HORNBEAM (D)

The best deciduous, formal hedge plant in temperate climates. Tolerant of most soils, it is planted at intervals of 45cm (18in). It makes good growth almost from ground level so that early training is easy, with clipping back in late summer after the first two years . The leaves, which turn yellow in autumn, are retained through the winter.

CHAMAECYPARIS LAWSONIANA (E)

Was a favourite hedging plant but shows a strong tendency to become bald in the lower part after a few years. There are many cultivars, among which is 'Green Hedger', an easily managed plant, though the bright green colour will not appeal to everyone.

CRATAEGUS

C. monogyna COMMON HAWTHORN and **C. oxyacantha** MAY (D), perhaps forms of one species, make the traditional English hedge. They are easy to grow from seed and plant out, arm themselves with repellent thorns and accept much pruning. They can be cut back as severely as is necessary when dormant. The slasher mounted on a tractor has become a sad necessity, but hedges recover fairly well in the next spring. The old practice of laying such a hedge is described at the beginning of this chapter.

× *CUPRESSOCYPARIS LEYLANDII*
(Cupressus macrocarpa × Chamaecyparis nootkatensis) (E)

Took many people by surprise when its vigour exceeded all expectations: it grows to 18m (60ft) in twenty-five years. In fact it makes an excellent specimen or screen when given plenty of space. As a formal hedge it behaves well, but should be transferred from open ground – not a container – and then attached to a bamboo which is tied to a wire stretched along the hedge site. Once the central leaders reach 0.3m (1ft) beyond the height required for the hedge they are cut back to 15cm (6in) below that height in early summer and the laterals are cut back moderately at this time and for each subsequent pruning. The Leyland Cypress and its clones are very hardy and tolerant of sea winds.

ELAEAGNUS PUNGENS (E)
The cultivar 'Maculata' is a popular shrub

whose green leaves have a patch of rich yellow in the centre. Admirably hardy and not unduly vigorous – but would you get tired of it shouting at you every time you opened the garden door? If not you should look out for reversion of the foliage to plain green, which is all too common and needs urgent action, cutting off all stems which show this change.

ESCALLONIA VIRGATA (E)
Has arching branches and white flowers. It is very hardy and should make an elegant informal hedge, but dislikes chalky soil.

EUONYMUS JAPONICUS
JAPANESE SPINDLE BUSH (E)

Most often seen as cultivar 'Ovatus Aureus', a gold-variegated form, only fully hardy in the mildest temperate climates and flourishing by the seaside. Grown as a formal hedge it is unattractive, but allowed some freedom to spread it is better. Predictably the type with dark, polished leaves makes a good formal hedge. Both are trimmed in mid-spring.

FAGUS SYLVATICA COMMON BEECH (D)
The most popular deciduous formal hedge, a little behind the hornbeam, not as healthy or prolific in lateral growth but splendid when the leaves open, their colour an unmatched fresh green. It needs well-drained but fertile soil and should not be pruned in the first three years after planting. Once established, pruning is due in late summer. Mixed hedges

LEFT:
Fagus sylvatica (COMMON BEECH) with *F. sylvatica* 'Riversii' together make a wonderful tapestry hedge of green and purple. A problem may arise because the rate of growth of *F. sylvatica* is considerably more rapid than that of 'Riversii', but there are examples with a good regular outline. Prune in late summer to shape

of the type with its form 'Purpurea' or 'Riversii', whose leaves open pale red in spring, becoming purple before long, have charm but seem to be difficult to manage. Perhaps this is because of different growth rates.

FORSYTHIA × INTERMEDIA (D)
'Spectabalis' can reach 3m (10ft) high and across and needs plenty of space, but the upright growth predominates and plants can be put in 1.8-2.4m (6-8ft) apart. Prune immediately after flowering, taking away all flowered stems except those which are two to three years old, and feeding to encourage the young shoots from the base.

FUCHSIA MAGELLANICA (D)
'Riccartonii' is a plant of uncertain origin but over the last 150 years has established itself as fully hardy in the mild areas of Britain and Ireland, particularly the south-west where the flowers with scarlet sepals and violet corolla, on semi-wild hedges, make an unforgettable impression. In many inland districts it is cut to the ground each winter but by the end of spring is growing strongly. It needs plenty of moisture, not unknown in SW Ireland.

GRISELINIA LITTORALIS (E)
From New Zealand, and only hardy in maritime areas where it makes a dense growth of stems. This characteristic, along with its tolerance of salt winds, makes it a good choice for a windbreak near the sea. Removal of some stems from the outside in early summer encourages growth near the centre.

BELOW:
A very handsome yew hedge with 'roofing'. Beautifully maintained, it is trimmed every autumn and in summer is decorated in front with tobacco plants

HIPPOPHAE RHAMMNOIDES
SEA BUCKTHORN (D)

A native of the British coast, tolerant of salt-laden winds but able to flourish in average conditions inland. Grey scaly twigs and orange coloured fruits (ignored by birds) are attractive in winter and the grey-green leaves in summer are equally so. As a hedge it may be cut to size in spring.

ILEX AQUIFOLIUM COMMON HOLLY (E)

Makes an excellent hedge, formal or informal, and is tolerant of pollution and of any type of soil. Some berries will form on the surface of the hedge but may have to be sacrificed if needs be in order to keep a formal outline. Unless the hedge is very long, use secateurs to avoid damaging leaves, cutting back longer shoots individually in spring. This is time-consuming but not boring. 'J. C. van Thol' is an excellent cultivar with dark green, hardly toothed leaves and is just as satisfactory as Common Holly as a hedge.

LAURUS NOBILIS BAY LAUREL (E)

Noble it is, but only fully hardy in the fortunate areas. However, neither is it wholly tender in many places, where it is cut to the ground in a severe winter but revives in the next spring. This would ruin a few years' topiary work. In the mild areas so often mentioned here it tolerates wind. Pruning is best done in midsummer to maintain shape.

LAVANDULA ANGUSTIFOLIA
COMMON LAVENDER (E)

This plant is often recommended for hedging but in most of Britain the uncertain climate makes it difficult to keep tidy. It should not be pruned after flowering but in spring, when new growth has appeared.

LIGUSTRUM OVALIFOLIUM (E)

Tolerates dim light, poor soil and neglect. This and its price explain its popularity as a hedge in town gardens. The flowers have an unpleasant odour. The gold-variegated form has a bright yellow margin reviled by good-taste gardeners. Hedges of either form need pruning two or three times a year, once in early spring and perhaps twice in summer .

OLEARIA TRAVERSII (E)

Performs very well in maritime areas, even on poor soil in exposed positions. It can reach 5.5m (18ft). The shoots and undersurface of the leaves are covered in a dense white felt. The leaves are oval, leathery and dark green. It needs cutting back by a half after two years in spring, after that as necessary at that time. Not worth trying inland.

POTENTILLA (D)

There are good hybrids and garden varieties, mostly related to **P. fruticosa.** The majority reach a height of 0.9-1.2m (3-4ft) but there are considerable variations in size and vigour. A hedge is therefore best when composed of one subject only and the following are well established in the trade:

'Abbotswood'	flowers white. A dwarf cultivar of *P. davurica*, 0.3m (1ft) high.
'Elizabeth'	flowers soft yellow. A large hybrid, *P. arbuscula* × *P. davurica*.
'Jackman's Variety'	flowers bright yellow. A *P. fruiticosa* var. *grandiflora* seedling.
'Katherine Dykes'	flowers canary-yellow. A *P. fruiticosa* cultivar.
'Primrose Beauty'	flowers pale primrose. A *P. fruiticosa* cultivar.
'Tilford Cream'	flowers cream.

Pruning is certainly valuable. In spring weak shoots are removed and strong healthy stems shortened by half.

PRUNUS
P. Laurocerasus CHERRY LAUREL (E)

Best grown as a specimen 'unmolested by

the pruner' (Bean, 1976 p378). However, the cultivar 'Otto Luyken' grows only to 1.2m (4ft) and makes a compact shrub and a hedge when planted at 0.9m (3ft) intervals and kept in shape by the removal of wayward shoots. *P. Lusitanica* PORTUGAL LAUREL (E) is very hardy. The dark oval leaves are handsome, the racemes of flower in summer not so. It makes a good hedge but is subject to silverleaf disease.

QUERCUS ILEX (E)

Makes an excellent hedge in the milder areas in any soil which is not heavy. It should be grown from acorns, which are abundant after a hot summer. They are planted in open ground and on germinating are put singly in pots and grown on for a season or two (not more). Then they are planted out where they are to grow. *Q. ilex* resents transplanting and at more than 15cm (6in) is unlikely to survive. No pruning is needed for two to three years and then only light trimming in spring.

RIBES SANGUINEUM (D)

Can make an informal hedge, using one of the lower-growing cultivars (1.2m or 4ft) such as 'King Edward VII', which bears scarlet flowers in mid-spring and can be pruned immediately after that, using secateurs. The weak shoots are cut away and the stronger ones retained as far as possible, only the flowered portion being removed. The outline of the shrub should be fairly symmetrical but not formal.

ROSMARINUS OFFICINALIS (E)

At first it seems a good idea to grow rosemary as a hedge but it does not readily lend itself to the discipline, however slight, of hedge life. A visit to Provence shows that it needs prolonged heat and sun to give its best. In cooler and wetter climates it cannot be relied on to produce a hedge of uniform quality. Pruning is necessary in spring, cutting well back into the healthy but not old

wood. A light trimming after flowering helps to keep the plants in shape.

SANTOLINA CHAMAECYPARISSUS
LAVENDER COTTON (E)

Grows 0.3-0.6m (1-2ft) high, with dense leafy stems, both stems and foliage covered in a thick white felt. The flowers are bright yellow, in a head on a stalk up to 15cm (6in) long. A row of the shrubs hardly qualifies as a hedge but makes an attractive line of planting 0.6m (2ft) wide. The flowers may have to be sacrificed in favour of pruning in spring, preserving a rounded shape. In a few years the plant becomes untidy and cuttings should be kept in readiness for replacement.

TAXUS BACCATA
COMMON OR ENGLISH YEW (E)

Yew makes the great formal hedges of Britain and has no rival among the evergreens. In the USA it is not considered reliable in regions more rugged than Long Island and the cultivar 'Repandens' is often used as well as the species *T. cuspidata*. The virtues of *T. baccata* are that it is hardy; it regenerates even from the oldest wood and survives annual pruning for many years (the hedges at Levens Hall in Cumbria with their topiary have been pruned every year since 1692); it is unrivalled in producing a regular formal outline of great beauty, austere but not gloomy.

The only serious problems arise from:
1 Waterlogged ground, which can be fatal.
2 Infestation by the yew scale insect, which can damage sizeable areas but will respond to spraying with malathion.
3 Honey fungus infection, which is not common but threatening if it does occur.
4 Gnawing by rodents can cause the death of moderate-sized stems and is thought to explain the wavy outlines of some ancient yew hedges.
5 It is widely but not universally known that yew, when eaten, can be fatal to cattle (and probably man) but it is also clear that

cattle can be seen to eat the shoots without coming to any harm. Semi-dried twigs and foliage are more dangerous than green ones. It appears that the poison – probably the alkaloid 'Taxine' – is virulent when the stomach is empty, and perhaps only then. The lesson is clear.

In spite of these problems a yew hedge is very little trouble apart from the rather tedious labour of pruning, but that occurs only once a year in autumn. Nowadays the task is made shorter, if no less laborious, if petrol-driven cutters are used. They are, however, very heavy to manipulate on the upper part of the hedge.

The renovation of aged yew hedges is now established as a successful enterprise, though the method was advocated as long ago as 1879 in *The Garden* (p432). There is an outstanding example at Powys Castle undertaken by James Hancock, the head gardener. The most important yew hedges were planted just before the outbreak of war in 1914. They suffered neglect in the two World Wars and, when the castle came into the care of the National Trust in 1952, many of the formal hedges had grown to a width of 2.4m (8ft). The process of repair began with cutting back (stem pruning) one side of the hedge to the main trunk, removing all branches and reducing the tops to the required height. In the following spring the yew started to sprout and after three years there was healthy and quite dense growth. Then the other side of the hedge was treated in the same way. The final, excellent result was hard to believe after twelve years. The hedge was, of course, well fed during the pruning operation.

TEUCRIUM CHAMAEDRYS
WALL GERMANDER (E)

Herbaceous at the top, woody at the base. The leaves are bright green and the flowers, on a terminal raceme, have a rose-coloured corolla with the lower lip with a darker shade.

The plant is useful as an edging 0.3m (1ft) high to a bed or border, seen at its best in midsummer. Cut it back in spring, preferably using secateurs to avoid destroying the natural outline, which is irregular.

THUJA PLICATA WESTERN RED CEDAR (E)

Makes a good hedge planted at 0.9m (3ft) intervals. In midsummer of the second season after planting light pruning of the whole plant is carried out, in time for the new wood to ripen before winter. After that the leader is only beheaded when the required height is reached, at which stage the sides of the hedge are trimmed.

VIBURNUM TINUS (E)

A variable shrub and one of the cultivars 'Eve Price' or 'Gwenllian', preferably propagated from a single plant by cuttings, is desirable. The leaves are dark green, the carmine buds open to pink flowers at any time from Christmas to mid-spring. Pruning is not often needed but the plant responds readily even from old wood, and such a measure is undertaken in late spring.

Parterre in Tuscany, Italy. Here, box encloses blue gravel – effective and laboursaving

PLANTS FOR HEDGES

			Distance apart at planting		Pruning time (approx)
			Inches	Cms	
I	D	*Acer campestre*, FIELD MAPLE	18	45	Dormant
I	E	*Aucuba japonica*	30	80	None. Shape in spring
I	E	*Berberis darwinii*	24	60	After flowering (berries)
I	E	*Berberis × stenophylla*	24	60	After flowering
F	E	*Buxus sempervirens*, BOX	12	30	Early summer
F	E	*Buxus sempervirens* cv 'Suffruticosa' (for edging)	6	15	Summer
F	D	*Carpinus betulus*, HORNBEAM	24	60	Dormant
I	D	*Chaenomeles speciosa* and cultivars	30	80	Spur in spring, long shoots in summer
I/F	D	*Crataegus monogyna*, HAWTHORN	24 (30)	60 (75)	Summer
F	E	*× Cupressocyparis leylandii* LEYLAND CYPRESS	24 (30)	60 (75)	Summer
F	E	*Cupressus macrocarpa* MONTEREY CYPRESS	24	60	Summer
F/I	E	*Elaeagnus pungens* 'Maculata'	24	60	Mid-spring
I	E	*Escallonia* 'APPLE BLOSSOM'	30	75	After flowering
I	E	*Euonymus japonicus*, JAPANESE SPINDLE BUSH	18	45	Mid-spring
F	D	*Fagus sylvatica*, COMMON BEECH	18	45	Late summer
I	D	*Forsythia × intermedia* 'Spectabilis'	36	90	After flowering
I	D	*Fuchsia magellanica* 'Riccartonii'	24 (30)	60 (75)	Mid-spring
I/F	E	*Griselinia littoralis*	24	60	Early summer
I	D	*Hippophae rhamnoides*, SEA BUCKTHORN	30	75	Spring
F	E	*Ilex aquifolium*, COMMON HOLLY	18	45	Spring
F	E	*Ilex aquifolium* cv 'J. C. van Thol'	18	45	Spring
F	E	*Juniperus communis*, COMMON JUNIPER	18	45	Spring
I	E	*Juniperus viginiana*, RED CEDAR	60	150	(Screen) Spring
F	E	*Laurus nobilis*, BAY LAUREL	24 (30)	60 (75)	Midsummer

PLANTS FOR HEDGES

			Distance apart at planting		Pruning time (approx)
			Inches	**Cms**	
I	E	*Lavandula angustifolia,* COMMON LAVENDER	18	45	Spring
I	E	*Lavandula stoechas,* FRENCH LAVENDER	12	30	None
F	E	*Ligustrum ovalifolium,* OVAL LEAF PRIVET	18	45	Spring and summer
F	E	*Lonicera nitida*	15	37	Several times, spring to late summer
I/F	E	*Olearia*	18	45	Late spring
I	D	*Philadelphus coronarius*	30	75	After flowering
I	D	*Potentilla* cultivars	24	60	Mid-spring
F	E	*Prunus lusitanica,* PORTUGAL LAUREL	24	60	Spring
F	E	*Quercus ilex,* HOLM OAK	18 (24)	45 (60)	Summer
I	D	*Ribes sanguineum,* FLOWERING CURRANT	30	75	After flowering
I	E	*Rosmarinus officinalis,* ROSEMARY	18 (24)	45 (60)	Spring and summer
F	E	*Taxus baccata,* COMMON YEW et al	18 (24)	45 (60)	Autumn
I	E	*Teucrium chamaedrys,* WALL GERMANDER	6	15	Spring
F	E	*Thuja plicata,* WESTERN RED CEDAR	24	60	Late summer
F/I	E	*Viburnum tinus* 'Eve Price'	24	60	Spring

I = Informal
F = Formal
E = Evergreen
D = Deciduous

TOPIARY

The word came originally from the Greek τοπος, a place, which the Romans adapted to 'topiarius', the man who looked after the place, hence the gardener. In the garden of the younger Pliny (AD61-113) box hedges were clipped into shapes, some spelling the name of the gardener or his master and trees were planted in patterns, notably the quincunx with one tree at each corner of a square and one in the middle, thus:

This appealed to the Roman liking for orderliness. Topiary spread even to Britain, but with the collapse of the Roman empire this kind of gardening ceased until the Normans brought it back after 1066. It had never died out in France (Gaul) and soon became fashionable in England.

By 1592 the word topiary was used for the training of trees or shrubs into ornamental or fantastic shapes, coinciding with the new commercial wealth and its display in Elizabeth I's reign. In the next century French and Dutch influence was absorbed, producing designs of increasing sophistication culminating in the garden of Levens Hall in Cumbria (Westmorland). This garden was laid out by Guillaume Beaumont, a pupil of le Notre, and has been maintained without a break until this day.

The short reigns of William of Orange and Mary Stuart (1689-1702) saw the high point of British topiary. Beaumont had already designed the semicircular garden at Hampton Court, the royal residence. Soon the landscape movement of Lancelot 'Capability' Brown and later Humphry Repton did away with much topiary and it did not revive until mid Victorian times. Again, new wealth with cheap labour encouraged ostentation, which topiary and massive bedding schemes could provide. Towards 1900 there was a strong surge of interest, recorded in the *Book of Topiary* by Curtis and Gibson (1904), the latter being the gardener in charge of Levens Hall. After the First World War increasing wages, cost of materials and taxation led to the disappearance of many topiary gardens, a loss much aggravated by the Second World War.

However, interest in gardening increased. It had always been a British 'thing' and the working class (no longer a term to be bandied about readily), with more money to spend, developed a taste for topiary along with their traditional bedding-out. This is well recorded in the book *Brilliant Gardens* by Candida Lycett-Green and Andrew Lawson (1987), which contains many examples of topiary in gardens all of modest size, but developed with great skill and feeling.

Requirements for Topiary

A hedge or shrub is often the starting point. Perhaps some wayward growth from a hedge suggests the beginning of a cone or ball, and one ball leads to another. We are not concerned here with the development of hedges (see p158), but must consider those plants which are suitable for the training which leads to an ornamental feature.

First, the site should be level with sufficient shelter from strong winds, which is best provided by a hedge which filters the air and reduces its speed for a distance about twice the height of the hedge. The effect of walls is discussed on p160.

Second, exposure to sunlight for several hours a day is necessary for, if part of a plant

A view of the ancient yew topiary at Levens Hall, Cumbria, maintained continuously for three centuries. Box hedges enclose annual and perennial plants. The yew is trimmed with electric clippers in late summer

is always in shade, its growth will be relatively retarded. When choosing a site, remember that a view from above is always effective, either from the house as at Chastleton, Oxfordshire and Lytes Cary, Somerset, or from a raised terrace as at Blickling, Norfolk or Athelhampton, Dorset.

Third, plants should be hardy, comparatively slow-growing, and dense in form and habit. When propagating, cuttings should be taken from a single plant. Seedlings may vary in colour and form. Most deciduous plants may be discarded, though they can be and are used for topiary, especially in the USA – but they are losing ground there. Hawthorn, *Crataegus monogyna*, and other species such as *C. phaenopyrum*, the Washington Thorn, are reasonably dense but not when leafless and their growth is not easy to control. They tend to produce long straggling shoots needing frequent attention, though this may be a specifically British problem.

Recommended Plants
BUXUS SEMPERVIRENS BOX needs a well-drained soil and some protection from northerly winds. It stands clipping well as long as no frost is threatened and can produce sophisticated shapes. It is slow in growth and may take ten years to reach four feet, which will discourage many.

FAGUS BEECH *F. sylvatica* in Britain, *F. grandifolia* in the USA, is only suitable for architectural subjects such as arches or pillars. It grows quite rapidly, can easily become too tall and needs a skilled topiarist. Hornbeam *(Carpinus betulus)* is similar to beech but the dead leaves are less attractive.

ILEX AQUIFOLIUM HOLLY is very hardy, tolerates poor soil and atmospheric pollution, and grows quite rapidly. It can be clipped in spring or in late summer and responds well with new growth. In the USA at Disneyland and elsewhere in the south *I. opaca* (East

Palutka) and *I. Vomitoria* (Yaupon) are much used, but neither of these succeeds in Britain.

LAURUS NOBILIS BAY is a fine plant, not fully hardy in Britain, except in coastal areas. Elsewhere it is cut to the ground in a severe winter, but almost invariably shoots in spring and can reach 1.2-1.5m (4-5ft) in two years. For topiary it needs clipping with secateurs to produce a good outline and is seldom seen in this role.

LIGUSTRUM OVALIFOLIUM PRIVET. Often despised by élite gardeners for its suburban image is a satisfactory foliage plant, with dark glaucous leaves. The cultivar 'Aureum' is the plant which gardeners really love to hate, but it is the most popular of all shrubs for dark corners. Slower in growth than the type and easier to shape, it produces a colourful picture, if not exactly golden. It will need frequent clipping.

Privet has replaced the common *L. vulgare* for hedging in difficult areas of the garden in Britain, mainly because it is evergreen except in really severe winters. It is of ungainly habit and the flowers have an unpleasant stink. Nevertheless there are fine examples of ambitious privet topiary even in Britain, but the best are found where the summers are really hot – Italy and the USA. Privet needs more frequent clipping than yew or box but the cultivar *L. ovalifolium* 'Aureum' is less vigorous than the type and well suited to topiary.

LONICERA NITIDA CHINESE HONEYSUCKLE. A dense evergreen shrub, tolerant of most soils and weather, and can be used for architectural shapes. It responds too quickly to clipping, which has to be performed frequently, and seldom grows beyond 1.2-1.5m (4-5ft).

Traditionally it was offered by nurserymen as cultivar 'Ernest Wilson', though named simply as *L. nitida*. However, in recent years the cultivar 'Baggesen's Gold' has been much more popular, though the colour is not of the best and the plant is low-growing which limits its use for topiary. The best choice may be the cultivar 'Elegant', named by Krüssman as _L. pileata yunnanensis_, but which is now suspected of being a hybrid – _L. nitida × pileata_. It is not easy to find but grows to 0.9m (3ft) with horizontal branches and leaves of matt green.

TAXUS BACCATA YEW is botanically a conifer except that it bears no cones, and for that reason appears here. This great plant, already described on p165, forms a dense outline and bears repeated clipping even if this continues for centuries, as at Levens Hall (see p171). Growth is rapid enough to produce a 1.8m (6ft) tree in ten years from 0.3m (1ft) pot-grown plant, yet clipping is only needed once a year. Feeding with manure is essential in the early stages.

The special virtue of yew for topiary is shown in the well-defined lines, edges and curves of the best geometric examples. Reference has already been made to the large number of golden forms raised in the nineteenth century (p157) and these are especially useful for the geometric designs. A plain _T. baccata_ with _T. aurea_ either grown through it, or grafted at 1m (3ft), became popular and was the trademark of the garden designer Thomas Mawson (1861-1933). Healthy examples survive at Duffryn Garden in Cardiff, South Wales.

Conifers

CUPRESSO-CYPARIS LEYLANDII LEYLAND CYPRESS. An extremely vigorous plant which needs no encouragement and stands up to wind and coastal weather. Rather surprisingly, it responds to clipping (not too vigorous) and can be restricted to a formal outline by trimming three times in each season. All the same, it is best confined to large and simple designs.

CUPRESSUS MACROCARPA MONTEREY CYPRESS is somewhat tender and performs best in maritime areas. It stands clipping well enough but is apt to be untidy.

JUNIPERUS COMMUNIS COMMON JUNIPER. Has upright growth to 3m (10ft) and will keep a regular outline without much clipping. It tolerates chalk and rather poor soil.

THUJA PLICATA WESTERN RED CEDAR is hardy and rapid-growing, making a dense head of medium green colour. It is used for topiary in the USA.

First Steps
The first rule of topiary for the amateur is to keep everything simple. Cylinders, cubes, cones, pyramids and spheres are straight forward. Do not distort the natural shape of the tree or shrub more than is necessary.

After planting, deciduous plants (eg hawthorn, privet), if upright, are cut down to 15cm (6in) from the ground in early spring. Repeat in the second year, again in early spring. Cut away less, say 10-15cm (4-6in), each year after that. Beech and hornbeam need less severe pruning, to 30cm (12in) perhaps in the first year, leaving 45cm (18in) of stem in the second year. When the desired height is reached prune each year, only to keep that height, but also cut back laterals to produce the required shape (see table on pp168-9 for timing).

Evergreen plants are not pruned in the first year, but straggly branches are clipped as necessary. Feed and water every month. Subsequently, during the first three to four years, do not allow too much increase in height – probably 15-20cm (6-8in) a year is enough. Clip three to four times each year. Box, holly and yew are first cut in early summer then every six weeks.

Beech and hornbeam are clipped in midsummer but, as they mature, defer this until late summer or early autumn. Use secateurs for bay, holly and laurel, and prune in late winter to early spring if strong growth is needed.

Free shaping of young trees

Keep the design broadest at ground level, ideal for cones or pyramids. Only use bamboo or wire if it cannot be avoided; such aids are mainly needed in complex designs. Clear out dead wood and leaves from the inside of the plant to promote air circulation and penetration of light.

A good shape for beginners is a cone or pyramid. The outline follows that of many trees, and allows further development from the main leader. Use string as a guide for cutting a straight line.

Spheres and cubes are not very difficult and can lead on to other shapes.

A circle or crown can be created as follows. First, produce a life-size or scaled drawing, from which a metal frame can be made, ideally using a local blacksmith. When the frame is complete, get him to insert a strong metal rod to fix the completed design to the ground. As the plant grows, tie it to the frame, spacing the branches evenly. As it expands through the frame start clipping, once more remembering to clear leaves from the inside.

Container-grown topiary plants

The best containers are wooden tubs of oak, cedar or cypress, measuring say 53×53×53cm (21 × 21 × 21in). There should be ten drain holes, each about 15mm (¾ in) in diameter, and the tub should be raised on blocks 5cm (2in) high. Put a layer of broken crocks and gravel at the bottom, and top this with a layer about 10cm (4in) deep of light-textured soil.

The plant should have a wrapping of sacking round the root ball. If so, do not remove or loosen the wrapping. Place the plant on top of the soil, making sure it is in the middle of the container. Fill the space round the root ball with a light soil enriched with compost and a little general fertiliser. Firm it down by treading. Let the soil level be a few centimetres below the rim of the tub.

Water well and add a layer of mulch to protect the roots from heat and cold and to stifle weeds.

Water daily for a week, then once a week.

Keep in partial shade for one year. No more fertilising.

Mature subjects are best pruned when the sun is lower and the effect of removing leaves will be diminishing; that is, late summer. Some plants will need clipping more than once, but that makes for tidiness and puts a strain on the victim. Spring pruning is indicated for plants that have been damaged, perhaps by frost, which is a serious threat to all topiary. Manuring, followed by a long-acting fertiliser should follow the pruning in this unhappy situation.

Preformed Topiary

This is an activity which has been developed almost but not quite entirely in America. To most English gardeners it is a closed book and, having visited Longwood and the Philadelphia Flower Show, I can only express admiration for its results but beg to be excused from offering any advice on this remarkable artistic craft.

Yew topiary at Hidcote, Gloucestershire. Lawrence Johnston never discussed the ideas behind his twenty-one 'gardens within a garden'. However, this kind of topiary was already common in both Europe and the USA by the time he began to create his famous garden, so the concept was not original

ROSES

PRUNING PHILOSOPHIES

It is easy to make rose pruning sound difficult. The subject *is* difficult because it requires a knowledge of the various kinds of rose and their habits and it takes time to achieve that. The act of pruning, however, is not difficult given the right tools, well maintained (see p13-16): secateurs, long-handled for some climbers; loppers for any stems over 1cm (½in) in diameter, and a pocket saw for any over 37mm (1½in). A very

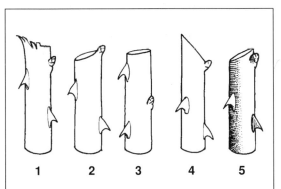

1 Rough cut too far from bud, may lead to die back
2 Cut too close to bud, may allow infection to enter and could damage bud
3 Cut too far from bud, may lead to die back
4 Cut sloping the wrong way. Bud becomes moist and may rot
5 CORRECT. Cut ends not more than 0.5cm (¼in) above bud

sharp pruning knife helps in tidying any untidy cuts, especially as these cuts are close, but not too close to a bud.

Do we have to prune roses? Roses that are never pruned may perform quite well for five years, but the stems will become long and spindly, the flowers smaller. All carefully recorded experience would support the assertion, that pruning once a year makes most roses perform well and enables them to live a long and useful life. But the questioning of accepted practices is always useful. When do we have to do it? In 1933 William Robinson, a most influential gardening author, wrote words to this effect in the preface to *The English Flower Garden*, his last major work (1933):

> A delusion is that the plants must be pruned late in the spring ... they are left all the winter to be knocked about [by the weather] . . . it is a much better practice to prune all our Roses before Christmas, if possible, and set them to work to make roots.

Combative as ever. There arises the matter of climate differences, especially noticeable in Britain with its wide ranges of temperature and rainfall, and of microclimates, often related to hills, plantations or lakes. Robinson's garden at Gravetye in Sussex had, and still must have, a benign micro-climate related to southerly slopes and woodland, with relatively mild winters. Under these conditions pruning at any time in the dormant period (October to mid-February in Britain) would be safe. For most gardens in this country, pruning before mid-February would run the risk of damage to the exposed shoots and leaving the pruning until April would involve a risk from late frosts to young immature shoots: hence the now accepted routine pruning for the majority of roses just before spring, which we take as beginning on 1 March. If the weather is unfavourable pruning may be delayed until mid-March. During this period new growth will develop slowly and is able to resist most late frosts.

CLASSIFICATION

Roses are classified below as suggested by the World Federation of Rose Societies, with a selection of good examples with their date of introduction. If this is not known, there is no entry.

Species Wild roses, mostly once-flowering.

R. foetida, R. glauca (rubrifolia), hugonis, paulii, pomifera, primula.

***R. spinosissima** (pimpinellifolia).* Burnet or Scotch rose. Naturalised on sand dunes in Britain. Leaves small, as are the flowers, but they have charm.

Varieties include Pink; Double Yellow; William III, pink-purple. *R.s. altaica* reaches 1.8m (6ft) and gave rise to a number of hybrids, including 'Frühlingsgold', 1937. 'Stanwell Perpetual', 1838, a cross between a Burnet rose and probably a damask, is hardly that, but it does repeat over a long period. All the Scotch roses flourish without routine pruning, but occasional thinning of shoots when overcrowded is beneficial.

Gallicas Old garden roses, Gallica. Summer-flowering only.

'Charles de Mills'; 'Gloire de France'; *Rosa mundi,* before sixteenth century; Tuscany.

Damasks Old garden roses, Damasks. Summer-flowering only.

'Ispahan', 'Mme Hardy', 1832; 'St Nicholas', 1950 (found in Yorkshire).

FIRST STEPS IN PRUNING ROSES

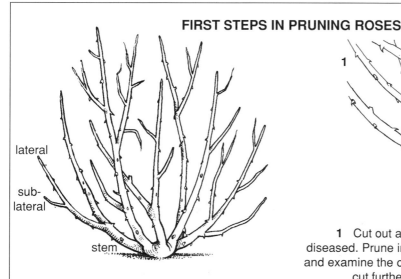

lateral

sub-lateral

stem

Look for stems which are likely to rub against others. Before they do so, remove the more expendable ones completely

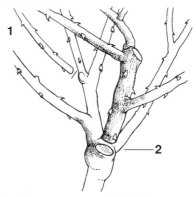

1

2

1 Cut out any wood which is dead or diseased. Prune into wood which looks healthy and examine the cut surface. If it is at all brown, cut further down into the stem
2 If you reach a point where there is no healthy bud above which you can cut, the whole stem must be sacrificed

China roses Old garden roses, China roses. Perpetual flowering.

'Fellemberg', 1857; 'Mutabilis', an amazing rose, date unknown, single flowers change colour from red to buff to pink to copper; 'Old Blush China', c1789, another remarkable plant, flowering in every month, always on Christmas Day at Tintinhull, almost disease-free, cut back by about one third in early spring, does well against a wall, reaching 2.4m (8ft).

Bourbon roses Old garden roses, Bourbons. Most and all those listed here have a second flowering in autumn.

'Boule de Neige' 1867; 'Mme Isaac Pereire' 1880; 'Zephirine Drouhin' 1868, the thornless rose, will reach 4.5m (15ft) against a wall. Coppery young leaves, double cerise flowers, fragrant, repeat flowering.

Portland roses Old garden roses, Portlands. Two flushes of bloom, often some at intervals as well.

'Portland Rose', *Portlandica*, c1790; 'Mme Knorr' ('Comte de Chambord'),1863, double pink with an edge of lilac.

Hybrid Perpetuals Old garden roses, Hybrid Perpetuals. Not, in fact, perpetual. Flower twice.

'Reine des Violettes', 1860; 'Souvenir du Docteur Jamain',1865; 'Mrs John Laing',1887, double fragrant pink flowers.

Tea Roses Old garden roses, Tea Roses. For greenhouse or conservatory, except in mild climates.

Hybrid Tea Roses Bush roses, large flowered, recurrent.

'Shot Silk',1924; 'The Doctor',1936; 'Grace de Monaco', 1956; 'Wendy Cussons', 1963; 'Peace', 1939, very large pale yellow flowers edged pink, leaves dark and glossy – very prone to blackspot, needs light pruning.

Albas Old garden roses, Albas. Summer flowering only.

Alba maxima; 'Celeste' , late eighteenth century, very fine shrubs with soft pink flowers; 'Königin von Danemark', 1826.

Centifolias Old garden roses, Provence (Centifolias). Summer-flowering only. Lax flowers and leaves. These are cabbage roses, developed in Holland in the seventeenth century and featured in Dutch paintings of that period.

'Rose de Meaux', before 1800, small leaves and pink flowers becoming darker on opening; 'Fantin Latour', pale pink double flowers, a tall bush – splendid.

Moss Roses Old garden roses, Moss Roses. Summer-flowering only.

'Common Moss' 1727; 'William Lobb', 1855, tall enough for a pillar, double purple-crimson flowers.

Rugosas Shrub roses, repeat-flowering, classed as modern garden roses.

Rugosa, c1796; *Rugosa* 'Alba'; 'Blanc Double de Coubert', 1892, white, no hips; 'Roseraie de l'Hay',1901, wine-red, no hips; 'Frau Dagmar Hastrup', 1914, pale pink, good hips. All these are in the top class, very healthy, reliable and with excellent foliage.

Polyanthas Bush roses, Polyanthas, recurrent.

'Little White Pet', 1829 (a sport of 'Felicité et Perpétue', but polyantha habit); 'Nathalie Nypels',1917, semi-double pink flowers, low but spreading, good repetition; 'Yvonne Rabier', 1910, double white flowers, well scented, robust.

'Old Blush China' (Parson's Pink China, The Monthly Rose) is an ancient rose, introduced to Europe in 1789. On a wall it grows to 2.4m (8ft) but makes a 1.2m (4ft) wide, 1.5m (5ft) high bush in the open. It flowers every month, always at Christmas at Tintinhull. The flowers are semi-double, two or three on a stem, beginning crimson then fading to pink. This wonderful old rose is hardy and free from disease and should be in every garden. Prune it early in the spring, cutting back stems by one third

Floribundas Bush roses, cluster-growing, recurrent.

'Rosemary Rose', 1945; 'Frensham', 1946; 'Iceberg', 1958, the best white rose, prune lightly; 'Arthur Bell', 1965, bright red flowers, dark purple foliage, tolerates some shade; 'Margaret Merril', 1977, white flowers tinged pink in the bud, very fragrant and easy to grow.

Grandifloras Bush roses, cluster-flowering, recurrent, average height 105cm (3ft 6in). A dubious class.

'Queen Elizabeth',1945; 'John S. Armstrong', 1961.

Hybrid Musks Shrub roses, recurrent. Two main flushes of bloom.

'Pax', 1918; 'Penelope', 1924; 'Buff Beauty', 1919.

Modern shrub roses Shrub roses, recurrent and non-recurrent.

'Nevada', 1927; 'Golden Wings', 1956; 'Cerise Bouquet', 1958; 'Constance Spry', 1961.

Ramblers Climbing roses, non-recurrent, summer-flowering only.

'François Juranville', 1906; 'Seagull', 1907; 'Albertine', 1921, *filipes* 'Kiftsgate'.

Climbers Climbing roses, recurrent and non-recurrent.

1 Noisette Climbers, all recurrent.
'Gloire de Dijon', 1853; 'Mme Alfred Carrière', 1879.
2 Large-flowered Climbers, flower more than once but later blooming seldom equals the first. 'Lady Hillingdon', 1917; 'Mermaid', 1918; 'Mme Gregoire Staechelin', 1927;'New Dawn', 1930; 'Guinée',1938; 'Parkdirektor Rigers', 1957; 'Helen Knight', 1977.

Miniature roses Miniature roses, bush and climbing, all recurrent. Height mostly 25-30cm (10-12in).

'Easter Morning', 1960;'Nozomi', 1972; 'Swany', 1978; 'Snow Carpet', 1980.

PRACTICAL PRUNING OF NEWLY-PLANTED ROSES

During the flowering period it is well worth visiting one or more rose collections , before deciding which roses to grow. The collections' plants are labelled and given the best cultivation and pruning, and it is possible to form an idea of the height and spread to be expected, apart from discovering the flower colour which is so often unrecognisable as that in a catalogue photograph.

If you are able to collect the plants from the nursery you have a better chance of planting in autumn which is the best time for putting them in the ground. Delivery by the nursery is apt to be uncertain, but it must be between autumn and early spring (in Britain, October to March). The ground has, of course, been well prepared and you pick a still, dry, fairly warm day. They do not happen at weekends. Equipped with secateurs, a knife, lopper and pocket saw, you are ready for action. If this is autumn or winter examine the root system, cut away any roots that are coarse (without rootlets) or damaged and then plant; that is all. Pruning of shoots follows in early spring and that applies also to any plants that arrive in the New Year. For the great majority, pruning is severe, cutting back main shoots to two to four eyes, about 15cm (6in) from the ground. At this stage it may be as well to name the exceptions to this apparently cruel first-year routine.

1 Any growing in poor, thin soil. Prune very lightly.
2 True ramblers, eg 'Dorothy Perkins'. Prune all strong shoots to 22-38cm (9-15in).
3 Ramblers, eg 'Albertine', with growth high on the plant and very little at the base. Prune to 22-38cm (9-15in).
4 Climbers and ramblers which are sports of Hybrid Teas and Noisette roses, all recurrent, eg 'Gloire de Dijon', 'Mme Alfred Carrière'. NO pruning, as they may revert permanently to the bush form.

SUCKERS

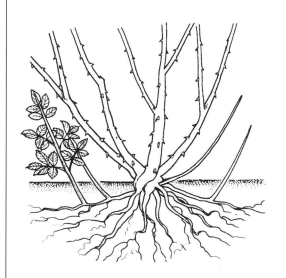

Suckers emerging from the roots of a rose grafted at ground level. Remove at their origin

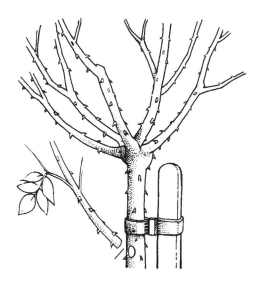

A sucker arising on the main stem of a standard rose. The foliage is that of the rootstock plant. Remove at its origin

5 Large-flowered climbers whose second or late flowering is poor, eg 'Lady Hillingdon', 'Mermaid', 'Helen Knight'. 'New Dawn' does repeat well. NO pruning.

Remember that these five exceptions to the rule of severe pruning refer only to the first year.

PRUNING OF ESTABLISHED ROSES

At any time look for dead wood and remove it completely (the pocket saw may be needed). Diseased wood is cut back to healthy-looking wood. Examine the cut end and if it is brown cut further to another bud, and so on until the pith is white. Even then there must be a bud above which to make the cut – if not the whole stem must be cut away. Do not overlook shoots which cross others and rub against them or look like doing so. One must be sacrificed. Look out for suckers. Most roses, (by no means all) grown in nurseries are grafted onto a rootstock, *R. multiflora* or a wild species. Shoots may arise below the graft and on suckers which may extend and may even take over from the grafted rose. As a rule the difference between sucker foliage and that of the grafted rose is easy to detect. The leaves are normally light green with several leaflets and thorns may be of a different shape. Cutting a sucker at ground level simply encourages new and diffuse growth. None of these tasks has to wait for a pruning session but can be carried out as soon as the problem is noticed.

SUMMER PRUNING OF ROSES

This is a subject of some importance and one of the commonest pruning operations. As with dead-heading of herbaceous subjects, it calls for some knowledge of the structure and habit of the plant, and unfortunately attracts the attention of eager volunteers who lack this qualification.

The object is to remove all flowers as they

OPPOSITE:
'Zephirine Drouhin', bred in France in 1868, is probably the best of the Bourbons and still widely available. This deliciously scented rose has no thorns and produces shoots 2.4m (8ft) or more long; it is best grown on a wall. The cerise-pink flowers are semi-double and produced continuously. It has a reputation for attracting mildew and blackspot, but that is probably exaggerated. It is nevertheless a lovable plant

BELOW:
'Adélaide d'Orleans', bred in France in 1826, is a hybrid of *R. sempervirens* from southern Europe and, like the latter, is evergreen with plenty of foliage. The flowers are small, semi-double and abundant on a climbing stem up to 4.5m (15ft). In great demand after it first appeared, 'Adélaide d'Orleans' was then neglected; however it is still available from specialist rose nurseries

fade – this also removes the seed or seeds. Once the seed-containing hips begin to form the energy of the plant is directed to their development, and the formation of new shoots and flowering stems is inhibited by growth-regulating hormones. There is also some danger of disease arising in the dead flower head if it is left to rot. As a rule, it is possible either to cut off individual roses at the origin of their stems or to remove a whole truss, for example of the floribunda rose 'Iceberg', carrying five or six blooms. In the latter case the stem should be traced down to a promising bud and cut off just above it. In all dead-heading, never leave an unsightly length of stem which may lead to dieback.

In some instances, and a good example is the polyantha-type rambler 'Little White Pet', individual blooms open and die after a very short life and dead-heading is indicated two or three times each day, unless brown is your favourite colour. *(continued on p186)*

ROSA CHINENSIS AND SOME OLD HYBRID TEAS
Pruning aims to encourage growth from the base

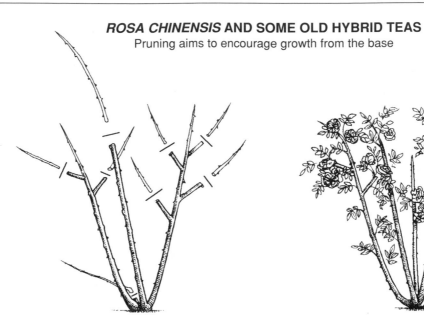

1 In early spring of the second year long growths are cut back by one third and laterals to 15cm (6in)

2 Flowering takes place on laterals of old wood. Summer prune

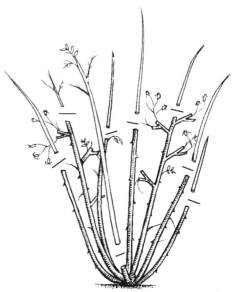

3 In the third and following years, long growths are cut back by one third and laterals to 15cm (6in) in early spring

4 Each autumn, cut back long growths by up to one third. Remove badly placed growths completely

ALBAS, CENTIFOLIAS, DAMASKS, MOSS ROSES AND SOME MODERN SHRUB ROSES

These flower mainly on lateral and sublateral shoots of second-year or older wood. Most do not repeat flower, but some will do so on laterals of the current year

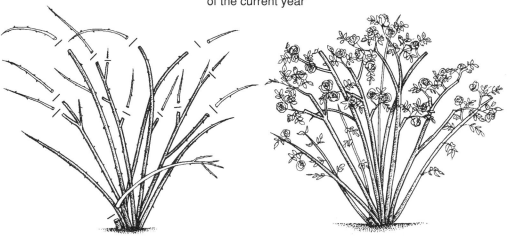

1 In early spring of the second year cut back any weak or damaged shoots

2 In the following summer, flowering takes place on laterals of old wood. Summer prune to encourage the formation of new laterals which may flower later in the season

3 In late summer, flowering takes place on laterals produced this season

4 In subsequent years, summer prune as before. Spring prune as necessary (see step 1), and shorten any overlong shoots

**SPECIES ROSES AND CLOSE HYBRIDS,
R. SPINOSISSIMA, R. RUGOSA,
GALLICAS, HYBRID MUSKS**

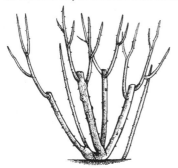

In early spring of the second year, lightly trim
the strongest shoots

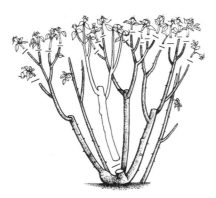

In autumn, cut out elderly shoots
which flowered poorly and shorten laterals
to 10cm (4in)

In subsequent years, summer prune and
cut out weak growths, especially in the
centre of the shrub

The contra-indication to dead-heading is the formation of attractive hips. _R. canina_, the Dog Rose, and _R. rubiginosa_, the Eglantine, are the oldest to carry distinguished hips, but in modern gardens _R. glauca rubrifolia_ is held in affection for its red young stems, grey-green leaves and red-brown hips. Rugosa roses vary. The following bear excellent hips: 'Alba', 'Frau Dagmar Hastrup', Rugosa itself, and 'Scabrosa'. Hips are negligible (so dead-heading desirable) on 'Blanc Double de Coubert', 'Roseraie de l'Hay' and probably most others.

Those which flower on the growth of the current season include China, Bourbon, Portland, Hybrid Perpetual, Tea and Hybrid Tea, Rugosa, Polyantha, Floribunda, Grandiflora, Hybrid Musk, and Miniature roses.

China roses are rather tender and are best grown against a wall, when they will reach 2.4m (8ft). Pruning is best done at the start of spring, cutting the main shoots to 20-25cm (8-10in) long and removing any thin stems (less than the diameter of a pencil).

Bourbon roses need to be pruned between late winter and early spring (mid-February to mid-March in Britain). The star of this group is 'Zephirine Drouhin' with no thorns, cerise-pink quite fragrant flowers, and a long flowering season. It produces shoots 2.4m (8ft) long, moreover the leaves are coppery. Pruning involves cutting back the side shoots by two-thirds and main shoots by one-third. Dead-head all fading flowers.

Portland Roses are not numerous. Perhaps 'Comte de Chambord' has undergone a sex change and emerged as 'Mme Knorr', none the worse. There are two flushes of bloom. Give the routine early spring pruning and dead-head immediately after the first flowering.

Hybrid Perpetuals Famous as exhibition roses in Victorian days but are still going strong in borders today. Make a note of 'Mrs John Laing', (1897) with soft pink, fragrant double

HYBRID PERPETUALS AND HYBRID TEAS

These flower on the current season's growth and need quite severe pruning

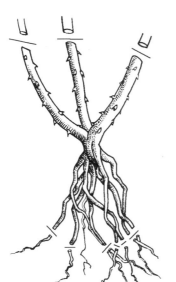

LEFT:
At planting, cut away any damaged roots and coarse roots with few rootlets. Cut main shoots back by a few inches

BELOW:
(a) In early spring, cut shoots back to around 15cm (6in) from ground level
(b) By early summer vigorous new shoots have been produced

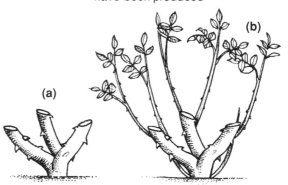

In autumn, flowered stems are cut back by one third. Any weak shoots are removed entirely

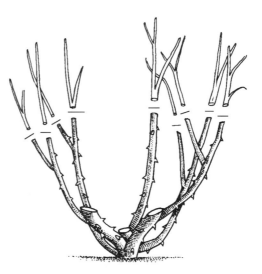

In subsequent years, in early spring cut out dead or diseased wood, and any inward-pointing, crossing or weak shoots. Cut remaining shoots back to 15-22cm (6-9in)

SUMMER PRUNING OF HYBRID TEAS

INCORRECT:
cut stems are too long

CORRECT:
cut stems are correct length, and are cut to a
strong, outward-facing shoot or bud

flowers. Prune those which are vigorous in early spring as you would Bourbons, others as you would Hybrid Teas but less severely. *Tea Roses* are tender and dislike hard pruning but should have a mild dose in early spring. 'General Schablikine' (1878), sounds sinister and is only picked out because his performance in the south of France is marvellous (not helpful to readers who do not travel). Prune in early spring. 'Lady Hillingdon', with double apricot-yellow flowers and coppery new leaves, is now grown in her climbing form as a rule and is given a warm place against a wall. Prune in spring.

Hybrid Teas need the routine early spring pruning. There do not seem to be any exceptions but there surely must be as there are thousands of these roses, with very variable characters.

Rugosas are indispensable. Life would be diminished without them for there is no substitute. Happily it is agreed that they normally only need light pruning in spring to improve their shapes, but if they go into a decline they respond well to drastic pruning to 0.6m (2ft). Then you must live without flower for a year. Dead-head 'Frau Dagmar Hastrup', which has pale pink flowers, with care as very good crimson hips follow. Leave at least half the hips to develop. Hips are negligible on 'Blanc Double de Coubert' and 'Roseraie de l'Hay'. Dead-head them as soon as the flowers fade – it can be a tedious job. *Polyanthas* accept the early spring pruning and none is better than 'Nathalie Nypels' (she was Dutch), who manages to produce fragrant pink semi-double flowers continuously through summer. That judgement was almost overturned by the arrival of 'Margaret Merril' (English) with not-quite-double, splendidly scented flowers, white with a shade of pink. Prune as for Hybrid Teas.

Floribundas (*cluster-flowered*) have a very strong team including 'Frensham' (1946) with

MINIATURES

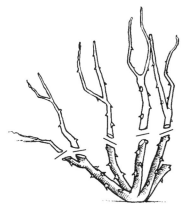

In early spring cut shoots
back to 10-15cm (4-6in)

Dead-heading means a visit to the plant two
to three times a day in the flowering season

In early spring, remove weak growth completely.
Cut back strong shoots to 10-15cm (4-6in)

POLYANTHAS

After planting, in early spring cut back strong
stems by one third. Remove any weak stems
completely

Flowering takes place in summer.
Summer prune

In early spring, cut back strong stems by half.
Cut out old or diseased wood completely,
In subsequent years, reduce strong stems by one
third or rather less. Cut out completely any weak
stems from the centre to keep it open

SUMMER PRUNING OF FLORIBUNDAS

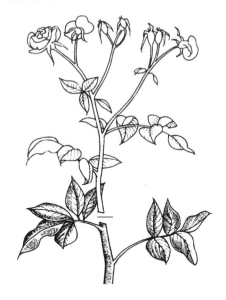

INCORRECT:
individual flowers only have been removed

CORRECT:
whole flower truss is removed to a strong, outward-facing shoot or bud

good, dark green leaves and clear red flowers in groups, hardly clusters.

It is not easy to calculate the extent of pruning but important to attempt it. Cutting off too much each year may weaken the plant, at first hardly perceptibly but within three or four years quite obviously. Being too gentle, on the other hand, leads to big bushes with thin, weak shoots. A compromise may produce a good collection of clusters, but not always. The advice of pruning some shoots lightly for early flowering and others severely to produce basal growths for flowering late in the season may solve the problem, but once more not always. This pruning must be done in late winter to early spring in the second year, and in the same period of each year thereafter. All the main one-year-old shoots are reduced by one third and any older wood cut to 15-22cm (6-9in), while any laterals which remain are shortened by 10-15cm (4-6in). 'Iceberg', justly famous for its

long and repeated flowering dislikes hard pruning (as does the Tea rose 'Peace'). This kind of pruning produces long shoots with few flowers. Given light pruning, taking off about 0.3m (1ft) from the main shoots each year, it makes a fine well-shaped bush to 1.5m (5ft) high, repeat-flowering but only slightly fragrant. 'Rosemary Rose' with dark, almost purple, foliage bears trusses of red flowers which recur reliably in partial shade, and that shade seems to have no bad effect. Instinct suggests that it should not be hard-pruned.

Grandifloras Mainly American, including 'Queen Elizabeth' USA, (1945). Very tall with large china-pink flowers in clusters, which last well after picking. It is probably *the* favourite rose, in Britain at least. The pruning of Grandifloras is the same as for Floribundas, from which they differ (mainly in height).

Hybrid Musks The pioneer was the Reverend Joseph Pemberton of Havering Atte

FLORIBUNDAS

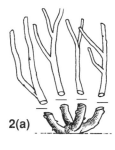

2(a)

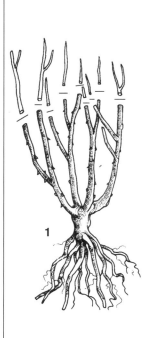

1

2(b)

3

4

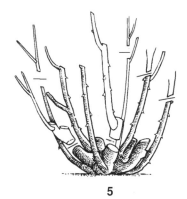

5

1   At planting, coarse and damaged roots are cut back. Main shoots are trimmed by a few inches

2   **(a)** In early spring all stems are cut back to 22cm (9in)
    (b) New growth appears in late spring

3   In autumn, cut all flowered growths back by 15-22cm (6-9in)

4   In early spring, prune back year-old shoots by one third, any older shoots to 22cm (9in) and laterals to 15cm (6in)

5   In subsequent years, prune in early spring as in step 4. Cut out any diseased and dead wood, and any stems likely to rub together or grow inwards

Bower in Essex. Soon after 1900 he started breeding, using two German roses 'Aglaia' and 'Trier', both with Moschata and Multiflora in their family tree. Crossing them with a selection of Teas, Hybrid Teas and Hybrid Perpetuals he produced an entirely new breed, first known as 'Pemberton Roses'. The best are not easy to pick out but 'Pax' (1918), 'Buff Beauty' (1919) and 'Penelope' (1924) are widely grown. The Hybrid Musks do benefit from pruning by living into a floriferous old age. In the late winter remove any stems that are filling the centre of the plant; the rest can be cut back by one third. These roses are successful in borders of perennial herbaceous plants as single specimens, and do well as an informal hedge .

Modern Shrub Roses A group of mixed character with a suggestion of Centifolia in 'Constance Spry' (1961). 'Nevada' (1927) arches to 2.4m (8ft) with round dark leaves and very large, creamy white single flowers in abundance. Only modestly repeating. 'Cerise Bouquet' (1958) has grey-green leaves and big clusters of semi-double, crimson, fragrant flowers. It blooms only in summer but for a long time and makes a beautiful arching shrub, 2.4m (8ft) high. These shrubs all benefit from pruning in early spring.

CLIMBERS AND RAMBLERS

True Ramblers Flower in early summer on the laterals of long shoots arising from the base. These roses include 'Dorothy Perkins' (1901), once the best-known rose of all, and 'American Pillar', both hybrids of *R. wichuraiana*. They are summer-flowering only, mainly on the wood of last year and slightly on older wood. The flowers are small.

At planting – if in late winter to early spring – prune all strong shoots to 25-38cm (10-15in) from the ground. If planting has been in autumn or early winter, delay pruning until the time just indicated. Strong

(continued on p196)

TRUE RAMBLERS
These flower once, on laterals of long basal shoots of the previous year

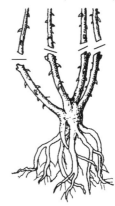

1 In early spring after planting, cut back shoots to 25-40cm (10-15in)

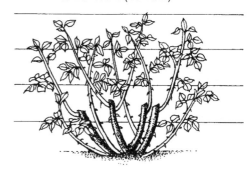

2 During the first summer, train new growth to wires as it extends. The plant will probably not flower this year

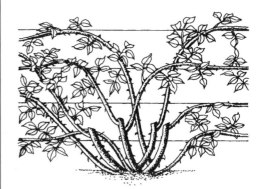

3 By the end of the first season, good growth has been made

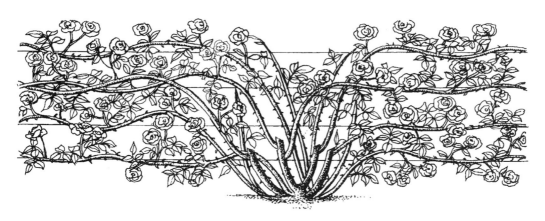

4 In the second summer the plant will flower well

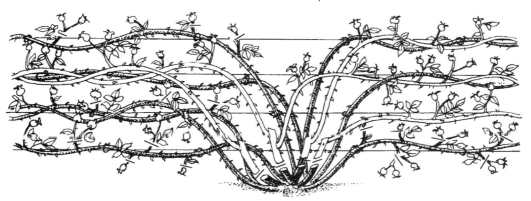

5 Flowered shoots are cut to the base as blooms fade, leaving several to fill out the framework

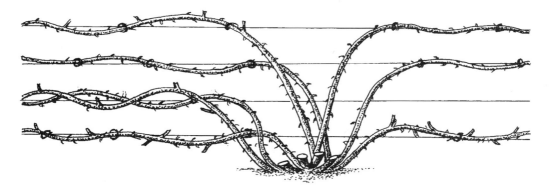

6 By the end of the season's growth, all stems are tied in ready for
the following year's flowering

CLIMBING ROSES, I
These flower on laterals from shoots of the previous year

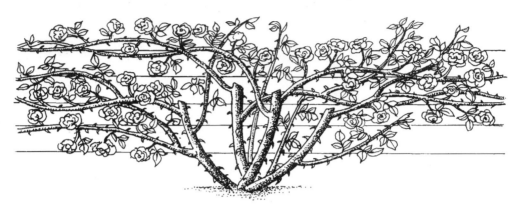

1 The plant flowers in summer, once only. New growth arises mainly
around 0.9-1.2m (3-4ft) from the base

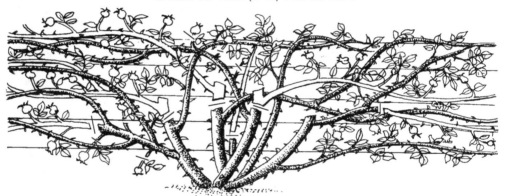

2 After flowering, flowered stems are cut back to the main leaders which will replace them.
These are trained in horizontally

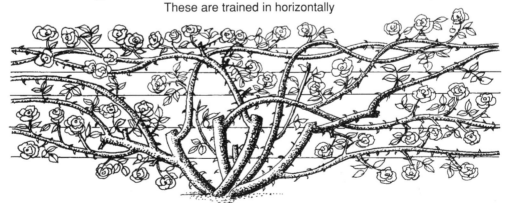

3 Flowering takes place the following summer along the leaders.
Repeat step 2 after flowering

CLIMBING ROSES, II

Climbing sports of the Hybrid Tea roses and Floribundas, and Noisette-style roses.
They flower on wood of the current year, usually repeating through the summer

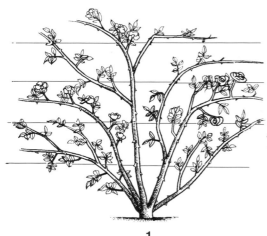

1

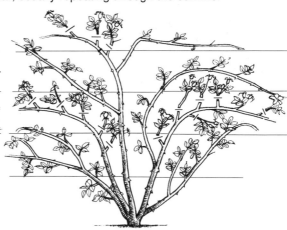

2

1 In the summer after planting new shoots are tied to their supports. A few flowers are produced

2 In winter, cut back flowered laterals to 15cm (6in). Secure leading shoots to wires

3 In the following summer flowers form on new shoots and laterals. Summer pruning encourages repeat flowering

4 In winter, cut back laterals to 15cm (6in) Repeat the cycle in subsequent years

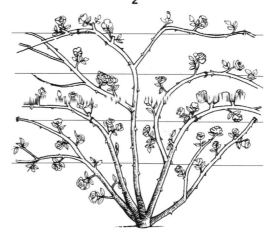

3

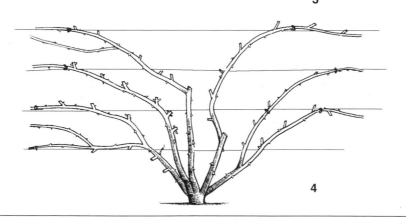

4

shoots will develop by early summer and they should be tied to horizontal wires at intervals as they grow. There will be no flowers. In the following summer, flowers will appear on short laterals from last year's growth. After the flowers fade all shoots are cut away at the base. If there are few basal shoots appearing, leave one or two of the flowered shoots but cut back their laterals to 10 or 12cm (4 or 5in). Tie in all new growth. Repeat the cycle each year.

Climbers Summer-flowering only, non-recurrent. Flowers larger than in those of the true Ramblers. The Climbers produce few shoots from the base, the new growth coming mainly from 0.9-1.2m (3-4ft) above ground, eg 'Albertine' (1921). Cut the stems back to a point just above the origin of a new shoot which has emerged from the old. Into this group has forced its way *R. filipes* 'Kiftsgate', an extremely vigorous form, climbing 9-12m (30-40ft) into a tree and bearing creamy white fragrant flowers most of the way. Pruning is almost impossible and fortunately not necessary.

Noisette Climbers and Ramblers All recurrent, and suitable for wall training or pergola. 'Gloire de Dijon' (1853) is the best example but there are poor forms around and it would be worth asking for a cutting from a plant you have seen to be of the best clone. Propagation under mist is easy – as a rule. This rose is certainly recurrent from early summer until autumn. A warning about pruning in the first year has been given (p180). After the first year all shoots can be shortened, leaving enough to allow horizontal training, if possible. Laterals are shortened to two buds.

Large-flowered Climbers Flower more than once but later bloom seldom equals the first. 'Lady Hillingdon' (1917) responds well to early spring pruning but is shy of flowering unless grown in a sunny place. 'Mermaid' is rather tender; pruning may be delayed until mid-spring and need not go beyond tidying

up. The flowers are single, sulphur-yellow in clusters. 'New Dawn' repeats its blush-pink double blooms until early autumn and needs only light pruning. 'Helen Knight' (1977) seems more like a wide shrub rose than a climber, with good yellow flowers for two months in spring. The long arching shoots may be cut back to 0.9m (3ft) when flowering ceases.

PILLAR ROSES

Repeat-flowering on wood of the current year. Usually of upright habit, not more than 3m (10ft) high. The pillar is best made of timber, failing the real thing of stone or good brick. Suitable plants include 'Aloha' (1949) deep pink, fragrant; 'Golden Showers' (1956) golden fading to cream, foliage dark green; 'Swan Lake' (1968) double white, flushed pink; and 'White Cockade' (1969) double pure white, good dark foliage.

For the first two years train the growths to surround the pillar and shorten laterals. Cut off leading shoots at the top of the pillar. Shorten laterals in early spring, to produce flowering spurs.

STANDARD ROSES

Hybrid Teas and Floribunda roses are the usual choice for standard roses in formal designs, not necessarily with bush or shrub roses. The site must not be exposed since the head is liable to be top-heavy, overweighted on one side. On planting the stake must be strong and driven in almost as far as the part which is above ground.

The base of the stem is not exactly elegant and is difficult to conceal without making access to the rose awkward. The weeping standard offers a solution. If a small-flowered (true) Rambler is used, the old growth is removed to a few inches after flowering. If a large-flowered hybrid such as 'Albertine' is chosen, it is cut back to a point immediately above the origin of a new lateral, but the weeping effect may be less easy to achieve.

PILLAR ROSES

Repeat-flowering on wood of the current year, upright habit to around 3m (10ft)

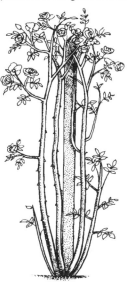

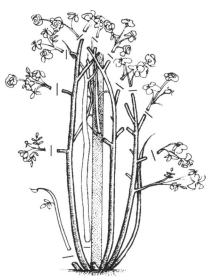

1 The plant is trained to surround the pillar. Summer prune

2 In autumn, flowered laterals are cut back to two buds. Cut out dead, diseased and weak growth

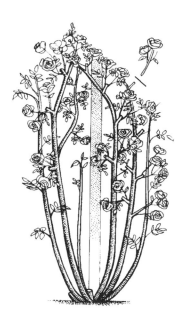

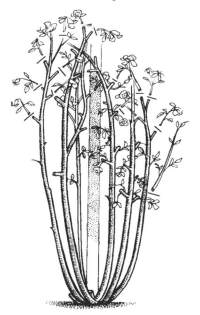

3 Flowering takes place on laterals of old wood. Summer prune

4 In the second and subsequent autumns, cut off leading shoots at the top of the pillar. Shorten laterals sufficiently to keep the plant more or less symmetrical

STANDARD

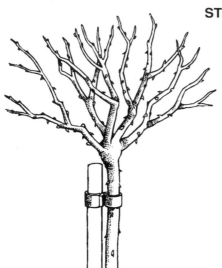

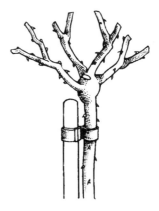

A standard rose at planting.
The main stem is secured to a stout stake

In late winter, cut back stems to 15cm (6in)
or 3-5 eyes, rather less for floribundas, say 6-8
eyes. This is repeated in subsequent years

WEEPING STANDARD

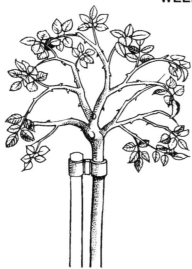

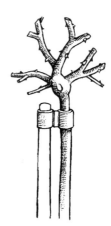

Weeping standard after grafting with
a rambler such as 'Excelsa' or
'François Juranville'

In early spring after planting, cut stems back to
two or three buds. After flowering, cut back old
growth to a few inches for small-flowered
ramblers, to immediately above the origin of
a new lateral for large-flowered plants

Strings attached near the tips of the long stems are then fixed to tent-pegs with slight tension. After two or three months they may be removed.

ROSE HEDGES

A first reaction to the idea of roses used for hedging is one of hesitation. Roses are deciduous, never really evergreen, though the *Sempervirens* sport 'Felicité et Perpétué' does its best. In winter they often look mournful, and after pruning offer only a forecast of pleasure to come. As boundary hedges they may be effective deterrents to intruders, but better plants are available for that purpose – hawthorn or, more sophisticated, the Japanese Bitter Orange, *Poncirus trifoliata*. This is slow-growing, admittedly, but impenetrable, bears fragrant flowers like orange blossom, and does not require pruning.

Only one group of roses springs to mind as hedge-forming: the Rugosas. Some of the best grow easily to a height of 1.2, 1.5, 1.8 or 2.1m (4, 5, 6 or 7ft) with the same spread, and here is a choice.

R. rugosa Many clones and a readiness to hybridise. A good form grows to 1.8 or 2.1m (6 or 7ft), its flowers scented and deep red, hips globular and also red; plenty of them.

R. rugosa 'Alba' Similar but with flowers pure white.

'Blanc Double de Coubert' 1.8×1.5m (6×5ft). Pure white flowers, faint scent, hips few and poor. It tends to be bare at the base, but is recurrent for four months at least.

'Roseraie de l'Hay' 1.5 × 1.5m (5 × 5ft). Big semi-double flowers, strong scent. A vigorous plant of dense habit. Hips negligible, but it flowers throughout summer; therefore remove dead flowers as soon as possible.

'Frau Dagmar Hastrup' 1.5×1.5m (5×5ft) but often lower. Pale pink flowers, faintly scented, over a long season. It is worth sparing some flowers from dead-heading to have a show of hips, which are like tomatoes and freely borne.

'Scabrosa' 1.5 × 1.2m (5 × 4ft). A dense, upright shrub, good dark foliage. Flowers much-scented, silvery pink (if there is such a thing) and freely carried.

On the whole it seems best to have a hedge of one sort only, not mixed, though that is tempting. Pruning of Rugosas is light trimming and that would make such a hedge easy to keep uniform, but not formal. Choose a rose which excels in scent.

HERBACEOUS PLANTS

It is not normal to include herbaceous plants in a discussion of pruning, but the secateurs and even occasionally the saw have worthy tasks to perform in the culture of annual, biennial and perennial plants.

1 Dead-heading by removing individual blooms as they fade in order to promote further flowering. It is thought that this spares the energy which goes into seed formation and directs it to further production of flowering heads. Examples are:

Chrysanthemum frutescens

FRENCH MARGUERITE, is grown from seed or cuttings under glass and is ready to be planted outdoors as soon as the risk of frost is minimal. Individual flowers are cut off as they die. The benefit of this is seen particularly well in cultivars such as 'Jamaica Primrose' with a yellow centre (as all these daisies have) and soft, yellow flowers whose fading is predicted by the darkening to almost black of the centre. If you keep at the job the reward is flowering which continues from midsummer till late autumn.

Dahlia hybrids, grown from tubers which can last for years if stored, away from frost each winter. These are potted up in spring and put out in the border in early summer, when they will flower from late summer until the first frosts. A daily inspection for dying blooms and removal of all of them

down to the foliage (leaving no stumps visible) is rewarded by repeat flowering. *D. merckii*, a hardy perennial in the south of England is treated in the same way.

Erysimum 'Bowles' variety – makes a superb bush of 0.6m (2ft) long stems studded with purple flowers in late spring. If each of these is cut right back to its origin as it fades from below upwards, new stems will soon appear and this process will be repeated until well into autumn, though never approaching the first flush of flower. This plant is perennial in the milder areas though short-lived, especially in rich soil. Cuttings under mist root readily.

2 Dead-heading the whole plant in the expectation of a second flowering. Examples are:

Astrantias have pleasant foliage from which their flower heads rise to 0.6m(2ft) .'Rubra', a form of *A. major*, has plum-coloured flowers and there are recent red cultivars of great promise. If dead-headed after their first flowering in early summer, they rest until the onset of autumn and then produce a crop of flowers as good as the first.

Delphinium hybrids. If the flowering stalks are cut right back after their first performance there is usually a second, less impressive but welcome display several weeks later. In the case of the Belladonna hybrids this repetition is uncertain.

Nepeta faassenii, especially 'Six Hills Giant', possibly a hybrid, which produces a mound of stems about 0.6m (2ft) high all covered in flower in early summer. All fade together and are cut well back in one rather tedious operation (thinking of a border 30 metres long), and by early autumn new growth is ready to repeat the flowering, which is less sumptuous than the first but still desirable. Discriminating cats chew the young growths and roll on them, but disdain the flowers.

Viola cornuta, from the Pyrenees, has evergreen foliage and produces flowers of white or various shades of blue in early summer. The plants like moisture and if that is not available they should be grown in light shade. Once flowering is over they should be cut back with secateurs, or shears if in a large clump. Include the leaves and give a feed so that new leaves and flowers should form

3 Cutting back flower-heads to prevent self-seeding. Examples are:

Chrysanthemum parthenium, FEVERFEW: a prime example. Left to itself it can produce seedlings 100 metres away in every direction. It is a pleasant plant, especially in its golden form, but this is not welcome in carefully designed colour schemes.

Heracleum mantegazzianum makes a huge plant 3m (10ft) high and seeds itself ruthlessly. Though alleged to be biennial, it seems to survive for years where it is not wanted. If it is a nuisance, cut back the main stem before the flowers develop – the Grecian saw makes this easy.

4 To delay flowering. Useful in the culture of some plants, such as:

Meconopsis betonicifolia. If you do not garden on acid soil do not read further, but if you do and enjoy a rather moist climate you should succeed. At the Savill Garden, Windsor it is grown as a perennial with a short life. It is prevented from flowering for one or two years after planting out and then has a flowering life of three or four years.

5 Dead-heading to give the plant a decent appearance. Examples are:

Alchemilla mollis. The flowers appear in early summer and the plant is then most beautiful, with very small greenish-yellow flowers in sprays over hairy rounded leaves of pale green. This is a great self-seeder and not at all easy to dig out from a rock wall, where it thrives. Flowers should therefore be cut off as soon as they fade, together with any leaves which show signs of age. New leaves will quickly form, but there will be no more flowers later in the year.

Doronicum 'Miss Mason', which flowers in spring after the daffodils. The dead flowers are sheared off and the pleasant, heart-shaped shiny leaves are revealed.

Helleborus foetidus is notable for leaf and flower. The leaves are beautifully cut, almost divided and almost black; the flowers are carried on the 0.3m (1ft) long stems in clusters of pale green with an edge of maroon in early spring. Once over they are cut to the ground and the evergreen leaves make a striking ground cover.

Helleborus orientalis has flowers which rise to 0.6m (2ft) above cut leaves of grey-green. It is treated in the same way as *H.foetidus.* A variable plant.

6 To remove foliage to display flowers. Example:

Epimedium pinnatum colchicum is almost evergreen and the leaves in autumn turn red and yellow. As winter ends you should begin to look beneath the canopy of foliage for signs of emerging flower heads. Once you have seen them, cut away all the leaves with shears or secateurs. The flowers will grow to 0.3m (1ft); they are yellow and pleasant but not exciting. New leaves soon appear and make a pleasing ground cover for a year. All epimediums do this.

7 To collect seed of worthwhile plants. There is always satisfaction in raising one's own plants from one's own seed. Examples are:

Hesperis matronalis, SWEET ROCKET, a perennial often treated as biennial because plants deteriorate and produce poor flower heads as they age. They should be 0.9m (3ft) tall and when raised from seed the colour varies from white to lilac on single flowers with good fragrance, which is most marked in the evening. After taking seed the flowering stems can be cut to the ground. The double forms are best avoided as they are unreliable (and not as beautiful). Sweet rocket has been in England since the sixteenth century.

Hibiscus trionum syn *H. africanus* is tender but when raised from seed, which it produces in abundance, sown under glass in spring it can be planted in the open ground when frost no longer threatens, and will flower on a stem of 0.45m (18in). The petals are white with a violet eye. The seed pods are rounded and prominent, attracting light-fingered visitors who cannot resist them. The race to be there before these can be exciting. The flowering season is long – from midsummer to autumn.

Lunaria rediviva. Perennial HONESTY is an unbelievably neglected plant, though introduced in 1596. It tolerates shade well and appreciates a good loamy soil. The flower heads rise to 0.6m (2ft) in spring, the petals being a very attractive white with a blue tinge. The seed pods are white and papery. Though it is barely perennial it also self-seeds freely, so there is no difficulty in maintaining a good group.

Salvia All of the many species need well-drained soil. Most satisfactory from seed is *S. patens* which occasionally survives the mild winters of recent years. The amount of seed varies but is greatest on the dark blue form, least on the pale 'Cambridge Blue'. A mauve form has appeared in the last few years and produced offspring of the same colour, as do the others.

Verbena bonariensis (from Buenos Aires) likes sun and makes a perennial plant 1.2m (4ft) high with branching stems, each with a tuft of lavender blue flowers from early summer until autumn. It seeds itself freely, and seed only needs to be collected as a gift for interested visitors. The plant can be cut down in autumn and is hardy.

Verbena rigida, also perennial, has violet flowers in the same period as *V. bonariensis* and is reasonably hardy – it seldom exceeds one frost.

There are plants which produce beautiful seed heads which might well be dead-headed if this habit was not known.

Actaea alba has light green leaves and small flower heads in late summer, unexpectedly turning into white berries, pea-sized on scarlet stalks. *Actaea rubra* is smaller but the scarlet berries rise above the leaves.

Arum italicum 'Pictum' produces narrow leaves with a marbled effect of very pale green, waved at the edges, which appear in autumn and grow slowly through winter into spring, reaching 0.3m (1ft) long. The pale green flowers appear on a spike and are surrounded by a spathe, a large bract, which is a modified leaf and is green, like those of the wild arum (Lords and Ladies). The flowers and leaves disappear by midsummer and in early autumn spikes carrying bright red berries appear apparently from nowhere. When they finally disappear the whole cycle is repeated. You may feel that all this is hardly worth waiting for, but many do.

Catmint, *Nepeta faassenii* 'Six Hills Giant'
will flower twice in a season if dead flowerstalks
are removed

FRUIT TREES &BUSHES

APPLES AND PEARS

It is said that no one today wants a standard apple or pear tree for a garden, and commercial growers find the smaller and more compact forms easier to manage and more rewarding. A few orchards (or their remains) with old standard trees still exist and very beautiful they are, even producing good clean fruits after eighty years. We, however, must address ourselves to the smaller forms which

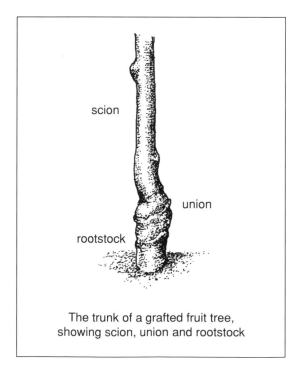

The trunk of a grafted fruit tree, showing scion, union and rootstock

have been made available by research at the John Innes Horticultural Research Institute, Merton, Surrey (opened in 1909, since moved) and East Malling Research Station in Kent (opened in 1913). After the Second World War these establishments were able to create a series of root stocks which could transmit to the scion grafted onto them varying degrees of vigour and produce a plant either dwarf, semi-dwarf, half-standard or standard size. These were the Malling-Merton or MM Stocks. In general use are:

M27	Extremely dwarfing – for vigorous varieties in good soil, kept weed-free.
M9	Very dwarfing – for dwarf bushes, dwarf pyramids and cordons.
M26	Dwarfing for average conditions.
MM106	Semi-dwarfing – widely used for bush, cordons, espaliers. Crops in three to four years.
MM111	Vigorous – on poor soil makes rather small trees; on good soil a large tree, perhaps.

All these stocks have a bred-in resistance to woolly aphids, and in both stock and scion

DISTINGUISHING WOOD BUDS AND
FLOWER BUDS ON FRUIT TREES

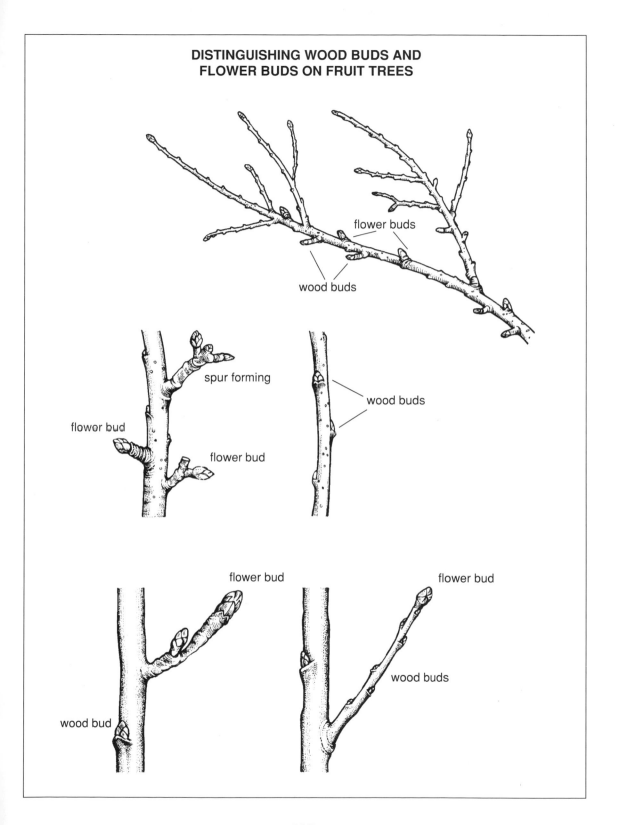

flower buds

wood buds

spur forming

wood buds

flower bud

flower bud

flower bud

flower bud

wood bud

wood buds

PRUNING FOR FRUIT
Spur pruning of mature apples and pears
After the fifth year the growth of the tree slows down. By judicious
pruning it can be encouraged to produce large crops for many years

1 In late winter maiden laterals are
cut back to four buds

3 In the following summer fruit is borne on the
buds which have formed

2 In late winter of the following year these shoots
are cut back to a flower bud

4 A spur system begins to form.
Eventually it will have to be thinned out

Renewal pruning
This depends on the ability of apples and pears to convert growth buds to flower buds on
two-year-old stems which have not been pruned

3 In the following summer/autumn fruit is
borne on this pruned lateral

1 In the first winter a strong lateral is chosen,
but left unpruned

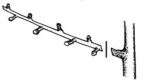

4 In late winter the fruited lateral is cut back
to 2.5cm (1in)

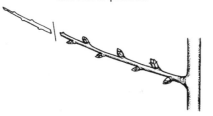

2 In late winter of the following year extension
growth is cut back to where it
joins the old wood

5 At the end of the growth period a strong new
lateral has formed – and the cycle continues

resistance to various viruses has been added by research at East Malling and Long Ashton Research Stations. Pears are grafted onto the Quince A root stock for garden use or Quince C for commercial orchards. There are three main styles of cultivation.

Bush (pruning diagrams pp212-13) The tree is usually grown in private gardens, grafted on M26 as an open-centre tree with main branches radiating from a stem. When planting (in the dormant period) make sure not to bury the stock-graft union (if you do so the graft may put down roots and grow away undwarfed). Next cut back the maiden stem to about 0.6m (2ft). At the end of the

Cordon pears. Those to the left (probably Conference) are bearing well. There is vigorous new growth, and this will be cut back to 7.5cm (3in) in midsummer. Growth of sublaterals from existing side shoots is cut to 2.5cm (1in): this lets light and air into the rather congested centre of the cordon. Note ivy encroaching

growing season (late autumn) there will be primary branches and in winter three or four of these are chosen, with as wide an angle as possible from the main stem and evenly distributed around it. These branches are cut back by half and any surplus, weak branches removed.

At the end of the next (second) season, secondary branches have formed and in winter all the leaders are cut back by one half, any weak ones by two thirds. Prune back any surplus laterals on the inside of the tree to four buds, hoping that they will produce spurs.

At the end of the third season repeat the pruning but leave laterals on the outer side unpruned. After this formal pruning may cease if growth is satisfactory. If flower buds have formed on unpruned laterals, cut back to the highest flower bud.

From now on the virtues of the form of growth will appear. All parts are accessible

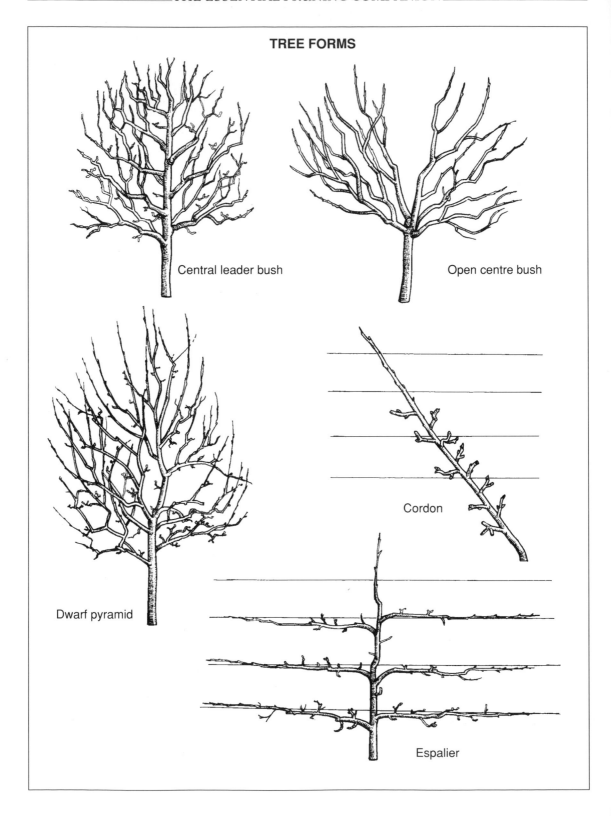

TREE FORMS

Central leader bush

Open centre bush

Cordon

Dwarf pyramid

Espalier

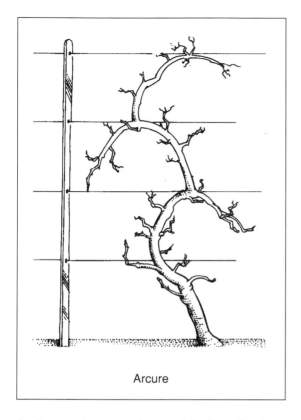

Arcure

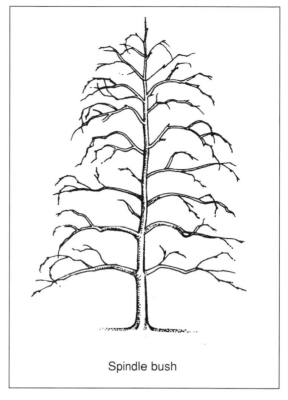

Spindle bush

for inspection, pruning and fruit-gathering.
Cordon (Pruning diagrams pp214-15) This
has the advantage that the stems can be
planted close to each other and thus several
varieties can be grown in a small space. A
dwarfing root stock is necessary and expert
advice is worth seeking locally. The cordon
is best grown at an angle of 45° from upright
so that all parts are handy. Bamboos are tied
to a wire fence and the cordon attached.
When planting see that the graft union is
pointing upwards (some say downwards!),
lest it should break.

At the end of the first season cut back
laterals to four buds and sublaterals to one
bud. Do not prune the leader. In the spring of
the second year remove any flowers as they
appear and in midsummer prune laterals to
three leaves and the basal cluster. Next winter
cut back laterals which were pruned in
summer to the highest flower bud, if any; if
not, to 2.5cm (1in). In the spring see whether

the leader has grown beyond the highest
wire – if so, cut away the new growth. In
midsummer reduce laterals and sublaterals
as before. In winter thin out any overcrowded
spurs.

Espalier (Pruning diagrams pp216-17) Same
principle as the cordon. If starting with a
maiden, plant in winter and cut back to 45cm
(18in). Train the top shoot vertically and the
shoots from lower buds at an angle of 45°. In
early winter depress these shoots to the horizontal and tie in to the wire fence. In the next
years the process is repeated until the three
or four tiers are completed, keeping unwanted laterals from the main stem severely
pruned as necessary.

An ingenious but simple variant of the
espalier is the single-tier or **step-over** form,
grafted on M27 root stock and used along-
side a path, perhaps in the vegetable garden,
or as a double edge to a path. It is best with
the same apple on each side, carrying a small

burden of fruit; only the choicest.

A brilliant and beautiful extension of the espalier system is the **arcure**, invented in Belgium and shown on p209. It seems to work well and is easy to manage.

Irresistible is the **Ballerina** or **Columnar** tree, which is upright and narrow and was born in British Columbia in 1964 as 'Wijerik', a sport of 'McIntosh'. It grows as if an upright cordon and the fruit is borne on short spurs quite close together. It should succeed.

Fan This method of training was originally devised to take advantage of the shelter and reflected warmth from walls. Those which are south facing are ideal for sweet cherries, apricots, greengages, peaches, nectarines and plums, as well as choice apples and pears, the latter two doing well in an open situation, as may be seen to perfection at the gardens of the Royal Horticultural Society at Wisley, Surrey. Today, fan training has largely given way in private gardens to cor-

ABOVE:
Espalier pear. Winter pruning has been carried out well, but the branches should be spaced a little more widely

OPPOSITE:
Fan training seems to have lost favour in private gardens, but is highly successful in the hands of experts, as with the fan-trained Conference pear at the Royal Horticultural Society's garden at Wisley shown in this photograph

dons and espaliers, which are more economic of space.

The technique is much the same for all the fruits mentioned above (pruning diagrams pp222-3, 226-7). A wall needs to be at least 1.8m (6ft) high and 4.5m (15ft) wide. It saves time to start with a feathered tree, which should have a branch on each side about

(continued on p219)

APPLES AND PEARS: bush tree

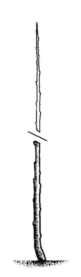
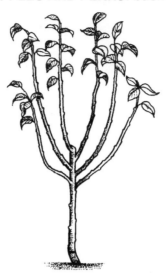
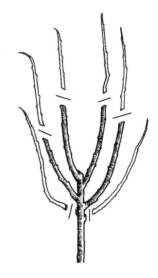

1 Maiden tree
at planting in winter.
Cut back by half

2 Vigorous new growth
has resulted

3 By the following winter
strong branches have formed.
Retain the best four,
cutting them back by half

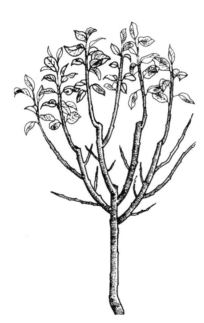
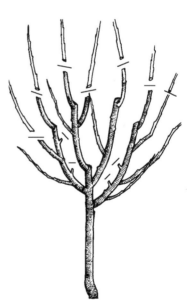

4 By the end of the second year
secondary branches have formed

5 Choose four more branches to become
part of the framework. Cut back strong leaders
by half, weaker ones by two-thirds.
Remove weak shoots

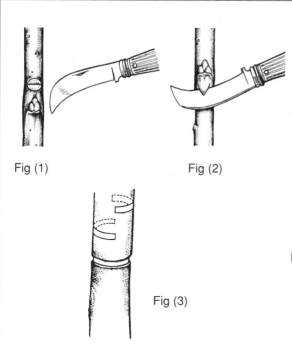

Fig (1)　　　　　Fig (2)

Fig (3)

Notching is the removal of a small triangle or semi-circle of bark above a dormant bud (Fig 1). It aims to stimulate the bud into growth by cutting off the flow of sap from the leaves and is carried out in late spring. It is used to influence the placing of active buds and to lessen the chance of unduly long stems without buds. Nicking is the same act applied below a bud and has the opposite effect, inhibiting bud growth. (Fig 2).

Bark ringing aims to promote the production of fruit buds and to cut down that of growth buds. This is achieved by interrupting the flow of food and hormones from the leaves and upper buds in the phloem channel. A ring of bark 0.5cm (¼in) wide is cut out as deep as the hard wood 0.6m (2ft) above ground level. This is done in late spring, making it possible for the ring to heal before growth ceases in autumn. A wider cut will probably kill the tree. If your courage fails, cut two semi-circles as in (Fig 3), and that may suffice.

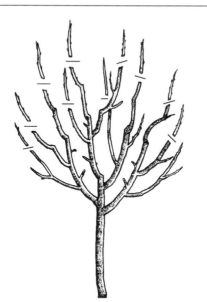

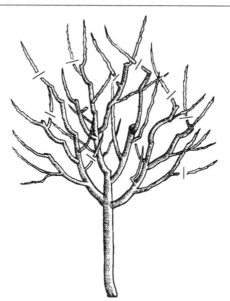

6 By the third year the main leaders are established. In winter strong leaders are reduced by half the current year's growth, weaker ones by two-thirds

7 Mature tree in winter. Pruning of the leaders is no longer necessary, and laterals on the outer growths are left unpruned. Laterals at the centre are cut back to a few inches, weak stems to 2.5cm (1in)

APPLES AND PEARS: cordon

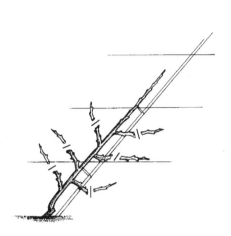

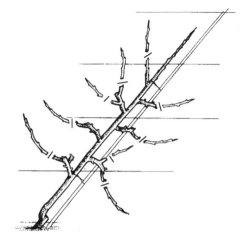

1 In the first winter, cut back any laterals to four buds. Do not prune the leader

2 At the end of the first growing season, cut back laterals to four buds, sublaterals to two buds

3 The following spring, remove flowers as they appear

4 In summer, prune laterals to three leaves and the basal cluster

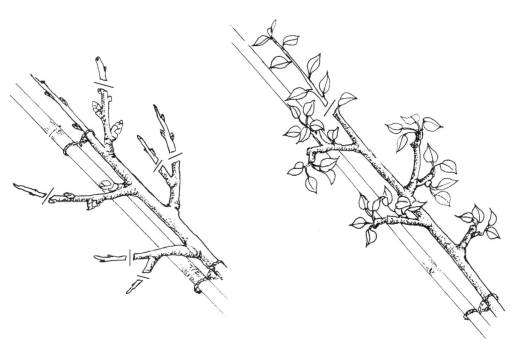

5 In winter, cut back pruned laterals to the highest flower bud, or 2.4cm (1in)

6 In spring, once the leader has passed the top wire cut the extension wood back to its origin

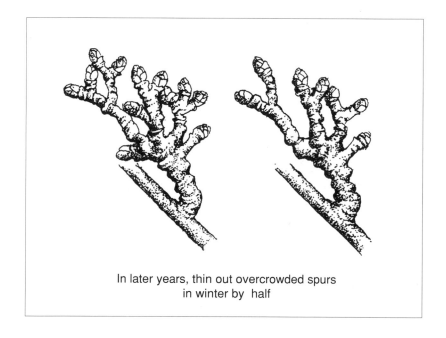

In later years, thin out overcrowded spurs in winter by half

APPLES AND PEARS: espalier

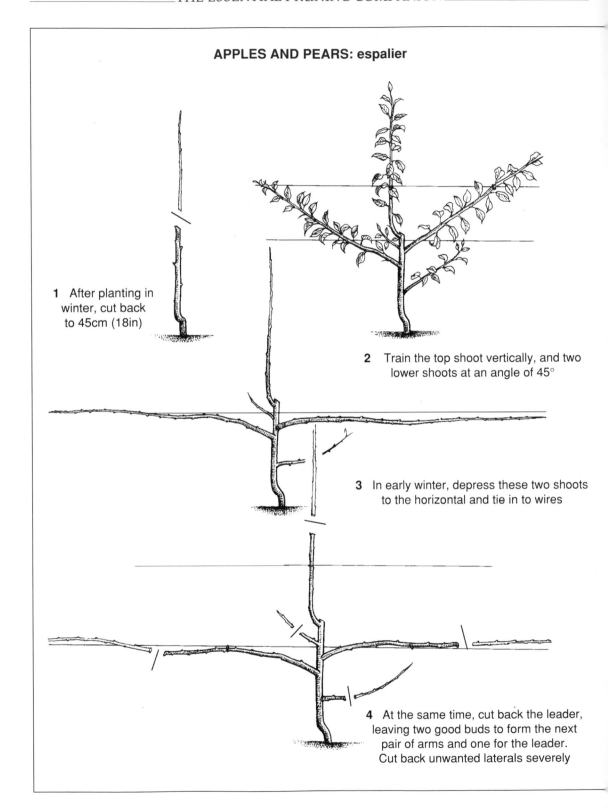

1 After planting in winter, cut back to 45cm (18in)

2 Train the top shoot vertically, and two lower shoots at an angle of 45°

3 In early winter, depress these two shoots to the horizontal and tie in to wires

4 At the same time, cut back the leader, leaving two good buds to form the next pair of arms and one for the leader. Cut back unwanted laterals severely

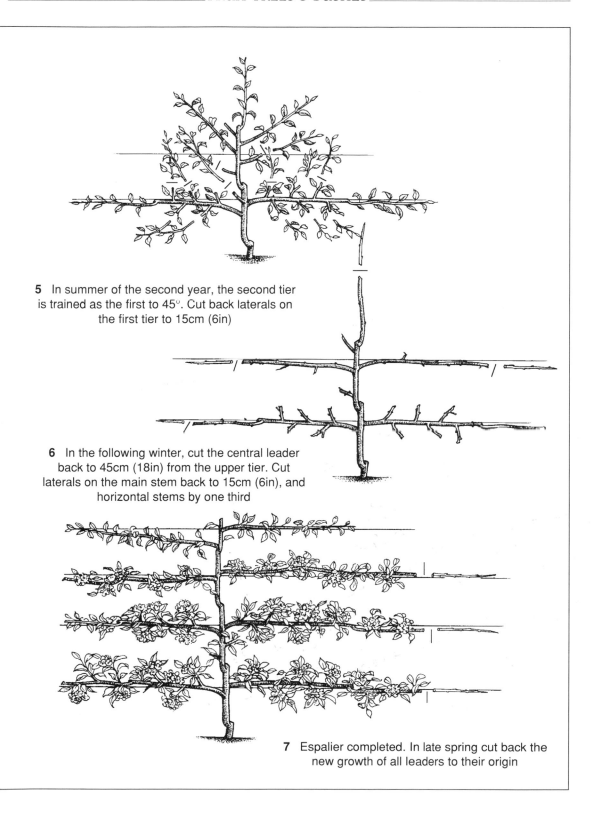

5 In summer of the second year, the second tier is trained as the first to 45°. Cut back laterals on the first tier to 15cm (6in)

6 In the following winter, cut the central leader back to 45cm (18in) from the upper tier. Cut laterals on the main stem back to 15cm (6in), and horizontal stems by one third

7 Espalier completed. In late spring cut back the new growth of all leaders to their origin

APPLES AND PEARS: dwarf pyramid

1 At planting, cut back to 45cm (18in)

2 In the following winter, cut back the leader to 22cm (9in) of new growth, the side branches to slightly less

3 The following summer, cut back any laterals not required to a few inches

4 In the second winter, cut back the leader to a bud facing the opposite way from before, to leave about 30cm (1ft) of new growth. Cut back laterals to 20cm (8in)

5 In the third and subsequent summers, prune laterals to 10cm (4in) and sublaterals as far as the basal cluster

6 In winter, cut back the leader to leave about 30cm (1ft) of new growth. Cut back branches as necessary to outward-facing buds to maintain shape

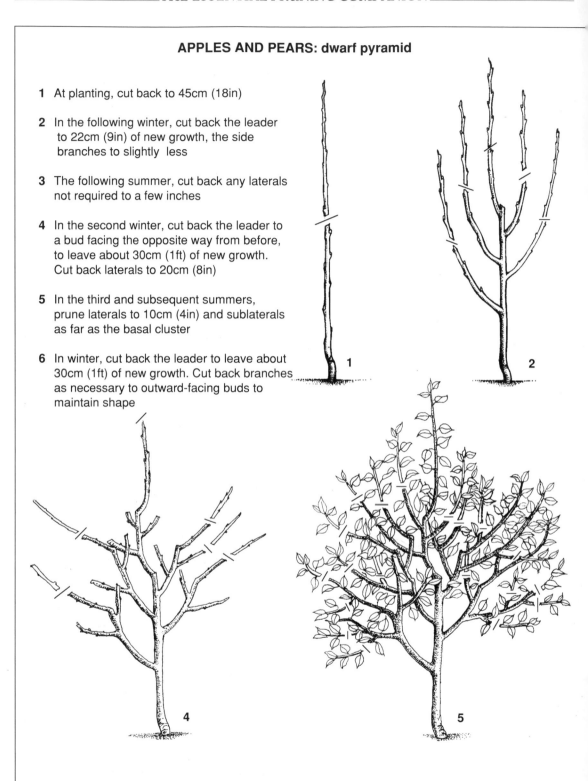

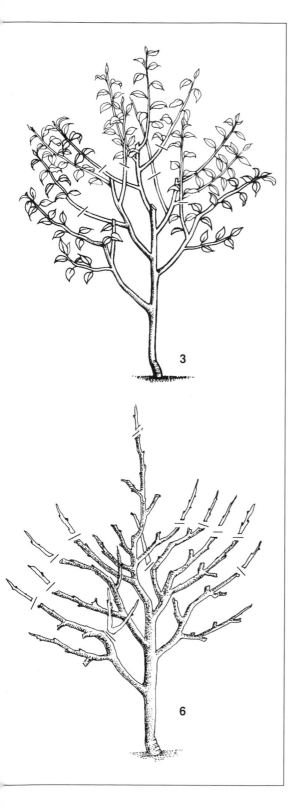

0.3m (1ft) above ground level. Other branches are removed and these two are cut back to 0.5m (18in). In the following season try to develop four good laterals on each side, two growing upwards and one downwards, leaving the centre more or less open. Side shoots will be shortened to 5cm (2in).

PLUMS

Plums descend from *Prunus spinosa* (sloe, blackthorn) and *P. cerasifera* (Cherry Plum, myrobalan), both of which come from Asia Minor where they have interbred for centuries. Their history in Britain is particularly concerned with the Laxton family of Rivers, Sawbridgeworth, Herts, who introduced a succession of plums and damsons from the 1830s for over a hundred years.

Plums are well suited to the average garden as long as they have a situation which is not north-facing and some protection from late frosts. Particular care should be taken to avoid frost pockets. Pruning has hazards, notably silverleaf disease, due to a fungus producing a toxic substance which circulates in the sap having entered through a wound, most often that of pruning. The leaves appear silvery compared with those unaffected, and that part of the tree will die. The only treatment is to remove all affected parts, cutting back until the cut surface is clear. Do this by mid-July as the risk has by then diminished. All the removed wood must be burnt at once. Naturally the pruning of plums and other plants of the *Prunus* genus should be restricted to late summer and autumn.

Some plums can be grown from suckers, for instance 'Pershore Egg', 'Warwickshire Drooper', and 'Cambridge Gage'. Most are grown on root stocks on which the growth is fairly compact. Two are now recommended, 'St Julien A' and more recently 'Pixy'. Plant a maiden tree in the dormant season. Cut the stem to about 1.5m (5ft), just above a bud.

Primary branches appear in summer but
(continued on p223)

PLUMS AND DAMSONS: bush tree

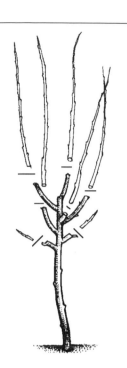

LEFT:

1 At planting the leader was cut back to 1.5m (5ft) and the laterals to 7-10cm (3-4in). Now primary branches have grown

RIGHT:

2 In early spring of the following year, choose four branches evenly distributed round the stem and cut back by half. Cut back laterals to a few inches

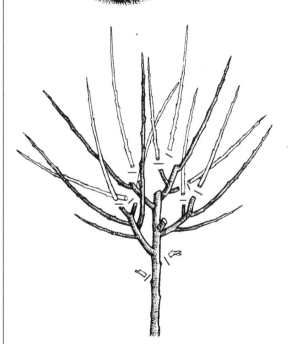

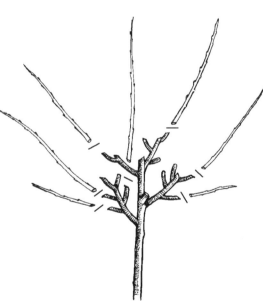

3 In winter of the third year choose four more branches and cut back all eight leaders by half. Remove all low laterals

4 At this time, also cut back laterals on the inside of the bush to 7-10cm (3-4in). In subsequent years, if growth is strong and branches pointing in the right direction, pruning of leaders need not continue. Weaker growth should be pruned as in the third year

PLUMS AND DAMSONS: dwarf pyramid

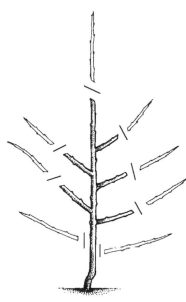

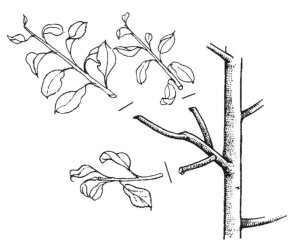

2 In summer cut back laterals to 20cm (8in), and sublaterals to 15cm (6in) above downward-pointing buds

1 A feathered maiden planted in winter. At bud break in early spring, remove laterals up to 45cm (18in) from ground level. Cut back laterals above this by half

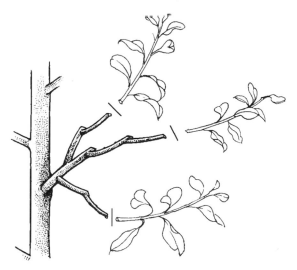

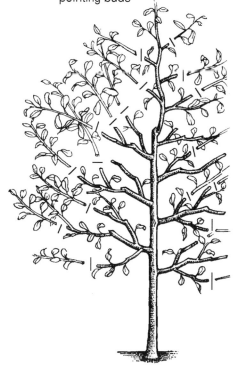

3 The following summer, cut back leaders to 20cm (8in), and laterals to 15cm (6in)

4 The following and subsequent summers, cut back branch leaders to 20cm (8in), and laterals to 15cm (6in)

SWEET CHERRIES: fan

1 In early summer of the first year, select two strong shoots and tie in to canes. Remove all other shoots

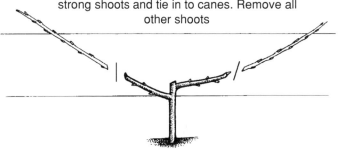

2 In the following spring, shorten each leader to about 30cm (1ft)

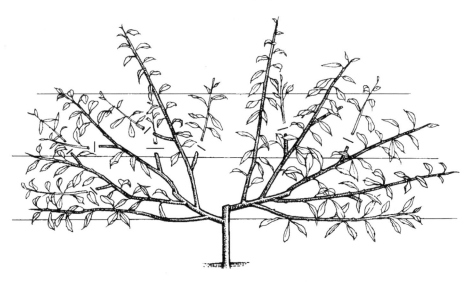

3 Tie in four to six strong shoots from each leader, leaving the centre of the plant empty. Cut back sublaterals to 7-10cm (3-4in)

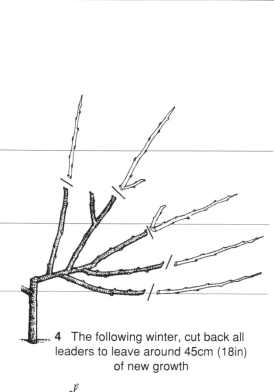

4 The following winter, cut back all leaders to leave around 45cm (18in) of new growth

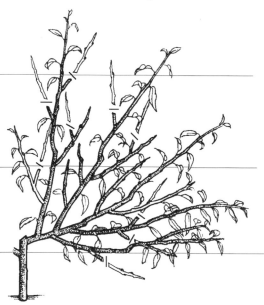

5 In summer, tie in shoots and cut back sublaterals to 7.7-10cm (3-4in)

no pruning is needed until early spring of the next year. Then cut back well-spaced branches by about one half, or rather more, to an outward pointing bud. Remove any surplus branches. Any laterals from the main stem are cut back to 7.5cm (3in) or so . In the third year prune as before in early spring, allowing some sub-laterals to develop, but cutting them back by one half. At the end of the season allow four more branches to remain but cut back laterals on the inside of the bush to 7.5cm (3in). Pruning then ceases.

Plums can also be grown as dwarf pyramids, in the same way as apples or pears. Damsons are grown in the same fashion as plums but with less severe pruning at every stage.

CHERRIES

Sweet cherries These present a problem for the average gardener. They make large trees, 12m (40ft) or more across, and need a dwarf-

A fan-trained Morello cherry: self-fertile, not too vigorous and does well on a north-facing wall. What more can you ask? As shown, it will flower profusely. If it fruits well, try to make sure that there is enough young wood to replace that which has fruited

SWEET CHERRIES: fan
Fruiting spurs

1 From the fourth year onwards, in summer cut out all breastwood and backward-growing shoots. Cut all sublaterals to 15cm (6in)

2 In early autumn, reduce all sublaterals cut in summer to 10cm (4in), to create spurs on which flower buds will form the following year

MORELLO CHERRIES: bush tree

For early training, follow pruning instructions for bush plums and damsons, p220

BELOW:
2 At bud break the following spring and in subsequent years, cut back some older branches to the origin of young shoots. Leave leaders unpruned

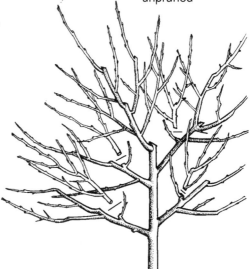

ABOVE:
1 In early spring of the third year, prune all leaders by half to outward-pointing buds to produce an even framework

ing root stock 'Colt' not yet widely available. Also one must have at least two different plants which are compatible, as all these cherries are self-sterile and cannot produce fruit on their own. Fan training can solve the problem of space up to a point, and is carried out in the same way as for apples. Starting with a maiden tree cut back to 0.3m (1ft). Pruning has to be severe in the period of forming the framework (see pp222-4).

Morello cherries are a relief to the gardener after the sweet variety. They are self-fertile, their growth is more restrained and they do perfectly well on a north-facing wall. As they flower on wood made in the previous year it is necessary to make sure that there is enough young wood coming on to replace that which has fruited. The early training of a bush tree is very like that of a bush plum, with an open centre. The bush is trained on a leg of about 0.9m (3ft) and the leaders cut back in early spring for four or five years. Some of the older shoots are pruned to one-year-old laterals on young growth just appearing. In time, perhaps ten years, the tree may need rejuvenation by cutting back main branches to within 1.5m (5ft) of their origin. Fan training is not often satisfactory.

PEACHES AND NECTARINES

It is difficult to be enthusiastic about a fruit tree which is more likely than not to produce a small, even negligible crop in most years in Britain. It is not difficult to form a framework by using lateral growths from a featured plant, by cutting back the leading shoots by one half at the end of the first and second seasons. If a wall is available, fan training may be a partial solution.

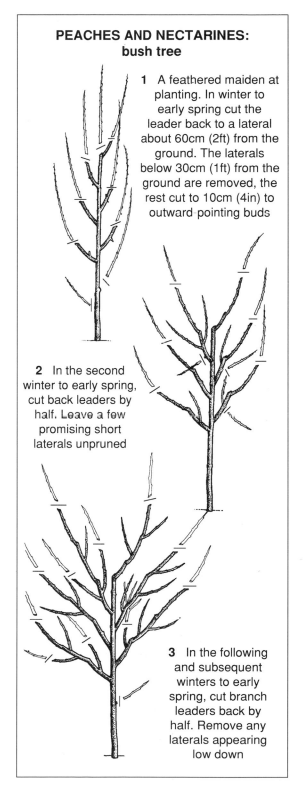

PEACHES AND NECTARINES: bush tree

1 A feathered maiden at planting. In winter to early spring cut the leader back to a lateral about 60cm (2ft) from the ground. The laterals below 30cm (1ft) from the ground are removed, the rest cut to 10cm (4in) to outward-pointing buds

2 In the second winter to early spring, cut back leaders by half. Leave a few promising short laterals unpruned

3 In the following and subsequent winters to early spring, cut branch leaders back by half. Remove any laterals appearing low down

PEACHES AND NECTARINES: fan

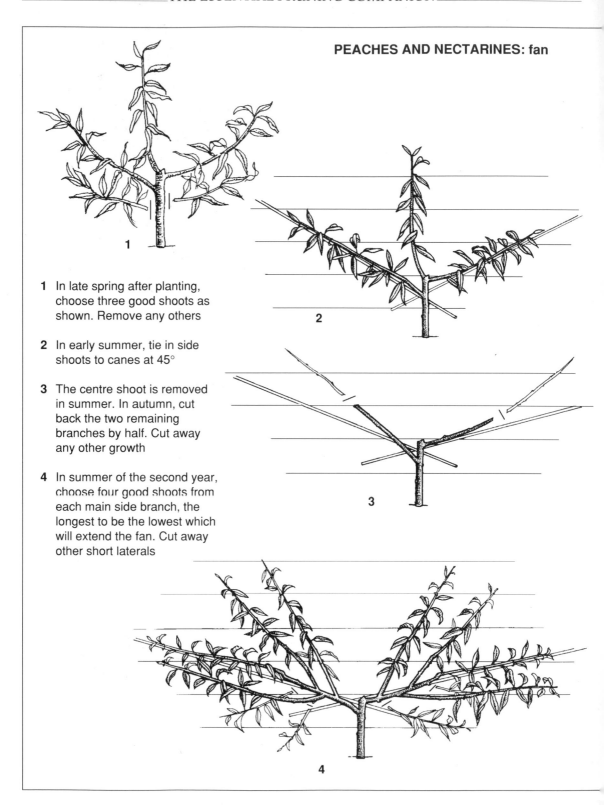

1 In late spring after planting, choose three good shoots as shown. Remove any others

2 In early summer, tie in side shoots to canes at 45°

3 The centre shoot is removed in summer. In autumn, cut back the two remaining branches by half. Cut away any other growth

4 In summer of the second year, choose four good shoots from each main side branch, the longest to be the lowest which will extend the fan. Cut away other short laterals

5 In late winter of the third year, shorten leaders by one third

6 In summer, choose three shoots from each leader. Cut out any others

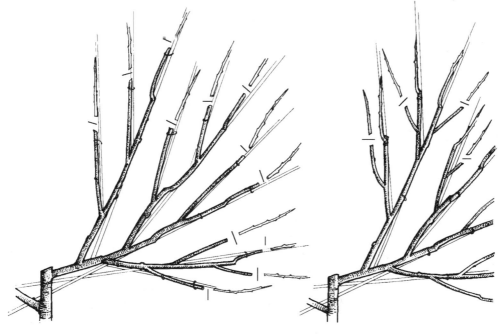

7 In the following winter, prune back the leaders lightly by one quarter

8 In subsequent years, prune any laterals which need to extend to form the fan by one third to one half

FIGS: fan

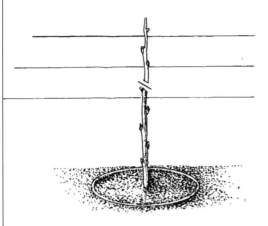

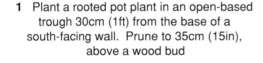

1 Plant a rooted pot plant in an open-based trough 30cm (1ft) from the base of a south-facing wall. Prune to 35cm (15in), above a wood bud

2 By summer, laterals have formed and are tied to supports. Remove misplaced growth

FIGS

The natural home of the fig is the Mediterranean basin from Syria to the Canaries. However, Smyrna figs and Capri figs have been introduced to California, together with the insect which fertilises them, and they are now well established there and in the Mexican Gulf states. In Britain they ripen in sheltered positions in the milder areas but are mostly grown under glass. Think twice before embarking on fig cultivation. Figs are not hardy, are very vigorous, and need careful and detailed pruning. Their fruit is damaged by birds and wasps. The young shoots can develop a grey mould in a wet year and canker at any time. They must be watered frequently in dry weather. However, figs are self-fertile and in a climate with little or no frost are worth trying.

The site must have all possible sun and the roots must be restricted if any fruit is to develop. An open–based trough 0.6 × 0.6 × 0.6m (2×2×2ft) with its top just above ground level will do, with the sides made of paving or bricks, while the bottom contains broken bricks or rubble to stop tap roots forming. This trough is built against a wall which must be at least 3m (10ft) high and as much wide. The trough is filled with good soil and a well-rooted pot plant installed.

It is pruned to 38cm (15in), cutting above a wood bud, in early spring. In summer tie in the laterals which will have developed, spacing them 45cm (18in) apart. Cut out any shoots coming forward from the wall, and any arising from the base. In the following spring cut back the shoots, now forming the framework, by about half. In summer tie in the laterals to canes and remove basal shoots. The canes should be at least 45cm (18in) apart and laterals should be 22cm (9in) from each other. In summer of the following (third) year, tie in extension growths and stop them *(continued on p231)*

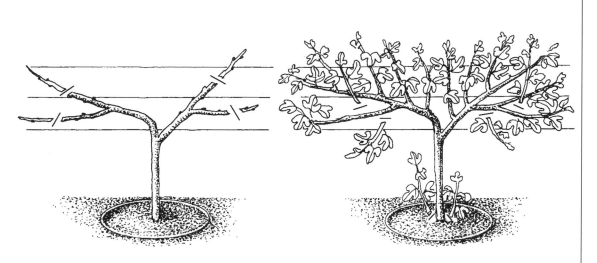

3 In early spring, cut back shoots by half

4 In summer, tie in laterals and remove basal and misplaced shoots

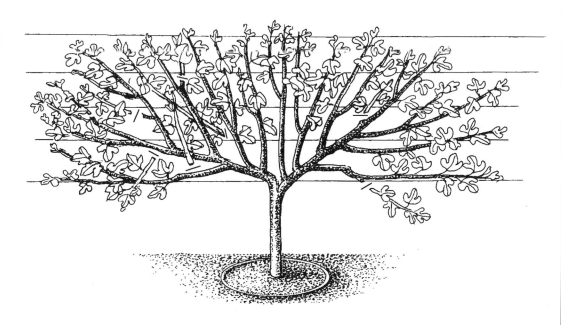

5 The following summer, tie in extension growths of the main ribs, and cut them when they have filled the wall space

FIGS: fan *(continued)*

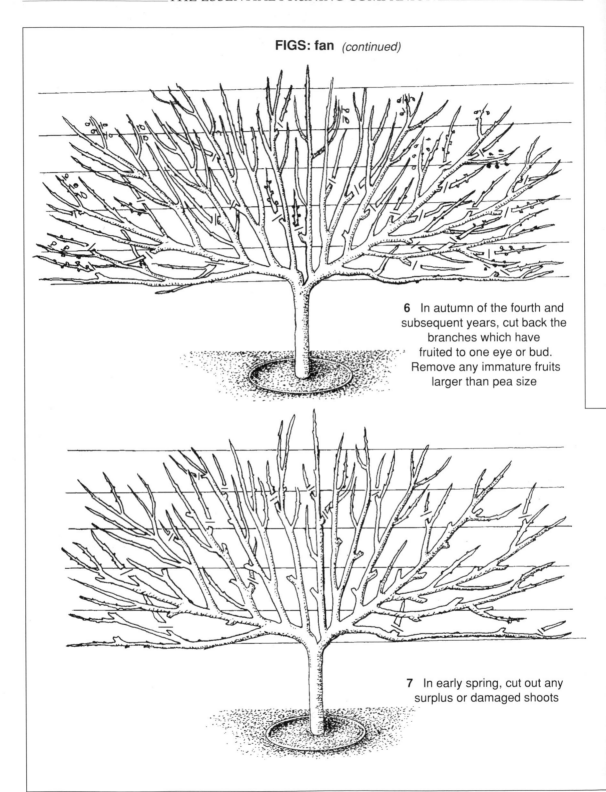

6 In autumn of the fourth and subsequent years, cut back the branches which have fruited to one eye or bud. Remove any immature fruits larger than pea size

7 In early spring, cut out any surplus or damaged shoots when the framework covers the allotted wall space. In late summer embryo figs, the size of a pea, will appear on young shoots and the best of them will survive and ripen. This is more likely if they are near the base of the plant, so it may be worth picking off those that are near the tip rather than at the base of shoots, as soon as they are seen. When the fruit crop is gathered only the best branches should be left unpruned and tied in after being spaced out to 15cm (6in), preferably more. From then on a succession of fruit and second-year growth should be maintained by cutting out some old and unfruitful stems from time to time.

CURRANTS

Red and white currants Can be grown on cordons, espaliers and fans. Cordons are simplest. On planting shorten the central leader by half and all the laterals to 2.5cm (1in). Next winter, and each subsequent one, repeat this shortening of the leader until it reaches 1.5 or 1.8m (5-6ft). In summer the laterals are pruned to about 10cm (4in), then in winter they are reduced to 2.5cm (1in) and will in time make fruiting spurs. Each winter the leader is cut back to a single bud, then in summer it and all laterals are reduced to 10cm (4in). And so on.

Bird damage is a serious threat to the crop of these currants and may delay the pruning programme. Both buds and fruit appeal to bullfinches, tits and sparrows. Only a fruit cage is really effective and it is as well to group all soft fruits under one cage. The top

(continued on p234)

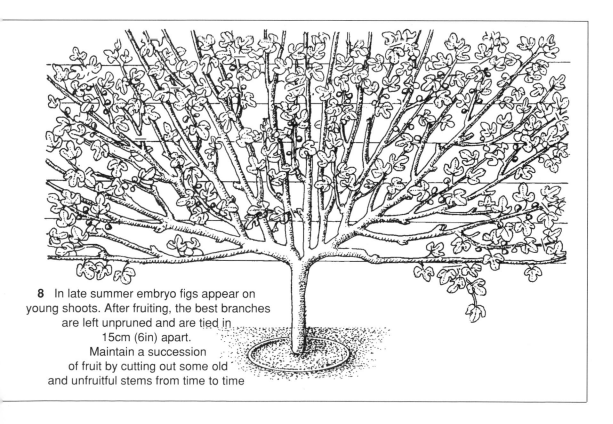

8 In late summer embryo figs appear on young shoots. After fruiting, the best branches are left unpruned and are tied in 15cm (6in) apart. Maintain a succession of fruit by cutting out some old and unfruitful stems from time to time

REDCURRANTS: bush

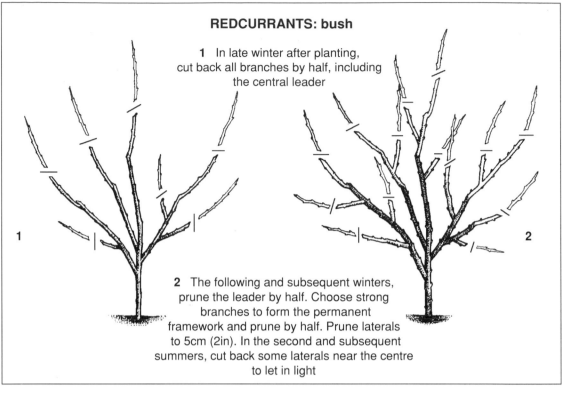

1 In late winter after planting, cut back all branches by half, including the central leader

1

2

2 The following and subsequent winters, prune the leader by half. Choose strong branches to form the permanent framework and prune by half. Prune laterals to 5cm (2in). In the second and subsequent summers, cut back some laterals near the centre to let in light

BLACKCURRANTS

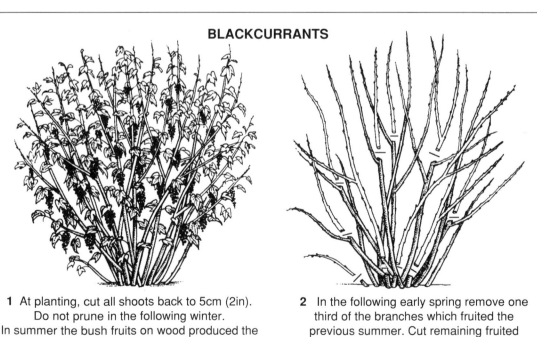

1 At planting, cut all shoots back to 5cm (2in). Do not prune in the following winter. In summer the bush fruits on wood produced the previous year. New growths appear at the base

2 In the following early spring remove one third of the branches which fruited the previous summer. Cut remaining fruited branches to vigorous new growth. Repeat this process each year

REDCURRANTS: cordon

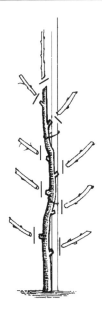

1 In the first summer, train the leader vertically, tying in to its support. Cut back all laterals to 10cm (4in)

2 In the following winter, prune the leader by half the previous season's growth. Cut back laterals to 2.5cm (1in)

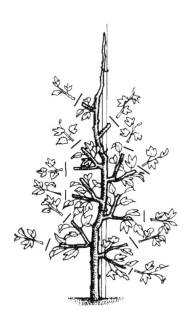

3 In the second summer, train the leader vertically. Cut back laterals to 10cm (4in). Repeat steps 2 and 3 until the cordon has reached the required height

4 Fully developed cordon. Cut back the leader and laterals to 10cm (4in) in summer. Each winter, cut back the leader to one bud of the summer's growth and all laterals to 2.5cm (1in)

of the cage can be covered by fish netting while the buds are forming, and the net can be removed at flowering time to be replaced as the fruits ripen. Insects avoid nets, which is not helpful to pollination.

Blackcurrants Need cultivation which is completely different from the above. They produce the best fruit on one-year-old wood, though some less good on older wood. They need plenty of manuring.

At planting, cut down the plant (one or two years old) to 2.5 or 5cm (1 or 2in) from ground level. Strong shoots will be made, up to 0.6m (2ft) long. In the following autumn cut away the weakest of the shoots. In the next year fruit is borne on all the shoots in midsummer, and then in the dormant season you should remove about one third of the branches to the base and any weak shoots. One year later again remove about one third of the old branches and cut others to a point where there are vigorous laterals. Continue this annual routine.

GOOSEBERRIES

Gooseberries are not demanding in their soil needs, but they can be very exacting for the pruner if the spur system is used. As they do not rate highly among fruits with most people in Britain – Lancashire and Yorkshire excepted – a simple method of culture is probably adequate. It produces more fruit than the spur pruning used in cordons, but the fruit will be smaller and have less flavour. I have to confess that an overdose of gooseberry fool as a schoolboy leaves the author with a lifelong distaste for the fruit.

The simple method is as follows:

At the end of the growing season, after winter planting, six or eight branches are chosen and cut back by one half to buds which point upward. In the winter of the second year leaders are cut back by one half, but laterals are left unpruned. After that there is no more pruning. Fruit is borne on two-year-old shoots and on spurs, if any form.

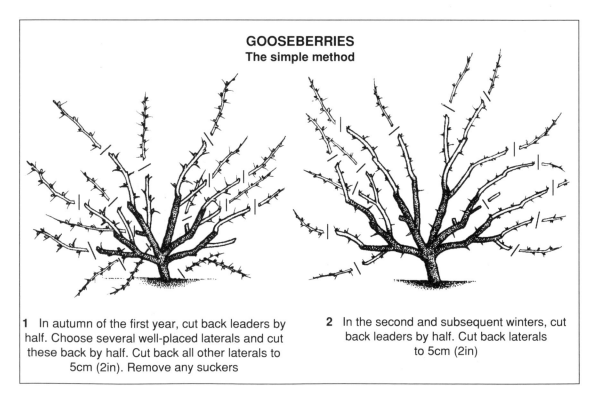

GOOSEBERRIES
The simple method

1 In autumn of the first year, cut back leaders by half. Choose several well-placed laterals and cut these back by half. Cut back all other laterals to 5cm (2in). Remove any suckers

2 In the second and subsequent winters, cut back leaders by half. Cut back laterals to 5cm (2in)

Triple cordons are ideal for gooseberry training, making the maximum use of the space available. Heavy crops may need thinning. In winter the side shoots are pruned to three buds, and are shortened in early summer to five leaves. The variety shown here is 'Whinham's Industry'

The close spur system used on upright cordons produces fruits of large size and better flavour. After planting in midwinter, branches are cut back by one half. At the end of the first growing season, the extension growth is cut back by one half. Choose shoots to make new branches and cut them also back by one half. Cut back other side shoots to 5cm (2in). In the following summer clear the centre somewhat by cutting back laterals, making it easier to gather fruit. Next winter, cut back leaders by one half. Cut back laterals to 5cm (2in).

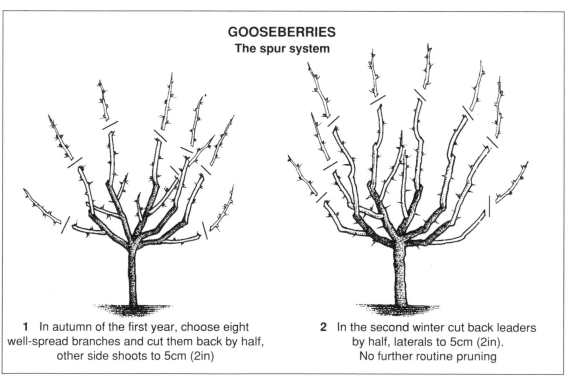

GOOSEBERRIES
The spur system

1 In autumn of the first year, choose eight well-spread branches and cut them back by half, other side shoots to 5cm (2in)

2 In the second winter cut back leaders by half, laterals to 5cm (2in). No further routine pruning

RASPBERRIES

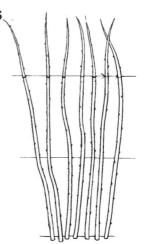

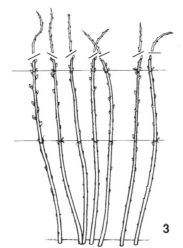

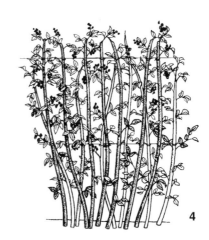

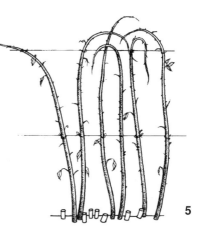

1 In the first season after planting canes are tied in 10cm (4in) apart. No fruiting

2 By autumn of the first year tying in is complete

3 In late winter, dead or failing tops are removed

4 In midsummer, fruiting takes place on last year's canes. New growth developing at the base is thinned to 10cm (4in) apart

5 In autumn, cut all fruited canes to ground level. Tie in new canes, and if growth is vigorous loop the canes over

RASPBERRIES

Need regular manuring and potash. The canes are supported by wires stretched between posts about 1.5m (5ft) high, only two strands being necessary. For short people the top wire can be at 0.9-1.2m (3-4ft), the canes arching over as the plants grow beyond this height.

Summer-fruiting raspberries are cut to about 25cm (10in) on planting in autumn or winter. There will be no fruiting in the following summer but new canes will appear in spring and the old stumps are removed. The canes are tied to supports as they grow, and any not required are removed. In the next early spring any shoots damaged in winter should be cut back to healthy wood. Flower-ing and fruiting occur in midsummer and any new growth is thinned to leave enough shoots to develop at 10cm (4in) intervals to fruit in the following year. In early autumn cut back the fruited canes to ground level. Tie in the new canes.

Autumn raspberries are not just a poor relation. The varieties 'Autumn' or 'Zeva' have excellent flavour, their only problem being the weather in early autumn, which can be excellent or the reverse. They need the same supports and the same pruning in the first year as the summer-fruiting raspber-ries. In the second year all canes are cut to the ground in early spring and should fruit in early autumn. Then the pruning of the pre-vious year is repeated, and so on.

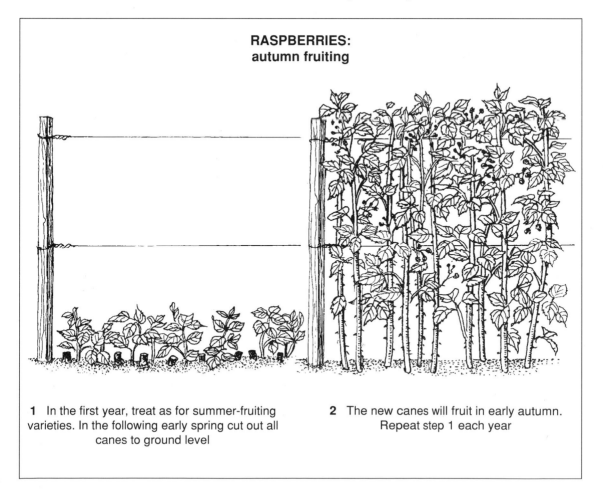

**RASPBERRIES:
autumn fruiting**

1 In the first year, treat as for summer-fruiting varieties. In the following early spring cut out all canes to ground level

2 The new canes will fruit in early autumn. Repeat step 1 each year

BLACKBERRIES

Some will feel that a good deal of the pleasure with blackberries is gathering them in the wild on hedgerows, where the choicest are only just within reach and pruning is not required. The easiest and most satisfactory system of training on wires depends on separating the canes that are flowering this year from those that will do so next year, and training one group to the left, the other to the right. This reduces handling to the minimum. After harvesting, cut the fruited canes down to ground level.

Loganberries can be managed in the same way. They are less vigorous than blackberries and easier to train.

BILBERRIES

Blaeberry, whortleberry, whinberry or blueberry is a British native, naturalised in the USA. The fruit is in season from late summer to early autumn, and is used in pies, tarts, jam and jellies. It may be mixed with another more acid fruit. The bilberry prefers an acid soil and produces shoots from ground level, or from a stool if pruned. The side shoots flower on growth of the previous year and fruit freely, and no pruning is required in the first two years. Manuring is advisable each year to produce berries of good size, while pruning after the first two years involves cutting away of the older shoots after fruiting.

QUINCES

The quince is the Golden Apple of the Ancients who looked upon it as the emblem of love and happiness (see p56). Native of the Mediterranean and Caucasus, it was introduced to Rome from Greece and then taken west, eventually to England. Chaucer speaks of it as growing here in his day. The fruit is either round or pear-shaped with yellow, woolly skin and flesh. The coating of the seed contains a gum with mucilaginous and demulcent properties, which explains why it

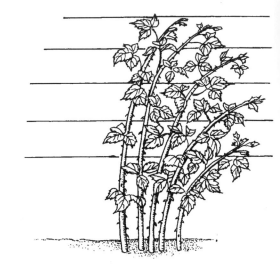

1 Tie all rods in to their supports. No fruiting

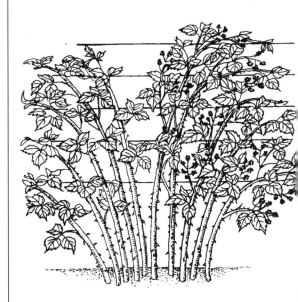

2 In summer, as new rods develop tie them in the opposite direction to the original set. In early autumn, fruit is borne on rods of the previous year

BLACKBERRIES

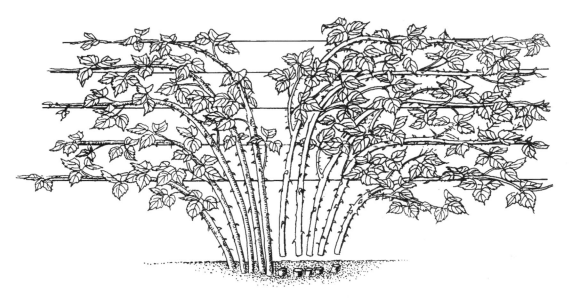

3 After fruiting, cut fruited rods to ground level

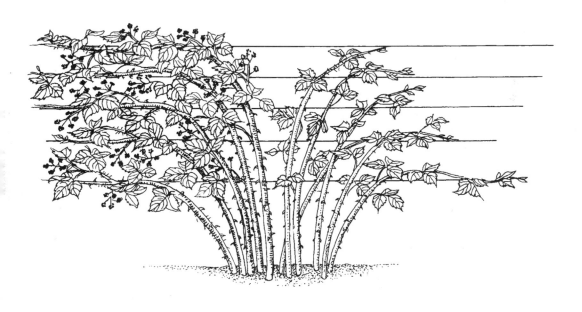

4 In summer, tie in new rods as they develop. In early autumn, fruit is
borne on rods of the previous year

LOGANBERRIES

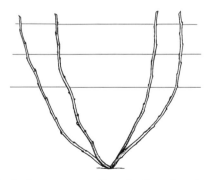

1 In the summer after planting, the stems are trained to wires as shown. In the following early spring cut back the tips so that canes are about 1.5m (5ft) tall

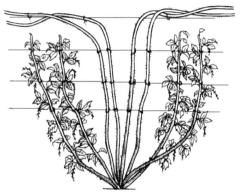

2 New canes are tied in to wires inside old canes as they grow during the summer. In autumn cut away the fruited (outside) canes

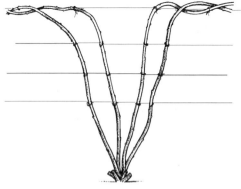

3 Tie in the new canes for fruiting the following year

makes good jam and marmalade. It was, and still maybe, added to apple pies as a routine. It is an excellent garden tree, growing no more than 6m (20ft) high, the head being dense because the branches grow in all directions. The removal of those that rub together is not easy and may damage the natural character of the tree. The flowers, white or pink, are 5cm (2in) across, solitary and produced in late spring. Quince is rarely damaged by frost. The only task is to attempt the control of suckers, which can be abundant.

MEDLARS

Mespilus germanica, comes from Europe and Asia Minor but is not native to Britain, though wild in the south. It makes a tree up to 6m (20ft) with an irregular habit of growth, which is attractive but difficult to describe. The flowers are white or slightly pink, solitary and appearing in late spring. The fruits, 2.5cm (1in) wide, are brown and apple-shaped with an open eye, surrounded by the persistent calyx, the whole again difficult to describe but unforgettable. They are left on the tree till leaf fall, then stored until 'bletted' – meaning about to decay. Pruning has little place but if vertical shoots arise from the branches, as they do at times, they should be cut away. The Latin name, _Mespilus_, derives from the Greek meaning 'half a ball', which well describes the shape of the fruit.

BLACK MULBERRIES

Morus nigra. Probably originated in Persia, but has been cultivated in parts of Europe for thousands of years, in Britain certainly since the early sixteenth century but probably long before. It makes a tree seldom above 6m (20ft) high but much wider, rugged and gnarled. The fruit clusters are dark red, about 2.5cm (1in) long. The taste when fully ripe is agreeable and the fruit can be used in the same way as blackberries. Mulberry gin is said to be far better than that made from sloes or damsons. No positive pruning is needed.

GLOSSARY

Acid See **pH**.

Acuminate Tapering to a sharp point; of leaves, the margins of which curve inwards.

Acute Ending in a point; of leaves, the margins of which are convex.

Adventitious Growth that appears on a plant at a position which it does not normally occupy; as on pollarded trees, or at the top of blackberry canes when they come into contact with the soil.

Alkaline See **pH**.

Alternate Leaves, buds or stems which appear singly, alternating from one side to the other.

Apex The tip of a stem. The apical bud is the uppermost on a stem, the apical shoot the highest on a branching system.

Axil The angle between a leaf stalk and the stem from which it is growing.

Bare-rooted Trees or shrubs lifted in the nursery and delivered without soil round the roots. Containers have largely replaced this practice but they are often less satisfactory, leading to rootbound and inadequately watered stock. The bare-rooted plant, if well looked after, suffers little shock from transplanting.

Bark The surface layer of the trunk and branches of woody plants, protecting the phloem and cambium *(qv)*. It is usually composed of dead, corky cells to which addition is continuously made from within and which allows for the expansion of the woody parts of the plant. Bark can vary in thickness from 1mm in cherries to 30cm (12in) in a Giant Redwood. Shredded bark is now widely used in making composts as an alternative to peat.

Bark ringing Used to encourage fruit trees to produce flower buds and to slow down growth. It involves cutting out a ring of bark not more than 5mm (¼in) wide round the trunk, about 60cm (2ft) above soil level in mid-spring (late April to early May in Britain). This allows the ring to heal during summer. The effect of the cut is to sever the downward flow of food and hormones in the phloem and this stimulates the production of flower buds. If you quail at the idea of this operation, a less drastic procedure is to remove a half-ring or semicircle on opposite sides of the trunk.

Batter The inward slope from base to top of a hedge, said to give a neater finish than a vertical surface, to prevent the hedge becoming top-heavy and to avoid damage from snow. There seem to be many fine hedges cut vertically which suffer no such problems.

Bracts are modified leaves and often resemble the normal leaf. They are found where a flower cluster or stalk arises, and in *Compositæ* form part of the flower itself. Coloured bracts surround very small flowers on some *Cornus* and *Davidia*.

Branch A limb or shoot arising from the trunk of a tree, or a smaller division of such a limb. A primary branch arises from the trunk and a secondary branch arises directly from a primary branch.

Breastwood Shoots which grow forward from fruit trees trained on a wall or as espaliers. Such wood should be removed during summer pruning.

Brutting Partly breaking a one-year shoot at about half its length and leaving it to hang down. It is done to prevent late-summer growth after summer pruning and is typical of hazel-nut cultivation. The brutted shoots are reduced to a few buds in autumn.

Bud A condensed shoot which may contain leaves, flowers or flower clusters, usually protected by scales. Growth or wood buds are usually smaller than fruit or flower buds and are pressed against the stem. The difference, important to the fruit-grower, is fairly easy to discern with practice.

Calcicole Describes a plant which tolerates or prefers an alkaline, limey soil.

Calcifuge A plant which will not tolerate alkaline soils, lime or chalk.

Callus Corky tissue which forms over any wound made on a woody plant and arises from the cambium *(qv)*. If a branch is cut from a tree the callous gradually covers the wound (if it is correctly made) and new bark forms. Callus is found at times at the base of cuttings and new roots may form from it.

Cambium See **Vascular system.**

Chalk Limestone, composed of calcium carbonate in a soft white formation, common in Britain. Calcifuge plants *(qv)* grow weakly and become chlorotic in a chalky soil. If you garden on chalk, spend a week in Cornwall visiting the great gardens and reconcile yourself to a life without rhododendrons or camellias.

Chlorotic Yellowing of leaves due to iron, magnesium or manganese deficiency. Iron deficiency is induced by very alkaline soil conditions; magnesium deficiency is usually due to it being leached from the soil by heavy rain (but also by excess potassium in the soil; manganese deficiency occurs in some sandy soils or clays). These three deficiencies can be corrected by adding the appropriate element, either directly to the soil or by spraying the leaves with ferrous sulphate (iron), magnesium sulphate (Epsom Salts) or manganese sulphate.

Cladode (Phylloclade) A stem which functions as a leaf and may look like one. It carries the flowers, which shows that it is a stem. Examples are Butchers' Broom *(Ruscus aculeatus)* and *Colletia armata.*

Clay An earth composed mainly of aluminium silicate, the basis being very fine particles of sand. In a pure form it is used for making bricks and pottery, but would be impossible for gardening. It does not break up when dry, retains water excessively and bakes hard in dry weather, but is quite fertile and retains fertilisers well. It can be improved by prolonged addition of leaf mould, compost or shredded wood.

Clean Of trunk or stem without shoots or branches.

Clone A clone is composed of plants all produced vegetatively from cuttings, budding, grafting or division from one parent plant, or a descendant using the same methods. These plants have the identical character of the parent and constitute a clone. Seed will never achieve this uniformity.

Coppicing Cutting away new growths arising from the base of a tree or shrub. In gardening it is mainly used to produce coloured young growth of stems (and sometimes leaves) on some willows or cornus, but also to provide very large leaves for ground cover when using ailanthus, eucalyptus, catalpa, and paulownia. It can be called stooling.

Crotch The junction of primary branches with the trunk of a tree. The branches are especially liable to break away if two limbs of equal size have formed the crotch.

Cultivar A plant variation which has originated in cultivation, not in the wild, and is sufficiently distinct to have a name of its own. In the wild such a novelty would be a 'variety' but the distinction is not always easy to make.

Dioecious Describes a plant which carries male and female flowers on separate plants. The pollination difficulty is solved in part by planting one male among several females. A nursery may help in deciding the sex of a plant (see **Monoecious**).

Entire Describes leaves with smooth margins.

Epicormic Such shoots (water shoots) are derived from adventitious buds which form beneath the bark of woody plants but move out with the cambium and are near the surface. When the main shoot is damaged they erupt and grow out from the bark. They are common on fruit trees but very few conifers produce them. They seem to occur for no apparent reason on European limes, at the base of the tree.

Eye A dormant bud, normally on a grape vine.

Fastigiate Of narrow erect growth, eg the Lombardy Poplar.

Feeding The application of elements essential for plant growth. Nitrogen, phosphorus and potassium are the basis of fertilisers, often with the addition of very small quantities of a few other elements, notably copper, iron and manganese (trace elements), which should be used with caution as they may be harmful in excess as much as in inadequate quantity. Carbon, hydrogen and oxygen are taken up from the air. Salts of the elements, dissolved in water, are taken up by the root hairs, and the extent to which this takes place depends on the texture of the soil, which should be loose and friable, ie crumbly.

It is not easy to calculate the amount of a fertiliser to be used, which depends to some extent on the weather and moisture in the soil, but it is wise to follow the manufacturer's instructions, which are carefully calculated. Generally speaking, nitrogen stimulates growth and leaf production, phosphorus helps to produce active roots, and potassium stimulates flower formation and ripening of fruit.

Form A difficult word since it is loosely used by gardeners, most of whom know what they think it means. Strictly it is applied to a plant which differs in some minor character, such as a white-flowered form of a red-flowered species. Form is one step lower than subspecies.

Genus A family of plants is composed of one or more genera. The similar members of a genus are species.

Glabrous 'Not hairy' (which is not the same as smooth). A glabrous leaf can be rough.

Glaucous Latin, 'bluish green or grey'. In Bean (1970, Vol 1) the definition is 'covered with a white or bluish white bloom'. The original meaning is surely to be preferred.

Globose Nearly spherical. Applied to fruits, shrubs and the crown of trees.

Habit Characteristic form of growth of a plant – upright, weeping, prostrate, etc.

Hairs Occur on leaves and stems and occasionally on flowers and fruits, as a cover or indumentum. Their main function is to insulate against heat or cold. The term hirsute is used botanically for coarse, dense hairs; pubescent means downy with short hairs barely visible. Tomentose means woolly or felted and villous refers to long weak hairs.

Hardy Indicates a plant that is able to grow outside without protection all the year round in a given area. In Britain there are obvious differences in hardiness between plants grown in the north and those grown in the south, and the Gulf Stream produces significantly warmer climates in coastal areas in Scotland and Northern Ireland. In the USA ten zones of climate are recognised, reflecting their degree of hardiness.

The lie of the land can influence hardiness considerably, producing microclimates both benign and hostile. In Britain mild spells in winter followed by frost undermine confidence in the weather pattern in most years.

Inflorescence The flowering part of a plant. There are three categories:

1 Cymose. A flower is produced at each terminal growing point and later flowers from lateral growing points.

2 Racemose. Having an active growing point and able, in theory at least, to develop indefinitely with the youngest flowers at the apex.

3 Mixed inflorescences, not belonging to either of the above categories. The most frequent kinds are:

Capitulum (racemose) – a tight collection of stalkless flowers, seen in *Compositae*.

Catkins – a mixed inflorescence of stalkless flowers, eg hazel.

Corymb – usually small flowers or flower heads, all about the same height. The flower stalks leave the main stem at different points (cf 'Umbel').

Cyme – a variety of inflorescence, all of which have growing points which end in a flower.

Panicle – a branching raceme in which each branch resembles an individual raceme. Branches may be alternate or opposite.

Raceme – an elongated inflorescence without branches. Each flower has a short stalk.

Spike – an inflorescence with a vertical axis and numerous stalkless or nearly stalkless flowers.

Umbel – an inflorescence in which the flower stalks arise from a central point at the top of the main stem. Umbels may be simple or compound.

Lateral A side-growth of any kind on a shrub or tree. Understanding of this term is vital to the pruning of fruit trees.

Leader The shoot which ends a branch and grows on in the same direction. The central leader continues the main trunk in a vertical direction and is not pruned unless damaged or misdirected, whereas laterals are pruned.

Leaves Considered here from the point of view of one who is seeking to identify a plant or at least place it in a genus. These are the most common arrangements:

LEAF FORMS

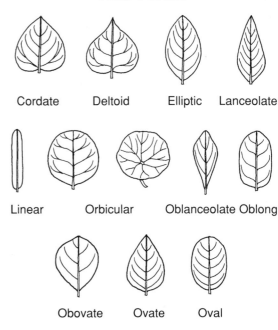

Cordate   Deltoid   Elliptic   Lanceolate

Linear   Orbicular   Oblanceolate Oblong

Obovate   Ovate   Oval

INFLORESCENCES

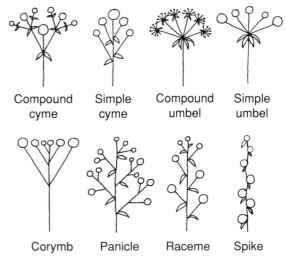

Compound   Simple   Compound   Simple
cyme   cyme   umbel   umbel

Corymb   Panicle   Raceme   Spike

Leaves may have a stalk (petiole) and are then petiolate; if without a stalk, sessile.

Leg The length of the main trunk of a tree from the ground to the lowest branch.

Maiden A tree or bush in the first year after grafting or budding. Term mainly used for fruit trees, but also roses. Feathers are the laterals of maidens. (cf **Whip**).

Microclimate See **Hardy**.

Monoecious A plant which has both male and female flowers, able to function in fertilisation (cf **Dioecious**).

Mouth The open end of a bell or trumpet-shaped flower.

Neutral The point of the pH scale (*qv*) at which soil is neither acid nor alkaline: pH = 7.0.

Nicking and notching See Fruit Trees & Bushes.

Petiole A leaf stalk. On some climbers the petiole will twine round the nearest support of a practicable size, eg clematis, nasturtium.

pH indicates hydrogen ion concentration and measures the acidity or alkalinity of soil, water or whatever. The scale is logarithmic so that the difference between pH 7.0 and 8.0 is much greater than that between eg, 5 and 6.

Phloem See **Vascular system**.

Pleach Originally meant hedge-laying by bending stems of trees or shrubs, then cutting them half through and interweaving them, using posts as necessary. It now commonly refers to a screen or hedge formed at some height, 1.8-2.4m (6-8ft) from the ground by branching of trees which are kept bare below this level. Limes or hornbeams are usually chosen for this purpose.

Pollard A tree which is cut back at intervals to a main trunk, often 1.2m (4ft) or so from the ground, which makes the work easy. The commonest reason for pollarding is to produce young pliable shoots, especially from willows. They are used in basketmaking and in forming hurdles, both active trades in marshy districts.

Raceme See **Inflorescence**.

Reversion Correctly used for:

1 Variegated (*qv*) plants which revert to producing leaves of their plain form, usually green, eg *Elaeagnus pungens maculata*, *Acer negundo variegatum*. Removal of the reverted stem is necessary but is not a cure for the tendency.

2 A virus disease of currants, causing the leaves to become smaller than normal with fewer veins. If the diagnosis is confirmed the plant should be removed.

Scion A shoot or bud removed from a plant for the purpose of budding or grafting to another, the stock, which provides the roots.

Shoot The growth of an emerging seedling. When leaves or lateral growths appear it is a stem. Unfortunately the word is also used for lateral growths, twigs or branches.

Shrub A woody plant with many stems and no trunk. A large shrub may become tree-like and may be persuaded to act like a tree by removal of side branches from the most upright stem, eg *Photina davidii*.

Species Plants of one species have characters which distinguish them from any other and they breed true. Subspecies are one step less well defined but in general resemble species.

Spur A short branch system which carries clusters of flower heads.

Standard Loosely used for any tree grown with a bare stem. Trees are trained as standards for fruit-growing with 1.8m (6ft) stems (half-standards, 0.9-1.2m (3-4ft) and shrubs, particularly roses, are often grafted on stems of 0.9-1.2m (3-4ft).

Sucker A word of ill-omen for gardeners, as it commonly refers to grafted plants on which the stock produces growth. This may overcome the desirable growth of the scion. The leaves on a sucker are often, but not always, easy to distinguish from those of the scion. These suckers must be removed, which is not an easy task. Advice to pull rather than cut them off is often valueless, as they are tenacious. Cutting off just below ground level tends to generate a forest of new suckers. One should attempt to trace each sucker to its origin on the stock root by gently digging, finally cutting the sucker away completely.

Tap roots A strong root growing almost or quite vertically downwards, presumably in search of water or nourishment. The Black Walnut, *Juglans nigra*, grown from seed is very quick to form a tap root and becomes very difficult to transplant within three years. In a permanent site it is best left to develop. Conifers behave in the same way. Well-behaved tap roots appear on carrots and parsnips, forming the edible part.

Tendril A modified leaf or shoot. Some branch and at their ends produce adhesive suckers which fix them onto a surface, eg ivy. Some are thready and twine, eg vines. Others wave about until they encounter something around which they can coil.

Thinning See Fruit Trees & Bushes.

Trellis A structure of light bars of wood or metal, crossing each other at intervals and fastened where they cross. Nowadays trellis is available in panels made of wood or plastic. If free-standing it needs support from posts at least every 1.8m (6ft) and can be partially draped with climbers. Against a wall it should be fastened to stand 2.5cm (1in) or a little more away from the wall surface.

Type Term used by long-suffering gardeners to differentiate a particular form of a plant from that more commonly grown, which they regard as the 'type'. Properly, the type is a plant described from the wild, the description being supported by a dried herbarium specimen. This 'type' plant may not be the commonest form of the species.

Umbel See **Inflorescence**.

Variegated Leaves usually, stems and flowers seldom, have markings in two or more colours in a variegated plant. The markings are, as a rule, white or cream, due to the absence of chlorophyll (which gives the normal green colouring), but other colours may be seen, as in the partially pink and white leaves of the climber *Actinidia kolomikta* (p137). Variegated plants are weaker than their plain green originals, and they tend to revert to that greenness.

Variety A variation in a wild as opposed to a cultivated plant. It must be sufficiently distinct to deserve a name of its own.

Vascular system A system of tubes in plants consisting of two series:

1 the *phloem*, which conveys foodstuffs made in the leaves to all other parts of the plant, including the roots, as necessary;

2 the *xylem*, which conveys water and minerals taken up by the roots to the leaves, where they are converted (with the aid of sunlight and the green pigment chlorophyll) to the complex substances needed for growth. This is the process of photosynthesis, as a result of which oxygen is given off into the air – just as well for us.

In herbaceous plants the phloem and xylem are in bundles scattered through the stem. In woody plants the xylem converts to wood, the conducting cells being arranged as a cylinder around this heartwood, which gradually dies from the centre outwards. A cylinder of active cells, the *cambium*, only a cell thick, expands to allow growth of the trunk and limbs, and also takes an active part in xylem transport. Outside this is a second cylinder of phloem cells, serving the same function as the inner phloem layer.

Vegetative propagation This is achieved by any known method other than seeds and includes offsets, runners, division, cuttings, budding and grafting.

Water shoots See **Adventitious.**

Whip A young tree (up to two years old) with an erect stem and no laterals (feathers).

BIBLIOGRAPHY

Arnold-Foster, W.
  Shrubs for the Milder Counties
  (Country Life Ltd, London 1948)
Bailey, L. H. *The Pruning Manual*
  18th Edition.
  (The Macmillan Co. New York 1934)
Bazeley, B.
  Tree Fruit Growing
  (Wm Collins and Son, London 1990)
Beales, Peter.
  Classic Roses
  (Wm Collins Co Ltd, London 1985)
Bean, W. J.
  Trees and Shrubs Hardy in the British Isles
  (John Murray, London; A-C 1970, D-M 1973, N-RL 1976, RI-Z 1980. Supplement 1988)
Brickell, C.
  Pruning
  (Mitchell Beazley, London 1979)
Bristow, Alec.
  How to Bring Up Plants
  (Harvill Press, London 1983)
Brown, George E.
  The Pruning of Trees, Shrubs and Conifers
  (Faber and Faber, London 1972)
Curtis, C. H. and Gibson, W.
  The Book of Topiarys
  (The Bodley Head, London 1904)
Dallimore, W.
  The Pruning of Trees and Shrubs
  (Edward Arnold Ltd, London)

Dallimore, W. and Jackson, A. B.
  A Handbook of Conifers and Ginkgoaceae
  4thEd (Edward Arnold, London 1966)
Fraser, H.
  The Gardener's Guide to Pruning
  (W. H. and L. Collingridge, London 1966)
Gibson, M.
  The Book of the Rose
  (Macdonald General Books, London 1980)
Grounds, Roger.
  The Complete Handbook of Pruning
  (Ward Lock, London 1973)
Hadfield, Miles.
  Topiary and Ornamental Hedges
  (A & C Black, London 1971)
Halliwell, Brian.
  The Complete Book of Pruning
  (Ward Lock Ltd, 3rd Edition 1988)
Hudson, J.
  The Pruning Handbook
  (Prentice Hall, New York 1971)
Huxley, Anthony.
  Huxley's Encyclopedia of Gardening for Great Britain and America
  (Universe Books, New York 1981)
Lacey, Geraldine.
  Creating Topiary
  (Garden Art Press, Northiam, East Sussex 1987)
Lloyd, Christopher.
  Clematis
  (Wm Collins, 1977).

The Well-Chosen Garden
  (Elm Tree Books, London 1984)
Lycett-Green, Candida and Lawson, Andrew.
  Brilliant Gardens.
  (Chatto and Windus, London 1989)
The Plant Finder
  Devised and compiled by Chris Philip,
  Editor Anthony Lord.
  (Headmain Ltd, Lakeside, Whitbourne,
  Worcester 1991)
Prockter, Noel J.
  Climbing and Screening Plants
  (Faber and Faber, London 1973)

Rehder, Alfred.
  _Manual of Cultivated Trees and Shrubs Hardy
  in North America_
  (Dioscorides Press, Oregon, 2nd Ed 1940)
Reid, John.
  The Scots Gardener
  (Glasgow 1683)
Robinson, William.
  The English Flower Garden
  (John Murray, London 15th Ed 1933)
Sackville-West, Vita.
  In Your Garden
  (Michael Joseph Ltd 1951)

ACKNOWLEDGEMENTS

This book is a 'companion' to encourage the belief that a knowledge of the form and character of plant species and their cultivars is necessary for the rational practice of pruning.

I have tried to keep up with the changes in nomenclature which are announced each year. _The Plant Finder_, edited by Anthony Lord, is most valuable in this respect and I am grateful to him for help and advice. (Some believe that _The Plant Finder_ is the greatest horticultural invention since the trowel.)

I have had valuable demonstration of the effects of pruning from Michael Hickson at Knightshayes and Roy Finch in Worcestershire. From Christopher Lloyd, too, at Great Dixter and through his writing, which shows the value of record-keeping every year.

Topiary has gone almost beyond my experience, and I am grateful to Geraldine Lacey for her excellent advice. Anthony Huxley has been most patient at a very busy time, both in answering questions and advising me on how to avoid pitfalls.

Vivienne Wells was my first editor and was succeeded by Sarah Widdicombe, who has patiently guided me to the end, with John Youé as designer. I have almost enjoyed writing for them.

Wendy Pearce bravely agreed to convert my manuscript to a typescript, and did so with remarkably few spelling mistakes considering my erratic handwriting. Am I the last author to _write_ a book?

My thanks also to Andrew Lawson for his wonderful photographs, which capture the essential character of their subjects so well, and to illustrator Maggie Redfern, for a difficult task stylishly performed.

And, finally, special thanks to Patrick Taylor, who advised throughout and encouraged me to persist despite the setbacks.

John Malins
Tintinhull House, 1992

INDEX